Cybers
Fundamentals

Understand the Role of Cybersecurity, Its Importance and Modern Techniques Used by Cybersecurity Professionals

Dr. Rajesh Kumar Goutam

Assistant Professor
Department of Computer Science
University of Lucknow
LUCKNOW

www.bpbonline.com

FIRST EDITION 2021

ISBN: 978-93-90684-731

LIMITS OF LIABILITY AND DISCLAIMER OF WARRANTY

Distributors:

BPB PUBLICATIONS
20, Ansari Road, Darya Ganj
New Delhi-110002
Ph: 23254990/23254991

MICRO MEDIA
Shop No. 5, Mahendra Chambers,
150 DN Rd. Next to Capital Cinema,
V.T. (C.S.T.) Station, MUMBAI-400 001
Ph: 22078296/22078297

DECCAN AGENCIES
4-3-329, Bank Street,
Hyderabad-500195
Ph: 24756967/24756400

BPB BOOK CENTRE
376 Old Lajpat Rai Market,
Delhi-110006
Ph: 23861747

Published by Manish Jain for BPB Publications, 20 Ansari Road, Darya Ganj, New Delhi-110002 and Printed by him at Repro India Ltd, Mumbai

www.bpbonline.com

Dedicated to

Professor Brijendra Singh
Who encouraged me to write this book

About the Author

Dr. Rajesh Kumar Goutam is an assistant professor in Department of Computer Science University of Lucknow. He has over 10 years of experience in teaching and research in the computer science field. He did his MCA from Uttar Pradesh Technical University, Lucknow, and earned his Ph.D. in Computer Science from Babasaheb Bhimrao Ambedkar University, Lucknow.

Goutam's interest lies in developing the framework to detect the true source of cybercrime and to track the criminals across digital infrastructure. He has contributed to the Cybersecurity field through his several publications in various journals of repute. The author is an active member of various professional bodies too.

About the Reviewer

Vignesh Balasubramanian has over vast of experience in performing Vulnerability Assessments, Penetration Testing and Digital Forensics Investigations. Prior to becoming a cybersecurity professional, he worked as a Systems Integration Tester at Reliance Jio Infocomm Limited in Mumbai. He is now working independently on cybersecurity training and consulting projects.

Acknowledgement

First and foremost, I am thankful to "Almighty God" and my parents too for their blessings and enabling me to complete this book.

I would like to thank Professor Alok Kumar Rai, Vice-Chancellor of the University of Lucknow, who believed in my capabilities and provided me congenial atmosphere and necessary infrastructure to write this book.

I am thankful to Prof. Brijendra Singh, Head, Department of Computer Science, University of Lucknow, for his continuous encouragement, regular guidance and motivations during the entire period of writing this book. I am indebted to Professor Sanjay Kumar Dwivedi, Head of Computer Science Department, Babasaheb Bhimrao Ambedkar University, Lucknow, who taught me the basics of research. I am also thankful to Dr Suresh Prasad Kannojia for his valuable suggestions on technical aspects of this book. We are fortunate to have Dr Sudhir Singh and his wife Mrs Ranjana who always encouraged me to do outstanding work in research and maintained healthy and convivial environment around me. I am grateful to the entire BPB publication team for providing me the opportunity to complete this book. I owe very special thanks to Dr Vignesh Balasibramanian for technically reviewing this book and to enhance the quality of chapters.

Finally, words fall short to convey my emotional sentiments from the deepest core of my heart to my wife Anupam Lata, brother Mr Rakesh Kumar, bhabhi Mrs Janki, and sisters for constantly supporting me and always being on my side whenever I needed their help.

Preface

Today, we have a virtual, parallel and essential world, commonly known as cyberspace, which enables us to perform our personal, social and economical activities online in an efficient manner and facilitates to store sensitive data over global network. Although the internet is considered powerful and indispensible tool for digital revolution, it is vulnerable and provides immense opportunities to criminals to earn illegal money and to get social and political benefits. Criminals launch attacks with their malicious codes to harass individuals, to breach confidential business data, to remotely control digital infrastructure, and to restrict legitimate access to devices. These attacks are rapidly growing in numbers across the world, are triggered by professionals in an organized manner to increase destruction coverage and for greater economical and societal damages. Cybercriminals are now presenting formidable risks for nations to protect their national critical infrastructures and pressurize the governments for their frail demands by paralyzing the functioning of their institutions and crucial sectors.

We are now living in digital age where the internet has a key role in our survival. The internet users, including school children, teenagers, adults and veterans are sharing cyberspace with criminals and publishing the crucial information over internet and are inviting risks. To avoid these risks, the internet users must understand its perils together with its benefits. It is time to be a smart user so that we can reap the benefits of information and communication technologies and can fail criminals' malicious attempts without any inconvenience to our safe access to cyberspace and internet enabled devices. This book has been envisaged to meet these requirements and is delivered to spread awareness about the inherent risks with internet technologies among its readers.

Cybersecurity is not a state, instead it is a long-term process that protects our digital infrastructure with its inherent software, hardware, networks and database with appropriate procedural and technological counter measures. Unfortunately, we are still dependent on firewalls and third-party antivirus software for the protection of digital infrastructure, which is grotesque. To tackle with cybercriminals' tactics to gain access to digital infrastructure and to make them failure in their malicious attempts, we need to devise our own defense strategies such as Intrusion Detection System, Prevention systems, and Response Systems that requires the fundamental knowledge of the Cybersecurity subject. This book has been written with these considerations and provides comprehensive knowledge of important topics ranging from basics of computer security to flooding attacks and Cyberwar. This book is useful for BTech/MTech, BSc/MSc, BCA/MCA students in Computer Science and Information Technology both disciplines. This book can be useful resource for researchers who are interested to pursue a career in 'Cybersecurity' area of research.

This book consists a total of six chapters.

Chapter 1 introduces the concept of data and information, and explores how data is transformed into meaningful information. Data communication model and its components have been elaborated. Further, we explain Internet, Networking and World Wide Web and differentiate from each other in order to prepare a solid background to understand the subject cybersecurity in deepen. The chapter classifies the word 'security' in term of Information security, Network security, World Wide Web security and cyber security and explains how cybersecurity has now been converted into common, global and shared problem.

Chapter 2 details about the history of cybercrimes and its expansion across the world. We talk about the various forms of cybercrimes used to threaten the people. Further, we discuss the challenges existing in the field for cyber security, which are acting as a barrier to reduce adverse impacts. We discuss how and why cybercrime are supported and are being adopted as a profession across the globe.

Chapter 3 discusses how the national critical infrastructures are important for any country and dependent on digital environment been elaborated. The need of intrusion detection system has been elaborated with its architecture, classification, and functions. The CIA traid and defensive life cycle has been explained in terms of intrusions detections and prevention. The chapter details the major types of intrusions and their categorization too.

Chapter 4 deals with the methods to identify the true source of cybercrime. It details various procedures through which cybercriminals hide their identity while they commit crimes and evade themselves from detection. The barriers that make identification of origin of cybercrimes difficult have been explained. This chapter details complete anatomy and classification of traceback mechanism, which are used to track and chase the cybercriminal.

Chapter 5 defines stepping stones in cybercrime. The algorithms used to detect the stepping stones have been elaborated together with its foundation assumptions. Further, intrusion response system has been defined and categorized on the basis of passive response and automatic response. The anatomy of actions taken in response to intrusions by IRS has also been summarized.

Chapter 6 defines COTS software with Vulnerability life cycle to highlight shortfalls in the internet structure. The main attraction of this chapter includes Cooperative intrusion traceback and response architecture (CITRA) that does not add overheads in the absence of intrusions. Further, this chapter details DDoS attacks and their classification too.

Downloading the coloured images:

Please follow the link to download the
Coloured Images of the book:

https://rebrand.ly/qkhcqzq

Errata

We take immense pride in our work at BPB Publications and follow best practices to ensure the accuracy of our content to provide with an indulging reading experience to our subscribers. Our readers are our mirrors, and we use their inputs to reflect and improve upon human errors, if any, that may have occurred during the publishing processes involved. To let us maintain the quality and help us reach out to any readers who might be having difficulties due to any unforeseen errors, please write to us at :

errata@bpbonline.com

Your support, suggestions and feedbacks are highly appreciated by the BPB Publications' Family.

BPB is searching for authors like you

If you're interested in becoming an author for BPB, please visit **www.bpbonline.com** and apply today. We have worked with thousands of developers and tech professionals, just like you, to help them share their insight with the global tech community. You can make a general application, apply for a specific hot topic that we are recruiting an author for, or submit your own idea.

The code bundle for the book is also hosted on GitHub at **https://github.com/bpbpublications/Cybersecurity-Fundamentals**. In case there's an update to the code, it will be updated on the existing GitHub repository.

We also have other code bundles from our rich catalog of books and videos available at **https://github.com/bpbpublications**. Check them out!

PIRACY

If you come across any illegal copies of our works in any form on the internet, we would be grateful if you would provide us with the location address or website name. Please contact us at :

business@bpbonline.com with a link to the material.

If you are interested in becoming an author

If there is a topic that you have expertise in, and you are interested in either writing or contributing to a book, please visit **www.bpbonline.com**.

REVIEWS

Please leave a review. Once you have read and used this book, why not leave a review on the site that you purchased it from? Potential readers can then see and use your unbiased opinion to make purchase decisions, we at BPB can understand what you think about our products, and our authors can see your feedback on their book. Thank you!

For more information about BPB, please visit **www.bpbonline.com**.

Table of Contents

CHAPTER 1
Introduction to Cybersecurity

Internet is a big source of knowledge and easily accessible to all. Interestingly, it has equal opportunities for criminals too. Cybercriminals leverage modern technologies to develop sophisticated tools and techniques, and use them to perform malicious activities aimed at distorting, disrupting and/or stealing sensitive data and information, primarily for financial gains. They are creating barriers to innovation, knowledge sharing, economic growth, and the free flow of information. In this chapter, it is assumed that you have some basic knowledge about computer networks, while the chapter emphasizes on understanding the terms data and information with reference to Cybersecurity.

Structure

In this chapter, we will cover the following topics:

- Data and Information
- W3 Consortium (W3C)
- Networking, W3 and Internet Relationship
- Information Security

- World Wide Web Security
- Network Security
- Cybersecurity

Objective

The aim of this chapter is to impart the basic knowledge of Data and Information in readers and making them aware of inherent risks and problems with our digital infrastructure. After reading this chapter, you would understand the necessity to protect digital infrastructure encompassing internet, networking and World Wide Web. You will be familiar with the key motivations behind the cybercrimes and understand the key concepts such as Information security, Word Wide Web security, and Network security. Our focus is to introduce you to Cybersecurity and its coverage, and help you understand Vicious Architecture and taxonomies of Cybercrime.

1.1 Data and information

Data can be defined as the facts, measurements, and statistics gathered in real-time environment[1]. This term is associated with scientific research and examined for reasoning, discussion and decision making. Initially, data was represented in text forms, numbers or in combination of both. After the introduction of multimedia, the term data expanded its boundaries and incorporated audio, images, graphics, and video in itself [2]. However, there are various types of data that exist but all get stored in digital form.

Information is the meaning of stored data in some context for its intended receiver(s). Information in any stage becomes data for computers. When data is accurately processed in an organized manner with a specific purpose and it presents some relevant meaning to its user, then it is called information. The information becomes useless if it does not lead a significant increase in end-user knowledge.

1.1.1 Data versus information

Both the terms *data* and *information* are often used in the same context by novices, which is technically not true. Data usually refers to raw facts or unprocessed facts, which contain numbers, letters, characters, and multimedia objects. It represents qualitative or quantitative measurements of a particular set of items during a particular time span. When data is processed to find some conclusions, then it is termed as information [3]. The major differences between data and information are as follows:

- Data is used as input for computer system to generate information.
- Data refers to unstructured and disorganized facts and when these facts are processed in some organized and structured way in a particular span of time, then we get information.
- Data is independent in itself, while information needs data for its own existence.
- Data is meaningless while information carries relevant meaning and becomes beneficial for end users.
- We can perceive data as raw material to generate information like product.

1.1.2 Characteristics of information

Transformation of data into information requires number of steps such as data processing, data cleaning, and data analysis and interpretation. Information remains irrelevant until it adds something new to users' knowledge. It has five major characteristics:

- **Accuracy**: It is the degree of analysis that provides correct facts to its users. It implies the state of being error free, clear, updated, and having no mistakes.
- **Completeness**: This is another important attribute which ensures that all the necessary data have been collected and processed in a right way to draw a conclusion.
- **Consistency**: It refers to a quality of information that is consistent, but not having conclusions in parts.
- **Uniqueness**: It refers to globally accepted facts in a consistent order without ambiguity.
- **Timeliness**: It enables users to make quick decisions on the basis of information that is delivered.

1.2 Data communication

Computers are basically used to collect data from different sources, convert that data in to meaningful information. Generated information becomes useless until it is delivered to the right person at the right time. It is equally important to transmit information quickly for the benefits of its users across the world. To transfer the information across the world, we use well-connected digitally networked infrastructure. In remote information sharing, communication needs to cover a distance. Data communication refers to exchange of information between two or more computers with the help of some communication medium. This communication medium can be either wired medium or wireless medium.

1.2.1 Data communication model

A data communication model contains five key components:

- **Source**: Source refers to device that generates the information to be transmitted. The source may be in the form of computers, mobiles, telephones, and so on.
- **Messages**: The message is the information that is to be transmitted for destination end. The message may include text, pictures, audio, videos or any combination of these.
- **Transmission medium**: The transmission medium refers to physical path or network connecting source and destination, through which message is transmitted from sender to receiver. The transmission medium path may consist of coaxial cable, twisted pair, fibre-optic cable, and satellite microwave.
- **Destination**: Destination refers to the device that receives the information coming from sender end through transmission medium.
- **Protocols**: A protocol refers to a set of rules and conventions that govern the digital communication between two parties. It represents an agreement between communicating parties in direction to how to proceed the communication.

1.2.2 Data communication system

The effectiveness of data communication system depends upon following characteristics:

- **Interface**: To communicate with the help of communication medium, devices at the sender end and receiver end must have an interface. As all the forms of communication depends upon the generation of electromagnetic signals, the interface in communication at both ends play a key role. Data signals generated from transmitter with its properties like its form and intensity are received by interface at communication end. Here it must be ensured that the channel interface is capable of receiving the signal generated from transmitter in its original form. Similarly, at the time of delivery from the communication channel, the interface should deliver the original signals to its destinations.

- **Delivery**: The system must transmit the information to its authorized receiver or correct destination.
- **Accuracy**: The data must be transmitted accurately from source end and must be received at receiving end in its original form as it was transmitted originally.
- **Synchronization**: The timing of arriving data packets and their order at destination is important. There must be synchronization between transmitter and receiver. In a good communication channel, the receiver knows when signals arrive at communication medium and how long they take to reach at receiving end. This can be easily understood with example of live cricket match. If the cricket match is being broadcasted and the data packets at our television sets are received in an unordered way with delay, we cannot enjoy the cricket match.
- **Error detection and correction**: To check the originality of signals at the receiving end, the communication must have error detection and error correction facility because in data communication the errors (numbers and ordering) cannot be tolerated.
- **Flow control**: Flow control is required to compensate the speed and capacity of transmitter, receiver and communication medium.
- **Security**: It is an essential measure for a good communication medium. The sender of the information will always wish to be assured that the information he is sending would be received only by the intended receiver and nobody else.

1.3 Computer network

A computer network is a set of computers that are connected to each other via wired or wireless medium. A computer in network shares information in its own network group and becomes remotely accessible from other computers existing in same network. Information sharing is the primary requirement for computers to be a part of a network. A computer connected to a network becomes accessible to other computers. Each computer incorporated in network is known as node or terminal. We form computer network for the purpose of data communication and resource sharing. The most common resource shared nowadays is connection to World Wide Web from which we retrieve the information across the world. Organizations are heavily relying on networking in order to share application software and to increase the productivity in limited expanses.

There are many ways in which network can be classified, such as their size, capabilities and geographical area they cover. Some of the most common types of ubiquitous network are detailed here.

1.3.1 Local Area Network (LAN)

This is the smallest and privately owned network that connects two or more computers in a relatively small coverage area like single office, building, and campus. Each computer in LAN has its own identification number through which it is recognized in communication process.

1.3.2 Metropolitan Area Network (MAN)

This is a network that spans in a geographic area larger than **Local Area Network** (**LAN**) and smaller than **Wide Area Network** (**WAN**). This term makes interconnection across the city and college campus with the help of a single larger network. A **Metropolitan Area Network** (**MAN**) is often formed by interconnecting several LANs together to cover an area of several kilometres.

1.3.3 Wide Area Network (WAN)

This type of network connects the computers or other networking devices across a much larger geographical area in comparison to LAN and MAN. Although WAN is not restricted to a particular geographical location, it might be confined to the bounds of a state or country. The networking devices such computers and mobile phones connected to WAN use the public network like telephone system and satellite system to facilitate the large-scale data transfer. A WAN interconnects various smaller telecommunication networks, including several **local area networks** (**LANs**) and **wide area networks** (**WANs**).

1.3.4 Personal Area Network (PAN)

A **personal area network** (**PAN**) is a network in which exchange of information and data occurs within the vicinity of a person. The systems in this network often use wireless technologies and communicate within the range of 10 meters. It allows devices like computers, smartphones and smartwatches to communicate and share the data. In our mobiles, the option *smart phone tethering* is the example of PAN network that allows the nearby devices to communicate if it is setup as personal hotspot.

1.3.5 Storage Area Network (SAN)

A **storage area network** (**SAN**) is a high-speed storage networking architecture that allows enterprises to access shared pools of storages connected to multiple servers. It is used for critical business applications where high throughput is required with low latency. It presents block-based storage and is accessible from all the applications running on any connected servers.

1.3.6 Enterprise Private Network (EPN)

Enterprise Private Network is designed to protect the data and making the resources shareable among different units of company such as offices, production sites, shops, and warehouses. Digital integration of different units ensures the mobility of resources while data protection is achieved through various security measures like encryptions and tunnelling protocols. Routers are programmed to complete registration process and to decide whether a device can access the EPN or not.

1.3.7 Virtual Private Network (VPN)

Virtual Private Network provides private network services to organizations using the public or shared infrastructure like internet.

These private network services are encrypted to ensure the delivery of sensitive data to right person sitting in private company safely. It is a controlled segmentation of communications provided to organization with specific needs.

1.4 World Wide Web

The World Wide Web popularly known as W3, was invented by English scientist Tim Berners-Lee in 1989. It is the virtual and borderless collection of web documents. It contains web pages, pictures, videos and other online content that can be accessed with the help of a web browser. It is the collection of network-accessible information that embodies human knowledge. World Wide Web is actually a virtual space where the websites are hosted. Web documents are pointed by **Uniform Resource Locaters** (**URLs**). World Wide Web is open to all and whoever wants upload the documents or websites can easily do with the help of **File Transfer Protocol (FTP)** and with its own domain name. The size of World Wide Web is continuously expanding with time with versatile information. There are few reasons behind its rapid expansion and these are detailed as follows:

1. The World Wide Web acts as a medium thorough which any person can advertise and popularize their business.
2. It removes the geographical boundaries and restrictions from distribution of information.
3. It is used as knowledge sharing platform.
4. It acts as a platform for freedom of speech.
5. Advertisement covers the whole world.
6. Fastest, Hi-tech and reliable medium for advertisement and communication.
7. Able to convey whole information about the business.
8. It requires very low cost compared to other alternatives available in the market.
9. It does not require much human effort.

Although Tim Berners-Lee invented the World Wide Web, whatever size and shape now exists is because of population. All of us enrich the World Wide Web because whatever we upload, whether documents or websites, to the web becomes information for all of us that is retrieved with the help of search engines after posing the appropriate queries. In this way, we can say the functioning of search engines depends on the documents available in the World Wide Web. Another reason behind the popularity of World Wide Web is that as it contains the information for all. People from various fields such as medical, engineering, and research upload the documents to the World Wide Web and these documents become the information for us.

1.4.1 Characteristics of World Wide Web

The major characteristics of World Wide Web are as follows:

- **Universal Coverage**: The tremendous growth of the Internet and W3 represents the most magnificent transformation in information technology. Now, we can experience the emergence of an open, distributed, global information infrastructure that works with the help of Internet and World Wide Web servers. World Wide Web covers all geographical areas where the internet connectivity exists. It is open to all to upload the text, picture, audio, and video and delivers the information when required. Its universal coverage makes it unique as it provides a common platform to share knowledge about various fields from various parts of earths without any intermediary.

- **Virtual**: World Wide Web is a hypertext-based globally scattered information system. In reference to World Wide Web the term *virtual* refers to qualities of persistence and interactivity. World Wide Web facilitates us with its services and provides us a common platform for knowledge sharing, but it is non-tangible in nature.

- **Borderless**: The construction of internet and World Wide Web empowers citizens to participate in the global digital economy, access knowledge without geographical boundaries and engage in lawful communication with the rest of words, regardless of location or type of device. All the information organized in World Wide Web structure can be thought at a central storage. It does not matter from which country it is being uploaded that means from the various parts of the world documents get uploaded to web and retrieved from this single repository regardless of physical boundaries and restrictions to satisfy searchers needs.

1.5 Internet

Internet is a heterogeneous collection of numerous different small networks, primarily owned and operated by small companies to cover whole geographical area. Small networks are able to interconnect with each other with the help of a common set of protocols explaining how to transform and exchange information. It is assemblage of variety of numerous networks that includes World Wide Web services to function properly. It is a medium through which the World Wide Web contents are made accessible and useful to users.

1.6 W3 Consortium (W3C)

The **World Wide Web Consortium** (**W3C**) is an international community that sets rules, regulations and standards to ensure long-term growth of the Web. W3C was formed in October 1994 to promote its expansion and evolution to provide a common world-Wide knowledge sharing platform. It functions under the supervision of its inventor and director Tim Berners-Lee and CEO Jeffrey Jaffe where around 450 organizations, 70 staff and public work together to develop W3 rules and software.

1.6.1 Functions of W3C

W3C mission is to bring the web in such form with which we can use its full potential. W3C creates specifications, guidelines, software and tools to provide a worldwide platform for information, commerce, independent thoughts and collective understanding. W3C performs the following functions:

- **Universal access**: W3C is doing continuous efforts to raise the standard of web as the universe of network-accessible information. This information is made available easily to users through computers, mobiles, television, or some other networked equipment quickly. Its priority is to provide a forum for human communication and opportunities for knowledge sharing to all people. This forum enables users to fetch the information and share what they like independently. It provides freedom to users about their hardware, software, network infrastructure, native language, culture, geographical location, or physical or mental ability.

- **Trust development**: The web is a collaborative platform, open to all to share whatever they feel and experience. The personal view of someone can divert the attention of population and create an explosive situation in society. To promote trustworthy environment, W3C efforts to create *Web of Trust* to maintain confidentiality, confidence, and integrity. It also develops trace back system to make a person accountable about whatever he publishes on the web.
- **Interoperability**: The need for information for all is vital and the web is a huge source of every kind of information freely available to all everywhere. It is a challenge for W3C to meet the requirements and supply the information to all seekers because they are using different platform, infrastructure, and software. All users cannot maintain similarity in software and interfaces. The W3C continuously efforts to adopt changes in its infrastructure so that it can support all kind of software users use to meet their information need.
- **Evolvability**: W3C believes that our knowledge and technology may become insufficient to tackle future problems. It keeps the future needs in its strategies and update infrastructure to adopt changes and meet current and future requirements. It follows basic principle of design and maintains simplicity, modularity, compatibility, and extensibility.
- **Decentralization**: W3C knows its responsibility well and believes that information on the web is the life and breath of Internet. It believes in distributed systems and decentralize the web for its safety and effective controlling. The web is partitioned and fragmented under single controlling system for better communication and quick maintenance, and to reduce the chances of vulnerability of web as whole.

1.7 Networking, W3 and internet relationship

The terms internet and W3 are often used interchangeably, and are considered synonymous of each other, but in reality, both are different. Internet is a huge network comprising of numerous small sub-networks, accessible to everyone from all the geo-graphical areas across the world. The inherent computers transmit data and communicate with each other with the help of a set of rules and regulations that is collectively known as 'protocol'. Internet provides e-mail, chat, and file transfer services over network to end users. Two or more than two systems are said to be in network if they are able to exchange the data and information with each other. In networking, inherent computers get connected somehow either with wired medium or wireless medium and use a particular topology to communicate. Networking helps to transmit the information form one server to another server existing at different geographical areas. World Wide Web is the virtual collection of interlinked web pages. The hyperlinks facilitate users to make navigation among the webpages. Nowadays, W3 can satisfy information seeker with relevant and desired information but only with the help of networking and Internet. It will be difficult or almost impossible to utilize the full potential of W3 if we do not use internet. Users connect with the internet with networking as intermediary and internet then takes the user to World Wide Web and help user to access the documents exist on the web. World Wide Web is formed with numerous servers scattered various parts across universe.

1.8 Information security

In this digital era, protecting our information is as important as protecting our physical assets. Information security is concerned to protecting digital information from destruction, stealing and unauthorized access. We might have medical reports or financial records that we want to keep it secret from others, even family members too. We also desire privacy with our mails and social media posts. We do not want to disclose internet passwords, credit card numbers and banking details with anyone and fear from getting into wrong hands. Due to quick and frequent requirement, we keep our documents, photographs and videos on online storage. Information security is also crucial for all organizations and enterprises as they conduct business with customers and traders listed that they want to keep secret. There are eight intertwined areas of information security as mentioned here:

- **Secrecy**: Secrecy deals with the protection of information from unauthorized hands.

- **Integrity**: Integrity ensures that received information is real and accurate as it was sent, without any modification from intruders.
- **Availability**: It is concerned with the ability of users to get access of information in its original form at desired location and time.
- **Authenticity**: Authenticity refers to the assurance that message, financial transaction or communication is from the source from where it claims. Authenticity is incomplete without identity.
- **Trustworthiness**: Trustworthiness is concerned with ability of system to produce authentic and reliable information.
- **Non-repudiation**: Non-repudiation refers to the ability of system to prevent the denial of authenticity from users participating in communication.
- **Accountability**: The term accountability refers the ability of system that allocates the person who uses interconnected environment for their activities on internet.
- **Auditability**: Auditability refers systematic evaluation of entire information system, measuring how well it meets the information security established criteria.

1.9 World Wide Web Security

World Wide Web is a system having large number of high storage capacity servers scattered across the world. Each server maintains the storage of information that is uploaded from particular regions. Furthermore, information from all the servers is merged to form a whole system through which information retrieval is performed with the help of search engines and web browser. Search engines are software that help information seekers to fetch the results from World Wide Web. Normally, information seeker cannot directly interact with World Wide Web. Search engines allow seekers to pose a query and match the query terms after cleaning, with the contents of web pages available in World Wide Web. In response to query, search engines present a list containing the links to the web-pages with snippets.

Due to versatile benefits of internet, governments, militaries, research and educational institutions, financial institutions, security agencies and even individuals are publishing millions of documents every day and sharing confidential information over the web. Most of the public services like e-commerce, transportation, communication, broadcasting, medical, and so on, are totally dependent on the internet. The most important thing about the internet is its availability and utility to all. Good people use its potential for social benefits, while some other use it to earn illegal profits, political and corporate benefits, distribution of restricted contents and for personal revenge as well. People are using it as a tool to create rumours and communal violence expansion. Cyber criminals pose the following problems:

1. They create malicious code to gain unauthorized access and exploit vulnerabilities.
2. They remotely control entire system and prevent legitimate users to make its utilization.
3. Breach the confidentiality to take political, corporate and social benefits.
4. Breach the secrecy and integrity of information during data transmission.

In the view of mentioned facts, the security of internet and World Wide Web becomes important and essential to keep this infrastructure beyond the reach of cybercriminals.

1.10 Network Security

Society has changed its way for communication. Now, we are using Internet-based communication channels to connect with family members, friends or co-workers. We use instant messaging, e-mailing and phone calls to communicate and conduct meeting through video conferencing. Information and data is transmitted instantly from one place to another through network. Once the data residing on your system is accessed from outside, then it becomes part of the network. This is another area where an intruder can steal, distort and disrupt your data and you will have only limited control. Network security is an activity that does not let the intruders access the network and maintain secrecy, authentication, non-repudiation, and integrity of network. Effective network security identifies legitimate users to let them access the network and stops variety of threats and viruses from entering or spreading over network.

Computer network is based on the **Open System Interconnection (OSI)** model and its seven layers. Layers communicate through interface in a fixed order to provide communication and data transmission between sender and receiver. Protocols are rules and standard created to guide how network application and layers shall function. After crossing a layer, protocols have some fixed states and each state results certain events in a fixed timeline. Frequently, intruders manipulate and disturb these events to disrupt information and its integrity. Although all the data traffic through network is not malicious, some of its packets may cause problem. It is very essential to identify those malicious packets and exclude them from normal data traffic. The identifications and denial of such packets is performed with the help of security policies that are applied to ensure network protection. Most frequently, intruders exploit the weakness in security policies and bypass the security rules to cause damage.

To understand the communication between two parties, it is essential to know the function of each layer and their internal structure where vulnerabilities exist. The vulnerabilities and risks at each layer of OSI model are as follows:

- The top-most layer in the OSI model is the application layer that is closest to end users. This layer is responsible for checking the authenticity of users and to protect the network from illegitimate access to maintain privacy of network. Once the authenticity of user is confirmed, the application services like file transfers, e-mailing and FTP services are granted usage permissions. This layer provides the interface to end users and deals with the syntax and semantic of action. Normally, web browsers cloning and e-mailing related crimes are committed with the help of this layer.
- The presentation layers are lower to the application layer and are responsible for encryption, decryption, compression and encapsulation of information and data. It transforms data as per application requirement. The vulnerabilities at this layer attract Unicode and steganography techniques-based attacks.
- The third layer from the top is the session layer in the OSI model. It sets up and terminates the connections to start and end a conversation, exchanges and dialogues among computers and applications. Session hijacking and spoofing

are most popular crimes committed due to vulnerabilities in the session layer.

- The transport layer is the fourth layer in the OSI model that ensures complete and error-free data transfer. It is concerned with data flow, reliable delivery, error detection and retransmission of transmitted information over communication channel. This layer supports **Transmission Control Protocol** (**TCP**) and **User Datagram Protocol** (**UDP**) to deliver error-free information at designated computers. As few ports in TCP and UDP are unprotected and invite cybercriminals to exploit vulnerability to cause harm.
- Network layer services include routing, addressing and error handling in transmitting data from node to node. Congestion control and packet sequencing are also integral part of its services. It converts logical address (IP) into physical address (MAC) during transmission. It supports ICMP, IP and ARP protocols. The vulnerabilities of this layer invite attack like flooding, sniffing and snooping which enable criminals to attain logins and passwords during data transmission.
- The data link layer in the OSI reference model has responsibilities to provide reliable and efficient communication between adjacent machines. It breaks data into frames and determines their frame boundaries for the physical layer to transmit over carrier. Kai-HauYeung et. al. [18] believe that data link layer does not have much security provisions and is highly vulnerable. It consists of switches with **Spanning Tree Protocol** (**STP**) and **Dynamic Host Configuration Protocol** (**DHCP**) to perform dynamic IP assignment. Switches at this layer are responsible to provide LAN connectivity and invites the threats from within the organization itself. Most common attacks at this layer are MAC flooding or ARP poisoning.
- The lowest layer in the OSI model is a physical layer that connects to hardware means for sending and receiving bit streams on a carrier. Data is transmitted and received with the help of protocols like Fast Ethernet, RS232 and ATM on physical layers. Most of the security threats cause **Denial of Service** (**DoS**) to enterprise network at this layer, preventing legitimate users to access information and resources. This disruption is achieved by disturbing the connections and manipulating wireless signals.

1.11 Cybersecurity

With the emergence of internet, it became possible to retrieve information quickly with minimum human efforts. As far as we know, it is the only medium that can advertise business in a very short time across the globe. Exponential growth of internet also affected the global economy positively as it has faced significant rise in web-related activities in last three decades. The growth in the usage of internet and networking has empowered the individuals and posed new challenges to governments and cyberspace administration as well. Cyber security is now being considered as a major concern across the world as it is being threatened by criminals, hackers and terrorists to succeed in identity theft and financial frauds. Terrorists are using internet as a weapon to carry out their activities and stealing information from different countries. The emergence of mobile phones also added more complexities in cyber world. Moreover, complicated and malicious software damage more often computer systems and block the network as well. All these established the cyber security as global issue for development of economy and national security.

1.11.1 Importance of Cybersecurity

The word "Cyber" has been taken from the world "Cybernetic" that means by using the computer [19]. Cybernetic covers the theory of communication and control of regulatory feedback. Cybersecurity includes technologies, processes and practices used to protect networks, computer hardware, software, programs, information and data from attack, damage or unauthorized access. The Cybersecurity covers preventative strategies applied to protect information from being stolen, compromised or attacked. It requires excellence to identify the threats and other malicious code that harm confidentiality and integrity of data and information.

The term cybersecurity covers the three things:

- Cybersecurity incorporates technical and non-technical activities and measures with intention to protect computers, networks, hardware and software.
- The degree of protection achieved through technical and non-technical activities and measures.
- Research and analysis of measures implemented to improve their effectiveness and quality.

Rossouw von Solms and Johan van Niekerk [12] define cybersecurity as the collection of tools, policies, security concepts, security safeguards, guidelines, risk management approaches, actions, training, best practices, assurance and technologies that can be used to protect the cyber environment and organization and users' assets. Organization and users' assets include connected computing devices, personnel, infrastructure, applications, services, telecommunications systems, and the totality of transmitted and / or stored information in the cyber environment [12].

As the importance of data is rising, the world is facing information war on global scale. It is expected to be more dominant in succeeding years. Data theft for social, political, financial advantage leaves people in a vulnerable position. Cybersecurity is a necessary consideration for Governments, militaries, research and educational institutions, financial institutions, security agencies, and even individuals. For families and parents, safety of children and family members is important as this digital interconnected environment is growing as invisible place of crime and frauds. Instant messaging, chat rooms, e-mails and social networking sites can bring serious troubles for children and family members in terms of financial frauds, emotional blackmailing and sexual harassments. Business organizations, financial institutions and small enterprises are now dependent on internet technologies for data access, information transfer and financial transactions. However, most of them are not much aware of the hidden risks and using internet without taking appropriate safety in consideration. The invention of internet changed our lives and affected surrounding social environment. Quick adoption of the technology made mobile-banking, online shopping, online trading and social networking possible that provides us with new opportunities and adventure. Vulnerability in personal and corporate environments can render a serious problem leading to damage of reputation and financial status of organizations. Better security awareness and planning helps organizations to protect their intellectual properties and trade secrets. There is a high possibility that Governments will maintain enormous amount of information, confidential records and its citizens' data on insufficiently secured computers and servers. Better security provisions will help government bodies to provide reliable governance, maintaining citizen-to-government smooth communications and better information security.

1.11.2 Cybersecurity – An international problem

Interconnected digital technology plays a crucial role in innovation, knowledge sharing and global trade for prosperity of nations around the world. It provides us opportunity for real-time borderless exchange of ideas. Cyber criminals create barriers to our path to progress and affect millions of people around the world, as well as countless businesses, entrepreneurs and the Governments of every nation. Cybercrime has now converted into business which exceeds a trillion dollars a year in online fraud, identity theft and due to some other online illegal activities. Cybercriminals take advantages of anonymity and build their enterprises to commit cybercrimes across the globe in the absence of trust among nations and law enforcement. To make the tracking and tracing difficult, sometimes groups of criminal's trigger attack in a particular sequence and in parts from different geographical locations across the world. Geographical boundaries of nations provide security cover to cybercriminals while amorphous and borderless nature of W3 provides them countless targets. Cybercrime is the biggest growing threat to the global society. The increasing global risk of cyber-attacks, create critical situations to the national, regional and international peace and security. It requires global framework as instruments to ensure security and stability in interconnected digital infrastructure across the world [5] [10].

1.11.3 Common and shared responsibility

Cybersecurity is now a growing concern across the world, the sophistication of cyber-attacks, sensitive information leakage and monetary damage are increasing at exponential rates in last two decades. The rapid development in technologies create intermediate gap between legislative and regulatory cybersecurity framework and this gap is due to delay in the recognition of newly emerged offences and adoption of amendments to the existing legislations. Cybersecurity is a cross-border and international problem, and legislation and provisions for cybercrimes cannot be drafted in isolation. The governments of all countries must do combined efforts in same direction to draft legislation, regulations, standards and necessary guidelines for effective regional and international framework development [6].

Cybercrime is very serious problem and most dangerous criminal threat to global economy. All nations are struggling with its appalling impacts. Most of the nations developed their own strategies to address the emerging security issues and to deal with cybercrimes but these are insufficient. Its complexity and international dimensions' demand multi stakeholder approach where the role and responsibilities of all nations, security agencies and other potential partners should be well defined to protect cyberspace. The participants must have clear set of principles about how to identify, manage and mitigate risks in order to draft legislation and develop security framework.

1.11.4 Cyberspace

The term "Cyberspace" denotes the fusion of all communication, networks, various databases and different information channels in large numbers. It is interconnected global digital infrastructure that comprises of internet, telecommunications networks, computer systems, processors and various controllers in different organizations [4]. Cyberspace not only comprises internet and computers together but also it connects electronic system or devices that can be either directly or indirectly connected to internet through some other devices. These devices may include **automatic teller machines** (**ATMs**), **Supervisory control and data acquisition** (**SCADA**) systems, and other telecommunication handlers [7]. Cyberspace includes software and data on computers. Carrier medium like cables and devices such as routers, bridge, servers are also part of it.

Cyberspace for particular nation becomes the part of global cyberspace. It cannot be isolated for a nation and controlled with its geographical boundaries. It has its own atlases and sophisticated electronic mapping techniques that help to manage networks and fault detection [7]. Its anonymous and borderless nature makes it unique. Unlike, physical world that is covered inside geographical boundaries, cyberspace is continuously expanding. Rapid technology development accelerating speed of data transfer and facilitating the activities like exchange of video, pictures and fund transfer to its users.

1.11.5 Cybercrime

Cybercrime refers to unlawful act that is performed using computers and internet in interconnected digital environment. It uses cyberspace for illegal acts and exploit its unique features such as speed, immediacy, and encryption to hide illegal activities and criminals as well. Cybercrime covers a wide range of offences including crime against data and systems, internet enabled forgery and frauds, disseminating sexual and pirated content. Cybercrime still does not have globally accepted definition. American lawyers are not able to justify cybercrimes with specific legal framework used in United States [8]. Cybercrime has tripartite theory that is crimes against the computer, crimes in the computer and crime via computer [11].

1.11.6 Vicious architecture of cybercrime

Cybercrimes are being sophisticated and have more severe economic impacts than conventional crimes. Information technology and skill dependent approach with worldwide coverage makes cybercrimes structurally different than conventional crimes. In comparison to conventional crimes against persons such as physical violence, robbery, theft, forgery, and so on, cybercrimes are very skill dependent that leave impacts long lasting. In conventional crimes, there is risk for physical evidences that help police and security agencies to reach to criminals but in cybercrime there are ample opportunities that let criminals go undetected and even suspected. Cybercrimes are now being complicated and even its detection and reporting too. Most of criminals who are very skilled, are adopting it as full time profession because of financial gain and low chances of their detection. In addition, Traditional law enforcement channels still does not have any internationally accepted guidelines and legislation that can determine cybercrimes and punish the criminals.

The vicious architecture as shown in *Figure 1.1* shows how characteristics of cyber-criminals, cybercrime-victims, and law-enforcement agencies support each other. Victims do not believe in law enforcement agencies and assumed that they will not get significant assistance. They do not have adequate skills and protected infrastructure to tackle with cybercrimes that encourage cybercriminals to commit crimes. Most of the time, cybercrimes go unreported this is because of fear to losing customer trust, damage in corporate reputation and in person due to fear of societal humiliation. Banks, financial institutions, defense organization and other businesses that have sensitive data and financial information do not highlight their victim related news against cybercrime:

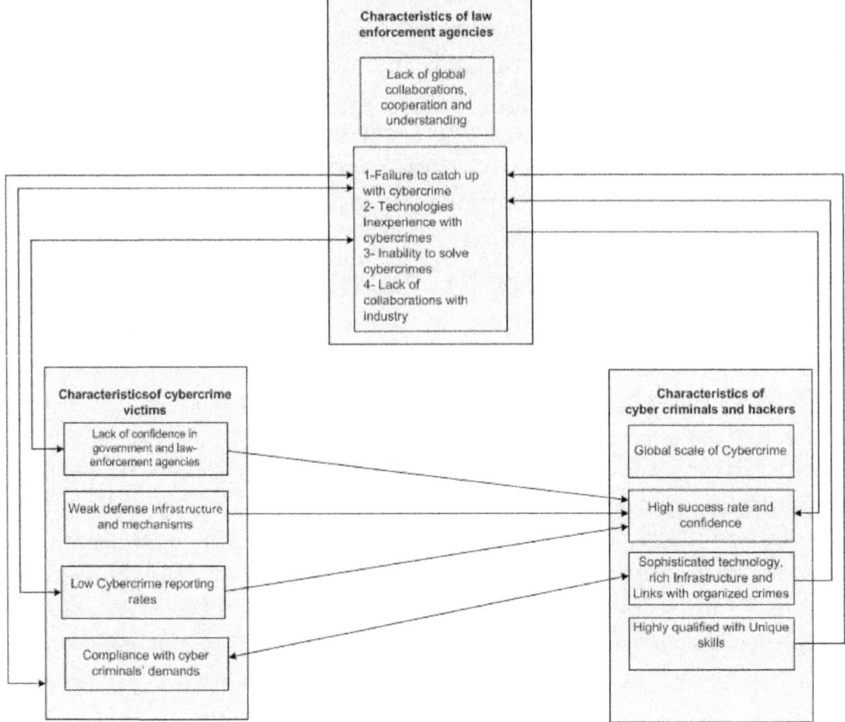

***Figure 1.1**: Vicious architecture of cybercrime*

Law-enforcement agencies such as Police forces and judiciary do not have adequate experience to deal with new forms of crimes. Police forces in most countries have their own local boundaries and legal barriers due to which they feel uncomfortable to deal with the global nature of cybercrimes. Rapid advancement in technologies and lack of inadequate response mechanism allows criminals to commit cybercrimes through use of sophisticated tools that help them to hide their identity and tamper, hinder or mislead investigations. Unfortunately, law enforcement agencies are not adopting advanced technologies as quickly as cybercriminals. Cybercrime investigations are highly complex and require rich set of resources and expertise to punish criminals. The lack of collaboration and coordination among various nations and their internal agencies also making the situations more severe.

Cybercrime is now fastest growing area of crime. Cybercriminals are using the speed, convenience and worldwide connectivity of the Internet to commit different criminal activities that know no borders, causing serious damage and posing everyday new challenges to world. The investigation and prevention of cybercrimes with international dimensions is very difficult as it requires skilled human resources and cross border cooperation. Few years back, cybercrimes were being performed by individuals or small group for their individual profits but now trends have changed, now networks of highly skilled cybercriminals selected from across the globe, are formed in real time to earn profit on unprecedented scale.

Wall defines cybercrime as transformation of criminal and harmful behavior through the use of network technology and classified cybercrime into three categories [8, 10]:

1. Crime violating integrity and working order of computer systems (Hacking).
2. Crime utilizing Cyberspace (encrypted communication among criminals and counterfeit and illegal selling of products).
3. Crime including illegal information transmission (theft of secrets, distribution of harmful contents).

1.11.7 Taxonomies of cybercrime

Cybercrime includes illegal use of cyberspace. The cyberspace features like speed, immediacy, remote operations, encryptions and obfuscation are exploited to make it difficult to identify the crime, its origin and criminals too [10]. The cybercrimes can be classified into two categories. In first category, computers are used as tools that help criminals to conduct cybercrimes while in other category computers become targets:

Access to and dissemination of contents	Malicious disruption or modification of data	Use of communications
• Secrets • Knowledge • Copyright contents • Sexual contents • Communal Rumors • Corporate information	• Identity denial • Financial statistics • EMP supply • Hardware sabotage • Account takeover • Image disruption	• Harassment • Spamming • Ransom • Business of forbidden material and information

***Table 1.1**: Cybercrimes with computers as tool*

When computers are used as tools, the following illegal activities are performed:

- Illegal access and dissemination of contents
- Malicious disruption or modification of Data
- Use of communications

The crimes under these illegal activities are mentioned in *Table 1.1.*

When computers become target for criminals the following illegal activities are performed:

1. Unauthorized access
2. Injecting malicious code
3. Disruption operation
4. Theft of services

The *Table 1.2* shows various crimes under second category of cybercrimes:

Unauthorized Access	Injecting malicious code	Disruption of operation	Theft of service
• Hacking • System hijacking • Network hijacking • IP spoofing	• Malware • Spyware • Virus • Ransomware	• DoS • DDoS	• Unauthorized use

Table 1.2: *Cybercrimes with computer as target*

1.11.8 Motivations behind cybercrimes

Cybercrimes are rising in numbers rapidly. Potential perpetrators find new opportunities to activate various forms of cyberattacks at different targets, at different scale with different motives. To reduce the number of cybercrimes, it is very essential to have an idea about the motivations behind sophisticated illegal cyber activities. Xingan Li [9] reveals various reasons due to which person commits cybercrimes. These are as following:

1. Financial gain
2. Political gain
3. To be prestigious as a goal
4. Negative Ideology
5. Taking technical Challenge
6. Curiosity of seeking new knowledge
7. Demonstration of Programming skills
8. Hacking to change academic results
9. Mobilizing political movement
10. Motivation for harassment
11. Hacking for the hacker community

12. Destroying evidence contained in information systems
13. Sexually motivated misuse
14. Psychological depression

1.11.9 Cyberattack, Threat, Vulnerability and Malware

A cyberattack refers to actions directed towards computer systems, networks and digital infrastructure to disrupt equipment operations, change processing, gaining unauthorized access and corrupting stored data. It is computer-to-computer and computer-to-network attack that breaches confidentiality, integrity and availability of a computers and disrupting information passing through them. Criminals trigger cyber-attack to have social, political and financial gain.

In cybersecurity, threat refers to a malicious code, agent or activity that has potential to cause serious harm to software installed on computers, network and its hardware too. Security experts' categories threats in two groups structured and unstructured. Structured threat becomes complicated and well supported with sophisticated tools. These are created under the sponsorship of nation having extensive funding and intelligence support to cause harm in digital infrastructure and disrupt services of enemy countries. In case of structured threats, tracking and tracing culprits requires adroitness and patience. The unstructured threat, on the other hand, is implemented to get hidden access to network with short term goals such as information theft, espionage, and Sabotage. These threats are created by individuals or small groups of people having limited funds and skills to irritate someone.

Vulnerability refers to flaws in computers, in networks and in digital infrastructure that causes risks and invites criminals to conduct crimes. Malicious users seek out ways through these vulnerabilities to have unauthorized control over computers and other networked devices. Interconnected digital environment contains two basic components; hardware and software, both may have design and operational problems. Sometimes, corrupted hardware and faulty software work well and meet users' requirements, but invite criminals at the same time through their vulnerabilities. It is very difficult to identify and fix hardware vulnerabilities in comparison to software vulnerabilities. Hardware vulnerabilities identification requires compatibility and interoperability testing before coupling the modules.

Malware is the combination of two words malicious and software. It is software or programming code that is inserted to a system to create vulnerability through which the system is controlled remotely. It can damage hardware, disrupt the stored data and deny access to legitimate users. Once malware resides in system, it conceals its presence and disables security measures to create a bridge between system and intruder. All the happening occurs without its owner permission and awareness [13]. Intruder access the information stored on remote system whenever required, encrypt it for its actual users to ransom money.

1.11.10 Cyberterrorism

Cyberterrorism is unlawful and violent activity that uses internet technology to damage critical infrastructure of a nation. Critical infrastructure includes essential services that government provides to its citizens and major public sector modules such as energy, transportation, education, health, banking, finance, and defence. Cyberterrorism is politically motivated act, more often having religious and ideological thoughts in its centre to cause enormous damage. Terrorist coax a large portion of population and impose the ideology on them to make them violent. They penetrate critical infrastructure to seize the government services. However, there is no globally accepted definition of cyberterrorism we found till date but Denning [15] define cyber terrorism as follows [14][15][16] [17]:

"Cyberterrorism is the convergence of terrorism and cyberspace. It is generally understood to mean unlawful attacks and threats of attack against computers, networks, and the information stored therein when done to intimidate or coerce a government or its people in furtherance of political or social objectives. Further, to qualify as cyberterrorism, an attack should result in violence against persons or property, or at least cause enough harm to generate fear. Attacks that lead to death or bodily injury, explosions, plane crashes, water contamination, or severe economic loss would be examples. Serious attacks against critical infrastructures could be acts of cyberterrorism, depending on their impact. Attacks that disrupt nonessential services or that are mainly a costly nuisance would not."

Cyberterrorism is the activity based on dependability of nations and its critical infrastructure over internet and communication technologies. Highly skilled terrorists know its potential and trigger cyberattack electronically to break into computers and network to control public sector modules such as energy, transportation, education, and health. It also interrupts essential services such as electricity supply, drinking water supply, cooking gas supply, fuel supply, and dams controlling. In this way, cyberterrorism puts national security in danger with millions of lives too.

There are several reasons due to which terrorists attract towards Cyberterrorism. These reasons are mentioned as follows:

1. It is cheaper than traditional terrorist's activities and does not require weapons and explosive materials.
2. It is safe as terrorists do not need to come face to face. They trigger the attack by hiding themselves behind a digital shield of anonymity.
3. Tracking and tracing is difficult in such huge digital interconnected environment.
4. Distance between terrorists and target is treated as almost negligible.
5. Removal of political, social and cultural barrier.
6. Number of targets and their varieties are enormous.
7. Terrorists do not need to go battle field instead they launch attack from their suitable and desired place.
8. Cyberterrorism leaves massive impacts than traditional activities.

1.12 Information security to cybersecurity

The term cybersecurity and information security is frequently used interchangeably, but there is significant difference between these two terms. Cybersecurity definition goes beyond the boundaries of information security and includes communication technologies with cyberspace utilities. Information security deals with the preservation of the confidentiality, integrity and availability of information, most importantly when it is not available on communication channels and accessible from W3 resources. *Figure 1.2* shows how information security converts in Cybersecurity in presence network devices and World Wide Web:

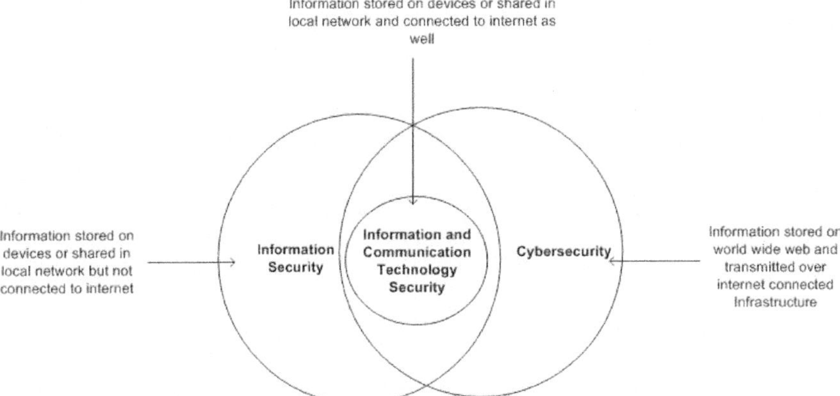

Figure 1.2: *Information security to cybersecurity conversion*

When information from computers is transmitted over communication channels and passing some other devices such as routers and switches, but not accessible through cyberspace, then it is termed as network security [12]. The term cybersecurity includes information security and network security, and adds few more dimensions such as security of common household appliances, interest of society, and critical national infrastructure. Cybersecurity is required to be seen as an extension of information security as well as network security. It is all about securing things that are vulnerable through the use of information and communication technologies. Information security deals only with the security of intangible assets while cybersecurity protects intangible and tangible both types of assets [12].

Cybersecurity is a complex problem, and rapid advancement in technologies and addition of new unskilled internet users are making the situations severe. We are still far away from permanent and effective solutions that can protect our information, network and assets. Cybersecurity incorporates a set of tools, technologies, risk management techniques, training and best practices that help to protect networks, communication devices, operating systems and data from malicious attacks and unauthorized access. When information resides to computers without having internet connections, then it is more secure and having less chances to breach but as soon as it passes through different communication channels and devices it requires more security measures and safeguards. In other words, information security requires comparatively less protection than the protection required in network security.

1.13 Role of risk analysis in cybersecurity

The role of risk analysis is to identify potential issues that can negatively impact security initiatives in an interconnected digital environment before their occurrence. It is the preparation to mitigate adverse impacts of threats and vulnerabilities in network and web environment.

A cyber security risk assessment process initially determines the assets that can be affected, thereafter risks that leave adverse impacts are identified. The organizations conducting the risk analysis seeks relative significance and interactions among various components: threats, vulnerabilities, assets, value, protection, and safeguards as shown in *Figure 1.3*:

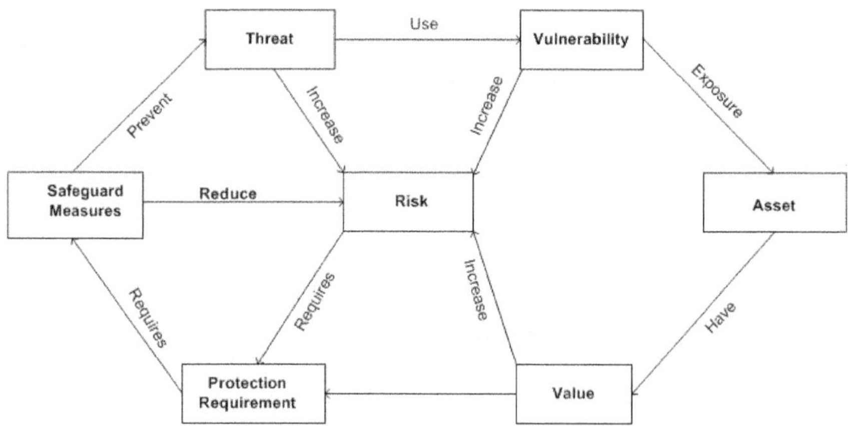

***Figure 1.3**: Risk analysis process*

Risk analysis is a continuous, multidimensional and forward-looking process that helps to predict the possible security threats and estimates related cost to have an idea about the security of digital infrastructure. Risk management has three stages: survey of possible risks, identifying, and analyzing existing risks with their associated cost and presenting remedies to identified risks in order to mitigate the adverse impacts on interest of society and critical national infrastructure. As security measures cannot assure full protection against all threats and vulnerabilities, the risk analysis endeavour probable consequences and suggest effective countermeasures that reduce the effects of risk up to acceptable level. The functions of Risk analysis include:

1. To set desired level standards that are required to protect information and interconnected digital infrastructure.
2. To identify the areas, weak zones, and assets that require protection.
3. To identify relevant threats with their functioning, in order to know its long durable adverse impacts on information and infrastructure.
4. Ensuring continuous and repeated risk assessments to produce consistent, valid and comparable results.
5. Estimating the loss and cost of business that is on risk due to vulnerabilities and threats.

Conclusion

In this introductory chapter, you have learnt about the basic concepts of data, information and data communication system. You have not only learnt about the basics of internet, networking and World Wide Web, but also about their relationships, characteristics and security aspects. The chapter details how intruders use the interconnected technology and its global reach property to generate multi-billion profits and to hide themselves behind the digital shield of anonymity. This chapter revels how landscape of security in computing is drastically changing. Initially, it was security about standalone system; thereafter, it has changed to information security and network security, and now merged and converted in cybersecurity.

In the second chapter, we shall know the historical development of cybercrimes and analyze its total costs. Thereafter, we shall focus on various forms of cybercrimes and describe major challenges in the field of cybersecurity.

Points to remember

- Data refers to the facts and statistics collected together for analysis. It includes numbers, letters, characters, symbols and multimedia objects. Data can be transmitted in the form of electrical signals and stored on magnetic and optical media.

- Information is facts about someone or something. It is processed, organized, and structured data in some context that becomes useful to humans.
- Information has following characteristics:
    - Accuracy
    - Completeness
    - Consistency
    - Uniqueness
    - Timeliness
- Data Communication refers to exchange of information between two computers or more than two computers with the help of some communication medium.
- Data communication model have the following five components:
    - Source
    - Message
    - Transmission Medium
    - Destination
    - Protocol
- Data Communication System has following characteristics:
    - Interface
    - Delivery
    - Accuracy
    - Synchronization
    - Error Detection and Correction
    - Flow Control
    - Security
- Two or more than two systems are said to be in network if they are connected through either guided media or unguided media and are able to exchange the data among themselves.
- Internet is worldwide network comprising many small networks with the ability to fetch and store data in World Wide Web.

- World Wide Web Consortium, popularly known as W3C was formed in 1994. It is an international community that sets rules, regulations, and standards to ensure long-term growth of the Web.
- Eight intertwined areas of information security are secrecy, integrity, availability, authenticity, trustworthiness, non-repudiation, accountability, and auditability.
- Cybersecurity is collection of tools, policies, security concepts, security safeguards, guidelines, risk management approaches, actions, training, best practices, assurance, and technologies that can be used to protect the cyber environment and organization and users' assets.
- World Wide Web facilitates the following:
    - Universal access
    - Trust Development
    - Interoperability
    - Evolvability
    - Decentralization
- Cyberspace denotes the fusion of all communication, networks, various databases and different information channels in huge. It is amorphous, borderless and virtual in nature.
- Cybercrime refers to unlawful act that is performed using computers and internet in interconnected digital environment.
- Cybercrime has tripartite theory that is crimes against the computer, crimes in computer and crime via computer.
- A cyberattack refers to actions directed towards computer systems, networks and digital infrastructure to disrupt equipment operations, change processing, gaining un-authorized access and corrupting stored data.
- A threat refers to a malicious code, agent or activity that has potential to cause serious harm to software installed on computers, network and its hardware.
- Vulnerability refers to flaws in computers, in networks and in digital infrastructure as well that leave those in risk.

- Cyberterrorism is unlawful and violent activity that uses internet technology to damage critical infrastructure of a nation.
- Critical infrastructure includes essential services that government provides to its citizens and major public sector modules such as energy, transportation, education, health, banking, finance and defence.

MCQ

1. **Information is:**
   a. Raw facts
   b. Unprocessed Data
   c. Processed Data
   d. Statistics
2. **Data is:**
   a. Information
   b. Input to form information
   c. Knowledge
   d. Meaningful Statistics
3. **Cyberspace:**
   a. Is amorphous in nature
   b. Has fixed boundaries
   c. Used for Cybercrime only
   d. Is owned by U.S.A
4. **Function of W3C includes:**
   a. Forms legislations
   b. Sets rules, regulations and Standards for web
   c. Ensures Network Security
   d. Protection from Cybercrime

5. **STP stands for:**
    a. Secure Transmission Protocol
    b. Secure Transmission Path
    c. Spanning Tree Protocol
    d. Simple Transmission Protocol
6. **DHCP stands for:**
    a. Definite Host Communication Protocol
    b. Dual Host Common Protocol
    c. Distinct Hosts Configuration Protocol
    d. Dynamic Host Configuration Protocol
7. **Which layer of OSI model determines the frame boundary of packets:**
    a. Physical layer
    b. Data link layer
    c. Presentation layer
    d. Application layer
8. **Web browsers cloning occurs on:**
    a. Transport layer
    b. Datalink layer
    c. Network layer
    d. Application layer

Answer

1. c
2. b
3. a
4. b
5. c
6. d
7. b
8. d

Questions

1. Explain the following:
   I. Data and Information
   II. LAN, MAN, WAN
   III. Internet, Networking, and World Wide Web
   IV. Information Security, Network security, and Cybersecurity.
   V. Cybercrime, Cybercriminal, and Cyberspace
2. Define World Wide Web consortium and its functions in detail.
3. Explain the major characteristics of data communication System.
4. Define information security and its intertwined areas.
5. Cybersecurity is an international problem. Explain.
6. Cybersecurity is common and shared responsibility. Explain.
7. Differentiate the following:
   I. Network Security Versus Cybersecurity
   II. Cyberspace Versus World Wide Web
   III. Vulnerability Versus Threat
   IV. Internet Versus Networking
8. Explain Vicious Architecture of Cybercrime in detail.
9. What do you mean by risk analysis in cybersecurity? Explain.

References

[1] **https://www.merriam-webster.com/dictionary/data**

[2] **http://repository.up.ac.za/bitstream/handle/2263/27367/03chapter3.pdf**

[3] **http://www.differencebetween.info/difference-between-data-and-information**

[4] A Comparative Analysis of Cyber Security Initiatives Worldwide, WSIS Thematic Meeting on Cyber security, International Telecommunication Union, Geneva, July 2005.

[5]A Report by Kamlesh Bajaj, *"The Cybersecurity Agenda"*, Mobilizing for International Action, East west Institute, 2010.

[6] Rajesh kumarGoutam, *"Challenges in Cyber Security"*, Bilingual International Conference on Information Technology: Yesterday, Today, and Tomorrow, 19-21 February 2015, PP. 108-113.

[7] Eric A. Fischer, *"Creating a National Framework for Cybersecurity: An Analysis of Issues and Options"*, CRS Report for Congress, Received through the CRS Web, February 22, 2005.

[8] Susan W. Brenner, *"At Light Speed: Attribution and Response to Cybercrime/Terrorism/Warfare"*, Journal of Criminal Law and Criminology, volume 97, issue 2, 2007.

[9] Xingan Li, *"A Review of Motivations of Illegal Cyber Activities"*, Criminology & Social Integration Journal Vol. 25 No. 1, 2017.

[10] LiorTabansky, *"Cybercrime: A National Security Issue?"*,military and strategic affairs, vol.4 No.3, December 2012.

[11] Stefan Fafinski, William H. Dutton and Helen Margetts, *"Mapping and Measuring Cybercrime"*, OII Forum Discussion Paper No 18, Oxford Internet Institute, University of Oxford, June 2010.

[12] Rossouw von Solms and Johan van Niekerk, *"From information security to cyber security"*, computers & security (38), ELSEVIER, School of ICT, Nelson Mandela Metropolitan University, Port Elizabeth 6031, South Africa, 2013, pp.97-102.

[13] A Report, *"Malicious software (Malware): A security threat to Internet economy"*, OECD ministrial meeting, Seoul, korea, 2008.

[14] Gabriel Weimann, *"Cyberterrorism: The Sum of All Fears?"*, Studies in Conflict & Terrorism, 28:129–149, 2005.

[15] Denning, D., *"Cyberterrorism"*, Testimony before the Special Oversight Panel of Terrorism Committee on Armed Services, US House of Representatives, 23 May 2000. (**http://www.cs.georgetown.edu/~denning/infosec/cyberter ror.html**)

[16] Sarah Gordon, "*Cyberterrorism*", White paper, Symantec Security Response. available at: **https://www.symantec.com/avcenter/reference/cyberterrorism.pdf**

[17] Gabriel Weimann, "*Cyberterrorism How Real Is the Threat?*", UNITED STATES INSTITUTE OF PEACE, 119, December 2004.

[18] Kai-Hau Yeung, Dereck Fung, and Kin-Yeung Wong, "*Tools for Attacking Layer 2 Network Infrastructure*", Proceedings of the International MultiConference of Engineers and Computer Scientists 2008 Vol II IMECS 2008, 19-21 March, 2008, Hong Kong.

[19] William Gibson, "*Neuromancer*", Ace Science Fiction Books, 1984 available at: **http://index-of.es/Varios-2/Neuromancer.pdf**

CHAPTER 2
Cybersecurity Landscape and Its Challenges

The scale, speed and sophistication of worldwide cybercrimes have tremendously increased in the past two decades. Criminals and computer professionals come together and conduct organized cybercrime as business to earn maximum profits with minimum risks. People are using internet and cyberspace without knowing the hidden risks and unknowingly helping criminals to succeed. All criminals are not computer professionals, but desire to participate in cybercrimes, underground black cyber market helps them and provides variety of malicious tools, hired skills and technologies. The products from underground black market, allow a common man to launch criminal activities and help to increase the landscape of cybercrimes worldwide. This chapter presents an overview of the historical development of cybercrimes and its consequences such as increased financial and legal liabilities as well as recovery costs. Further, the various forms of cybercrimes are described due to which world economy is at risk.

Structure

In this chapter, we will cover the following topics:

- History of computers and cybercrime
- Cybercrime –As a profession
- Cost of cybercrime
- Various forms of cybercrimes
- Challenges in cybersecurity
- Cybercrime underground black market

Objective

The objective of this chapter is to introduce you to various phases of internet development and to detail out how criminals started using internet technologies to launch their malicious activities. After reading this chapter, you shall understand the cost of cybercrimes and knowthe framework used to analyse it. You shall know major challenges due to which cybercrimes are uncontrollable and being opted as a popular medium to generate illicit profit. Knowing cybercrime underground black market would be interesting as it presents its structure, details its participants, and describes its popular products and services with the price ranges.

2.1 History of computers and cybercrime

A cybercrime is a malicious activity that is conducted with the help of internet and telecommunications channels. It differs from conventional crime in a variety of ways such as it is easy to commit remotely and requiring minimum resources for potential damage. Most importantly, it can be performed across the globe without being physically present in the concerned jurisdiction. Computers, networking, internet, and **World Wide Web**(**W3**) were invented to facilitate creation, storage and rapid transfer of government, corporate and personal confidential information to the right people. The digital era and development of electronic communication channels constitute a wonderful medium for knowledge transfer and benefits to researchers, scientists, businessman, academician, and students. Unfortunately, all these facilities are available for criminals too.

In 1642, famous mathematician Blaise Pascal constructed first non-electronic and mechanical machine that facilitated addition and subtraction of numbers to its users. This machine was able to perform multiplication and division too, but only through repeated addition and subtraction operations. In 1813, another English mathematician named Charles Babbage designed a mechanical calculator that was capable of performing calculations up to 20 decimal capacities. In 1833, he chalked out design for analytical engines to perform mathematical calculations, but after two phases of working, it was still incomplete [1]. In 1801, Joseph-Marie Jacquard, a French textile weaver and merchant, produced a machine where punched cards were used to form an endless loop for repeating pattern in the carpet textile design. This machine was capable to make repetition of waving steps up to desired number of times. The invention of this machine created fear amongst employees as they were worried about their job security. Thereafter, this repetition of events became the baseline in computer programming. The invention of this machine is known as first recorded cybercrime in its history as it negatively affected public interest indirectly. In the middle of 1880s, Herman Hollerith played a crucial role in computer development and introduced mechanical and electrical data processing systems for census in USA. He continued the experiments and invented the first automatic card-feed mechanism and keypunch machine around 1896. In 1911, Herman Hollerith and four others jointly formed Computing-Tabulating Recording Company and later it was renamed as International Business Machines Corporation, which is popularly known as IBM.

In February 1946, at Moore School of Electronics, University of Pennsylvania, the first electronic and digital computer was launched in which the electronic computing concept was introduced. This electronic machine is popularly known as **Electronic Numerical Integrator and Computer** (**ENIAC**) in the history of computers and the persons who invented such a masterpiece product were J. Presper Eckert and John W. Mauchly [2]. Thereafter, they worked with the proposal of the US government and developed a more modified version popularly known as **Universal Automatic Computer** (**UNIVAC**) and delivered it to government in 1950. This is now remembered as first commercially marketed computer that had the ability to process many types of information economically with rapid speed. Universal automatic computers were applicable to advanced mathematics and also to routine office work. These computers were capable of processing numerical and alphabetical information and to store the results automatically in its memory.

In 1960, commercial computers like **Programmed Data Processor (PDP-1)** were developed. However, due to the heavy size, expensive pricing, and shortage, their installation was difficult and as a result these were being used in time-sharing basis allowing authorized and unauthorized users to work on same computers. Thus, data and programs created by authorized users were vulnerable and accessible to disruption from unauthorized users. This was a dangerous situation. Thus began computer related crimes. In 1970s, computers were being adopted across the globe, especially in the communication infrastructure. A group of curious people from **Massachusetts Institute of Technology** (**MIT**) wanted to interrupt telephone lines to get advantage of free phone calls. Stewart Nelson from MIT succeeded to breach the communication channels with its own program to make free calls and this unauthorized act to access telecommunication system to connect someone without making payment became popular as **Phreaking** in computer's history. As aconsequence, the USA government declared intrusion into the telecommunication system as a punishable offence.

In 1957, President of United States of America Dwight Eisenhower was interested to develop a communication infrastructure using new technology for quick interaction and approved **Advanced Research Projects Agency** (**ARPA**) for conducting research in this direction. J.C.R Licklider was appointed the first head of the computer research program. He convinced his successors Ivan Sutherland, Bob Taylor, and MIT researcher Lawrence G. Roberts about the networking concepts [3]. In 1961, Leonard Kleinrock at MIT published a paper on packet switching theory, which became baseline for data transmission in the form of packets. Another problem was still persisting:how will a group of computers be connected to each other for communication. In 1965, Roberts resolved this problem and connected TX-2 computer with Q-32 computer in California with a dial-up connection [3]. In 1969, US Defence Department and ARPA-Net came together and installed two nodes for the communication purpose. The first node was configured at University of California, Los Angeles, while another was installed at Stanford Research Institute, University of Utah, to communicate with each other. On October 29, 1969, at 10:30 PM, the node configured at University of California sent a message to the node at Stanford Research Institute [4]. In October 1972, Robert E. Kahn successfully represented ARPANET at the **International**

Computer Communication Conference (ICCC). This was the first demonstration in public domain about networked technology [3].

In 1970s, the Altair 8800 computer was launched in the market, which was available for individuals at an affordable price. Now, the platform was ready to breach computers with programming skills. If we observe the early attacks with computers, we shall find that these were not for financial gain instead for fun or to irritate someone. The standalone systems were more secure because to get access or for file sharing, a user was required to login to that system. It was networking that enabled attackers to get unauthorized access remotely to someone else computer without permission. Robert Tappan Morris, a student at Cornell, created the first worm and unleashed it on the internet [5]. The worm replicated itself across the network, clogging the memory of infected computers. In this incident, several thousands of computers on which research contents were stored got adversely affected, but interestingly, Morris realized his mistake and halted the worm with minimal efforts.

2.2 Cybercrime – As a profession

Cybercrimes are growing in sophistication and frequency each day, putting billions of dollars, reputations and data at risk. People, especially youngsters, are adopting cybercrimes as a profession because it is now being developed as the easiest way to make huge amount of money in very short span of time illegally and chances to be caught are very less. Cybercrimes have now been converted into big economies, consisting of people with a varieties of skill sets working together to have financial and political advantages. Professionals and many different individuals are joining hands together to run sophisticated operations to compromise people'scomputers and to launch attacks.

Cybercrimes are now being committed by gangs from different geographical areas with the same objectives. The most organized criminal groups are operating cybercrimes as legal businesses with the help of teamwork to achieve common objectives. The participant criminals undergo proper training and get guidance from related professionals to sharpen their skills. Sophisticated cybercrime groups pose as legitimate organizations as these are operated across the globe with networks of partners, franchise, distributors and associates to gain maximum profit. Cybercriminal groups share tools, software, technologies and coordinate their actions to achieve common interest such as phishing campaign, stealing and cloning card data, and so on, cybercrime organizations are leasing out or franchising their malicious software, tools, and infrastructure as a service to its partners to capture large share of the hacking market. The partners work with well-framed terms and conditions and take these malicious services to different places to generate maximum profit.

2.3 Cost of cybercrime

Cybercrime is the area where risk-to-payoff ratio is leading [21]. A criminal can make millions of dollars within a minute with minimum probability to get arrested. Tracing the criminals across the web and holding them responsible for a malicious activity is a difficult task. Due to favourable environment for criminals, malicious activities are increasing on a much broader scale resulting in the increase of cybercrime costs.

Steve Morgan [20] describes cost of cybercrime as follows:

"Cybercrime costs include damage and destruction of data, stolen money, lost productivity, theft of intellectual property, theft of personal and financial data, embezzlement, fraud, post-attack disruption to the normal course of business, forensic investigation, restoration and deletion of hacked data and systems, and reputational harm."

Cybercrime costs can be categorised into four parts named anticipation cost, consequence cost, response cost, and indirect costs [22][23]:

- **Anticipation cost**: This cost refers to an expenditure on defensive measures taken for the protection from cybercrimes. The expenditure on antivirus software is an example of anticipation costs.
- **Consequence cost**: This cost refers to total damage cost, occurs immediately as a result of cybercrime. Property damage and money lost falls under this category.
- **Response cost**: Costs used to generate appropriate response after the occurrence of cybercrime is referred as response costs. The expenditure on investigation agencies, police forces, and judiciary is the example of response costs.

- **Indirect cost**: This cost includes reputational damage to organisations and firms, loss of confidence in online transactions by individuals and businesses, reduced revenues, and the growth of the underground black market economy.

2.4 Framework for analysing the cybercosts

The total cost of cybercrimes defines the severity of cybercrimes. The crime cost includes the damage it does to organizations and to national economies. The data about theft of intellectual properties, financial assets frauds, sensitive business information disclosure and securing network costs requires proper estimation in order to have prediction of budgets needs to be allocated to minimize the risks due to cybercrimes [25]. Ross Anderson et al. [23] [24] developed framework shown in *Figure 2.1* for the estimation of total cybercrime costs:

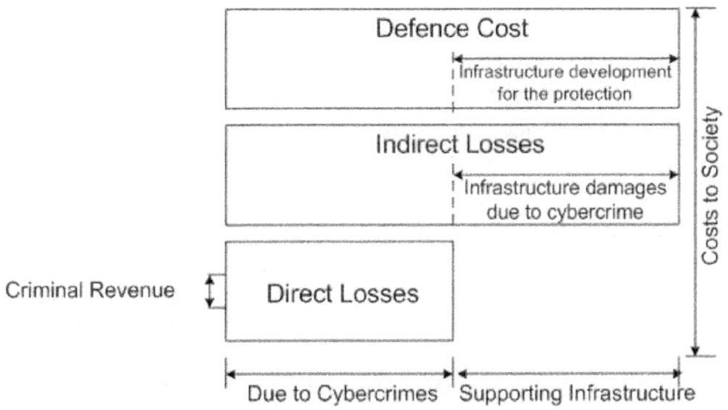

***Figure 2.1**: Framework for analysing the cybercosts*

In the framework, the cost categories can be summarized as follows:

- **Criminal revenue**: Criminal revenue refers to gross receipts from crime in monetary equivalent. The criminals' *lawful* expenditures are excluded to have an accurate measurement of revenue [23].
- **Direct losses**: These refer to the value of losses, destructions and damages due to cybercrime. Following are some examples of direct losses:
    - o Illegal withdrawn of money from victim's accounts.

- Time and efforts required to regain account details and credentials.
- Victims' distress.
- Secondary costs such as inability to have money when it was needed.

- **Indirect losses**: It refers to the value of the losses and opportunity costs imposed on society because of malicious activities. Indirect cost does not belong to individual victims instead a group of people or organisations are affected to bear costs. Suppose a bank lost reputation from online banking due to a malicious attack, the bank may experience reduced revenues from online transactions and shall bear overhead costs to manage human resources and facilitating cheques clearings. More funds will be required to replace damaged digital infrastructure and devices with new ones [23] [24].
- **Defence costs**: Defence cost refers to monetary equivalent of prevention efforts. It includes direct defence cost such as cost of creation, deployment and maintenance of prevention measures. Indirect defence cost includes inconvenience and opportunity costs that occur due to security measures [23] [24].

  Defence costs comprise the following:

  - Expenditure on security products such as spam filters, antivirus and firewalls
  - Expenditure on security services such as training and awareness program to individuals and employees
  - Crime detection, tracking and tracing costs
  - Monetary equivalent to law enforcement
- **Costs to society**: The totality of direct losses, indirect losses, and defence costs is known as costs to society.

2.5 Various forms of cybercrimes

Cybercrime denotes criminal activity, including Internet, computers or any other inter-connected infrastructure. This term also covers crimes such as phishing, credit card frauds, illegal downloading, industrial espionage, child pornography, scams, cyber terrorism, creation and/or distribution of viruses, spam, and so on.

2.5.1 Cyber stalking

Cyber stalking is basically a technology-aided stalking in which assailants harass the people with Internet technologies such as e-mails, social media account, instant messaging, chat rooms, and much more. It is an act of threatening people to cause distress, anxiety and fear [7]. It is repetitive behavior of criminal in which he writes abusive comments about someone publicly on the Internet to make a person feel scared and insecure. Cyber stalkers intrude into the personal life of victim and harass him psychologically that is why it is also known as **psychological rape** or **psychological terrorism** [7]. Criminals pursue and follow the victim on internet and start to campaigns of denigration against him by spreading false accusations, gossip and sexual contents.

Cyberstalking covers:

- Sending unwanted, frightening, or obscene emails, messages, or videos
- Harassing or threatening someone with abusive words on social media
- Tracking and tracing someone's activities on internet
- Tracking locations through the use of GPS technology
- Creating fake accounts on social networking and dating sites with someone else's photo, identity, and address, and making contacts on the behalf of victims

Cyber-stalkers usually suffer from anxiety, depression, stress or another addiction, most frequently becomes isolated from society and feel uncomfortable in their friend circle. Due to lack of social support and partner's ignorance, they spend most of their time with internet and peer to others' life with their daily online activities. More often, they use Social media platforms such as Facebook, Twitter, and even Instagram to perform the act and uploading fake or real offensive images of the victim or their loved ones. It is interesting that cyber-stalkers are not usually strangers to victims instead these are acquaintances such asex-partner, friends, fellow students, colleagues, and relatives [26]. Studies demonstrate that women are frequently victimized and share around 80.5% cases of cyber stalking while men are dominating as perpetrators [7, 19].

Gisela Wurm [30] described the various categories of stalkers as given follows:

- **Rejected stalker**: A person who starts stalking after the breakdown of close relationship is known as **Rejected stalker**. These stalkers desire for reconciliation and revenge with partner.
- **Intimacy seeking stalker**: A stalker who desires a relationship due to loneliness in life is called **Intimacy seeking stalker**. These stalkers reciprocate one-sided love and affection towards strangers. The single objective behind this kind of stalking is to establish an emotional connection with someone [31].
- **Incompetent suitor**: The stalkers of this category desire a non-emotional relationship either for a date or to meet sexual needs.
- **Resentful stalker**: These are mistreated people and victim of injustice and humiliation. This type of stalking emerges out due to the desire of revenge from a person they assume as culprit.
- **Predatory stalker**: Predatory stalkers are usually male stalkers that pursue females over internet for sexual gratification.

2.5.2 Intellectual property theft

The intellectual property refers to unique intangible human creation such as innovation, literature, art, model, symbol, scientific formula, logo and image with its commercial value. The protection of intellectual property requires owning to its true creator that legally enables its owner to use them to earn money for his hard work. With intellectual property rights, a person is rewarded for his time and efforts he/she put into the innovation and unique creation. These rights prevent the replication and theft of unique creation by potential competitors.

There are various types of intellectual property theft as described here:

- **Copyright theft**: To motivate the creators and innovators copyright protection is important because it ensures the royalty payments for their creative pieces. Copyright laws protect the rights of creative workers and helps creators to get handsomely paid for their art. Basically, it is a legal protection that is granted to creators for their authorship and prevents others from copying originality. Copyright laws protect books, software, literature, music, paintings, electronic games, movies, and so on:

Copyrights laws permit creators to:

- o To generate desired number of copies of their piece of work
- o It allows modification and extensions to their original work
- o It allows copyright owners to sale, rental, lease, lending, or ownership transfer
- o It allows presentation of copyrighted work publicly

- **Trademark theft**: A trademark refers to a unique symbol, logo, word and quote that belong to a company or its product. Trademark theft is said to be occur if a registered trademark is used by a person who is neither registered owner nor have license for distribution of concerned product. Trademark and company name are frequently used as synonymous of each other that removes the confusion in choosing original product from several reconcilable products available in the market. Once a company registers its trademark, then it owns right to legally protect itself if someone else makes attempt to use something similar enough to deviate customers.
- **Trade secret theft**: Trade secret is a broad term that covers more than manufacturing, industrial and commercial secrets. It also encompasses sales procedure, distribution procedure, advertising and list of suppliers, partners and clients too. If someone else uses such information without its owner consent, then it is regarded as an unfair practice and comes under the violation of trade policy.

2.5.3 Salami attack

Computations are sometimes rounded off to get converted in round figure and this is the factor due to which salami attacks succeed. Criminals steal insignificant amount of money from millions of accounts and sum up these tiny amounts to convert in huge robbery. The bank account holders become the victims of this attack, but amazingly neither they notice these deductions nor report it to banks. Suppose a criminal creates a software that deducts Rs. 0.01 from each account and transfers it to criminal's bank account, the customers do not notice such tiny deductions and collectively transfer a huge amount of money to criminals.

2.5.4 e-Mailbombing

It refers to sending large volumes of unsolicited e-mails to a targeted account with intention to fill up the recipient's inbox on the mail server. The uncontrollable deluge of e-mails presents a pandemic situation and makes a person unable to find relevant e-mails in his account. e-mail bombing is commonly carried out with *zombie* or *bot* computers and results consumption of resources, loss of network bandwidth, and system crash [8][9]. The e-mail bombing, which is also known as e-mail flooding, targets the hosts, which are engaged to run commercial website and handles corporate business e-mail account.

2.5.5 Phishing

Cyber criminals always look for information with economic value and *Phishing* is indispensable malicious activity for perpetrators to capture personal and financial information. Phishing refers to a fraudulent attempt to steal sensitive data and useful information such as banking details, login credentials, financial data, and corporate information through e-mails. These attacks begin with an e-mail that seems to come from a trustworthy source and entice victim to take an immediate action like clicking on an incorporated malicious link, opening an attachment, responding with a message, and downloading a file. The phishing succumbed organizations sustain severe financial losses, market share downfall and customer trust.

2.5.6 Identity theft

It is the most common type of crime in which a victim of identity theft does not have idea about the crime against him until he receives a notice or informed by an agency. Identity theft occurs when a criminal illegally uses identity of someone else and commits crime with his name [10]. The personal identity includes name, address, social security number, birth certificate, death certificate, debit and credit cards, bank account number, driving licence number and passport too [11]. Criminals use these stolen identities to commit frauds such as opening new accounts, taking apartment on rents, applying for loans, owning passport, and for other benefits government provides to its citizen's time-to-time.

2.5.7 Spoofing

Spoofing refers to technique in which criminal acquires a networked computer with its IP and impersonates as it by replacing its originals services and communications with its own. The criminal pretends to be a genuine person to communicate with others to know secrets, to accessing other systems, to stealing data, and much more. With spoofing, criminal deceives systems, individuals, and organizations and impersonates itself as a legitimate user to participate in communications. David A. Wheeler et al.[8] detail some methods, which are applied by the criminals to acquire someone else's place in the interconnected digital environment and commit the cybercrimes as a legitimate party.

Normal internet users do not care for source of information. The information they want to get is the primary concerned regardless of how they are retrieving the information or getting services. The cybercriminals often make changes in sender's identity or forge sender's identities and communicates with users as authentic source or service provider called **Spoofing** [5,6,8]. In other words, Spoofing is fraudulent and malicious practice through which one communicating party is masked and its activities such as responding and acknowledging are performed by cybercriminals to show other party that communication is in progress with known and trusted source.

2.5.8 Worms, Trojan Horses, Virus

Virus is created and used to create and exploit vulnerabilities in computers in order to have unauthorized control and illegal access remotely. These are the malicious programs spread across the computers and networks and cause potential damages from corrupting software to ruining stored data. Computer virus spreads itself through removable media, downloads and attachments with e-mails and creates multiple copies of itself in the targeted system without the user's knowledge. Virus is required to be executed at least once to create its multiple copies and attaches itself with system files to initiate the replication process. A worm is capable of replicating itself and does not require human efforts to cause damages. It sends multiple copies of its own computer-to-computer and does not attach itself with system files. Trojan Horse is malicious code but looks as legitimate [12]. It does not replicate itself and spreads across the network with human efforts such as opening e-mail, downloading a file and installing software. Indeed, virus, worm and Trojan Horse follow different approaches in their replication but work for common objectives. These common objectives are as follows:

- Generating irritating messages and popping up windows
- Deleting, modifying, renaming, hiding and replacing stored files
- Depleting attached resources such as drives storages and network bandwidth
- Overloading the whole network
- Vulnerabilities creation and exploitation
- Transferring controls to remote computers and criminals
- Disrupting control and security settings
- Damaging computer attached hardware resources
- Damaging network resources

2.5.9 DoS and DDoS

Online shopping, e-Commerce and social media websites deal with heavy traffic, people share their emotions, activities on social media, do business and financial transactions with e-Commerce and fulfil their routine needs with online shopping. Interruption in these websites can cause trouble for its users and ruin its owner goodwill and trust. A **denial of service** (**DoS**) attack refers an attempt to make computer, server or network resources unavailable to its authorized users usually by using temporarily interruption or suspension of services. If a particular website is now slowdown, then there may be chances of DoS attack. A DoS attack prevents users to utilize web resources by flooding the targeted URL with more requests than the server can handle. The DoS attack is achieved through flood attacks.

Popular flood attacks are given below:

- **Buffer overflow attacks**: It refers to most common DoS attack in which more traffic is diverted to network address than its handling capacity. A buffer is a sequential block of memory allocated to contain data from numeric values to an array of integers. A buffer overflow, or buffer overrun, occurs when large amount of data is put into a fixed-sized buffer than the buffer can handle. This additional data, which has to be adjusted somewhere, can acquire adjacent memory blocks that results corrupting or overwriting data already present in that space. This overflow leads system to crash and also creates the opportunity for attacker to run malicious code to breach the system.
- **ICMP flood**: **Internet Control Message Protocol (ICMP)** refers to a connectionless protocol that is used for IP operations, error diagnostics and fault detection. ICMP flood attack that is also popular as ping attack in which a large number of ICMP packets make request simultaneously to server repeatedly to hinder its ability to process the requests.
- **SYN flood**: The term SYN refers to synchronization in making connection among clients and servers. It is another type of DoS attack in which server is engaged to make connections with several non-authentic clients. If a server receives a SYN request from clients, then it process the request and completes the connection by sending acknowledgement "SYN-ACK" to clients. In a SYN flood attack, client's single SYN request is converted in Multiple SYN requests that seem to be coming from multiple different sources to single server, keeping the server busy in identifying the true source and its authenticity that delays connection establishment process. In most of the cases, server fails to send "SYN-ACK" back to legitimate clients and becomes incapable to process request.

A DoS attack refers an attempt to make computer, server or network resources unavailable to its authorized users usually by using temporarily interruption or suspension of services. In *Figure 2.2*, the criminal communicates with the server with fake IDs which are activated for very short span of time to make requests. After sending requests, these IDs are removed and server searches these

IDs for responses and wastes the time resulting inability to process legitimate requests:

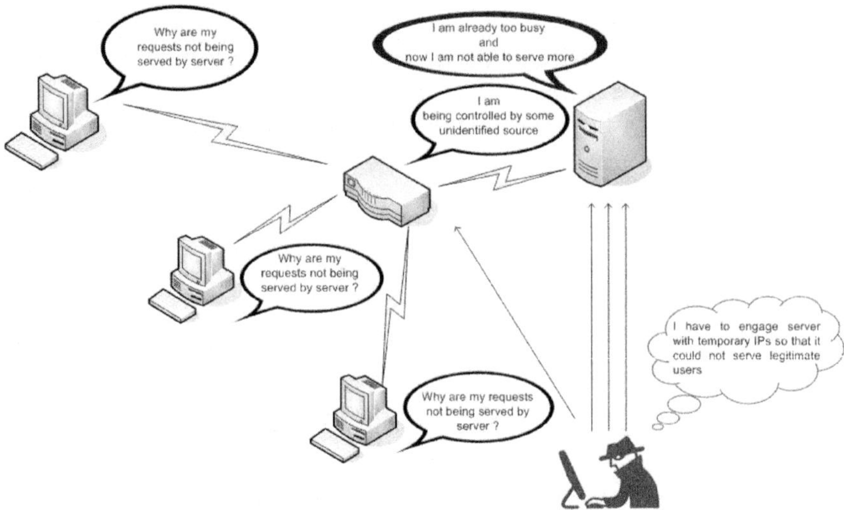

***Figure 2.2**: Denial-of-service attack*

Distributed denial-of-service (DDoS) attack refers to an attack in which large number of maliciously affected computers targets a single system, prohibiting legitimate users to access the target system. The massive incoming requests and messages force the target system to shut down resulting denial of services to authentic users. Initially, attacker uses the vulnerability of a system in network and prepares this system as botmaster to launch the attack. Botmaster further identifies number of vulnerable systems that can be remotely controlled and act as intermediary systems between the target and botmaster. These intermediary remotely controlled systems, which are popularly known as 'slave agents' or 'Zombies', follow the instructions from botmaster and communicate the victim directly. Normally, websites are preferred targets for the denial of services because customers, partners and followers interact with organizations through websites.

DDoS is not concerned about the hacking or data stealing instead it is procedure that keeps busy server all the time so that it cannot serve clients further more. Cybercriminals launch DDoS attack to bring a website and online services of particular organization down to hamper its reputation in customers. Suspension of online services also creates negative impacts on search engines ranking that reduces customer traffic towards it. Potential competitors in business use the DDoS as tool to win in throat-cut competition. Attackers also make websites disappear with DDoS and demand ransom to resume the online services. The following *Figure 2.3* shows the procedure to launch DDoS attack:

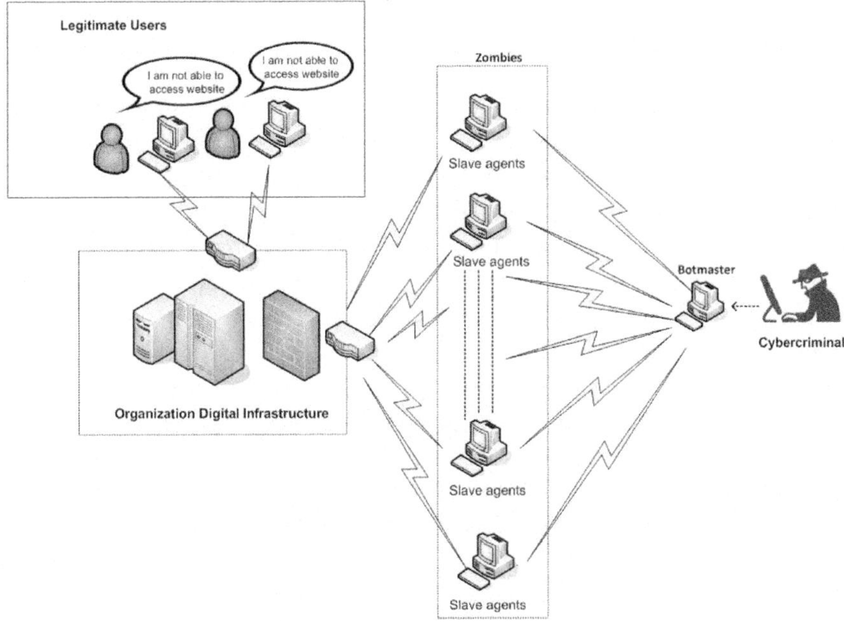

***Figure 2.3:** Distributed denial-of-service*

2.5.10 Pornography

Pornography is sexually explicit material in textual, visual and audio-visual form, used to arouse and provide sexual satisfaction to audience. Pornographic material includes books, magazines, photographs and video-clips in electronic form containing naked men, women and even children who expose their sexual organs and perform sexual acts. The porn industry is most lucrative for criminals and does business in billions with the help of internet. The cybercriminals provide the porn materials to audience in the desired format and charge handsomely.

2.5.11 Defacement attacks

A defacement attack is carried out by replacing the original webpage of particular website with its almost similar one but having some hidden changes without its owner's consent. The defacement is performed with popular and trusted websites as users do not hesitate to deliver own data on these websites. In such an attack, the intentions of cyber criminals are to collect the users' personal information such as credit card number, mobile number, password, and so on.

2.5.12 Ransomware

Ransomware is a threat that encrypts files and documents, and holds a computer / Data hostage until a ransom money is paid as fee. Ransomware not only encrypt files and folders on single computer, but has capability to infect entire network, including servers. The first case of ransomware was detected in Russia between 2005 and 2006 that was capable to do compression and then password protection of files [19]. Initially, this ransomware infected general files such as .DOC, .XLS, .JPG, .ZIP, .PDF, and kept on hostage. Later on, it captured **Master Boot Record** (**MBR**) and prevented operating system from loading. Ransomware deals with money and targets business instead of individuals. Apart from infecting computers and mobile devices, it also infects shared, removable drives and servers [19]. Some families of ransomware target tax-related files and database files to ensure bigger profits.

2.6 Challenges in cybersecurity

As the use of information technology is growing rapidly worldwide. Significant increase in digital activities and large utilization of internet resulted more chances for cybercrimes. The lack of adequate knowledge about system protection and possibility of anonymity results in cybercrimes in society. Several countries have witnessed significant increase in spamming, virus infection and worm infection. India is also experiencing the cybersecurity problems with various challenges [17]. These challenges are as follows:

2.6.1 Cybersecurity is borderless

For most of us the internet is essential part of our daily routine to keep in touch with social media, academics, online shopping and paying bills. In our profession, we also use internet and other information technologies to enhance efficiency, quality of services and to access new markets across the world. As internet offers large number of benefits, there are also security challenges related with its use. Rapid use of internet has established new opportunities for criminals and terrorists to access our personal and corporate information. The major problem with the cybersecurity is its borderless nature [13]. As the cyberspace connects the system across the world, so it often becomes difficult to locate the origin of attack.

2.6.2 Anonymity of actors

Although we are actively fighting and preventing cybercrime-related activities from damaging hardware and infrastructure, but it is difficult to locate the origin of cyber attack. In the virtual cyberspace, it becomes difficult to locate the political borders and culprits as well [13]. The major problem in cybersecurity is the identification of actors in a virtual space where acquiring anonymity is easy and where period gap between the intruder action and its effects exists [18]. In addition, the continuous rapid growth of sophisticated computer technologies among the skilled population also makes attackers identification extremely difficult.

2.6.3 Fuzziness of terminology

The fuzziness of terminology is also a major problem in reference to develop global rules for cybersecurity that diminishes the capability of policymakers to prepare the rules for world population [14]. In addition, cybersecurity is defined in different ways and several different cyber terms are being used with the same intention. There is no globally accepted definition of cybersecurity and cybercrime, various terms are in use with related meanings.

2.6.4 Large and amorphous

Cyberspace is large, amorphous and continuously growing in nature. It is virtual and interconnected worldwide. It does not cover any physical or geographical area. The complexity of cyberspace is mounting day by day because of links between computers, mobiles, tablets, servers, routers and other components of the Internet's infrastructure. Cyberspace includes complex technologies, whose expansion, construction and existence are imagined only during the process of maintenance. It is difficult to chart or map to cyberspace.

2.6.5 Speed of technology development

IT is still considered as an innovative and dynamic sector that is continuously emerging new technologies rapidly. The time period between evolution of new vulnerability and the development of a sophisticated tools or techniques that fail the cyber attacks are getting shorter. In other words, the technologies we develop are not efficient for a long term. We are still unable to develop a technology that can permanently prevent the cyber attacks. We required continuous efforts to tackle with this problem. As it is confirmed that world is facing a problem in creating strong cyber army, very few experts are able to present the solution of sophisticated cyber attacks. On the other hand, cyber attackers, criminals, hackers and cyber terrorists are executing their planning in a much more organized manner. It becomes very essential for us to form a capable cyber army that can save us from financial frauds and information loss.

2.6.6 Tracking the origin of crime

The tracking and tracing of users' behaviors across the internet is still a big problem and requires permanent solution to attach users with their activities and timeframe [8]. The basic idea behind the internet construction was to provide a common platform to scientists and researchers for knowledge sharing and not to linking each person as it is now [16]. It was constructed to expand the different possible usage of networking. It is very important for a nation to track and trace the origin of any cyber attack and infrastructure to block such types of attacks for nation's long-term survival and prosperity. A better cybersecurity tracking and tracing infrastructure can restrict future cyber attacks. The process of tracking and tracing a cyber attack often results sufficient details about the technologies being used in the attack and about criminals as well. Time is also an important factor during the identification and tracking of cyber threats. How quickly you identify the cyber attack and present solution to interrupt the progress of attack is also important.

2.6.7 Shortage of cyber expertise

Today, world is facing rapid increase in the number of cyber attacks in government offices, private organizations and companies. Requirement for skilled cybersecurity experts who are capable to protect organizations from cybercrime is high worldwide, but the shortage is particularly severe in the government organizations that often fail to offer salaries as high as the private sector. It is highly required to fill the gap between supply and demand. Martin C Libickiet. al. [15] carried out semi-structured study with representatives of five U.S. government organizations, five educational institutions, two security companies, one defence organization, and one outside expert. Authors made following conclusions.

- The cyber experts who are capable enough to detect the presence of advanced threats often claim compensation more than $200,000-$250,000 a year[16].
- Normally, the organizations avoid to provide expensive cyber training to their employees because of the fear that employee will take out the skills to other employer[16].
- Now, organizations do not wait for individuals to become graduate with specialized degrees. They are now more concerned with those personality characteristics that correlate best with the requirements of cybersecurity.

On the basis of these three points, we are able to say that because of expensive and advanced training, nations often fail to form strong cyber army.

2.6.8 Lack of international cooperation

Internet is very large network comprises millions of computers scattered across the world provides opportunities to cyber criminals to obtain and exchange information rapidly. The invention of electronic money, online banking, electronic financial transactions and e-business became the crucial factor for the appearance of new cybercrimes. Today, law enforcement agencies are facing cross border challenges in investigation and counter action against cybercriminals. Crime scenes and culprits may belong to different territories in such cases the cooperation among territories is essential for investigation and punishment for cybercriminals. Unfortunately, most of the countries do not cooperate each other in investigations and may instead use cybercriminals skills against enemy countries. Law enforcement agencies most frequently confront obstacles such as the extradition issues during investigation.

Cybercriminals conduct crimes with sophisticated tools and well-planned strategies that make it difficult to trace them. Crimes are fragmented into shards and triggered through cross border routes that make it difficult to investigate crime scene and need permission from concerned government and administration to reach criminals. There is an urgent need for cooperation among states to reduce cybercrimes, protecting critical infrastructure and preventing electronic espionage, bulk data interception and offensive operations that results massive economic and societal damage.

2.6.9 Lack of international legislation

Cybercrimes are exponentially growing and posing everyday economical and societal challenges before each country across the globe. Business organizations, government agencies and financial institutions, and so on, are being hacked to gain political and financial advantages. Most importantly, cybercrimes are being triggered in rapid frequency, every time with unique and sophisticated technology having capabilities to paralyze the economies and damage national critical infrastructure. In the view of its global scale and worldwide adverse impacts, it is very essential to develop international legislations to fight against cybercrimes.

Unfortunately, we still lack globally accepted cybercrime definition and effective legislations that create obstacles in investigations and prosecution against cybercrimes. Anonymity and absence of borders turns internet into easily accessible, efficient and dangerous weapon for cybercriminals. Due to amorphous and borderless nature, no nation can cope with cybercrime independently. The effective fight against cybercrimes needs well-framed international legislations and cooperation against the criminal activities. Although some nations-states are taking affirmative action and cooperating in the investigation and prosecution, but remaining countries are still showing lax approach against cybercrime beyond their own boundaries.

2.7 Cybercrime – As a Service

It is not a secret now that crimes are being committed online. Cybercrimes are now a central concern and identified as biggest risks to society and world economy. Major reasons behind the boom in cybercrimes are the ease of availability of hacking tools in low cost and development of the cybercrime-as-service industry. It is our perception that to launch a cyber attack one should be technically sound, having programming and networking skills but reality is something different. The *Figure 2.4* shows the hierarchy of employees with their level of skills.

Cybercrimes are not only considered a nefarious hobby instead it is a way of earning a living for cyber criminals. It turned into business, in which skilled attackers co-operate with each other, work together and maximize their profits and minimize the risk of being arrested. Cybercrime in terms of profession has ability to attract youths and engage them to malicious activities. In last two decades, cybercrime has turned into a matured industry and it is estimated that it generates around $1 trillion annual revenues [27]. Cybercriminals are now empowering the novice criminals with attack code and services, who lack technical intelligence. They charge sheer amount of money from novices to get their malicious task to be accomplished:

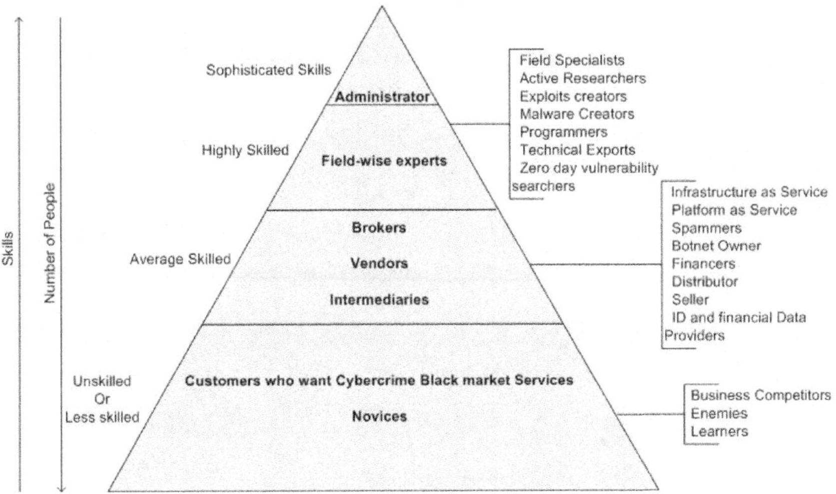

Figure 2.4: *Hierarchy of employees*

The following *Table 2.1* shows the popular categories of tools and services offered to novices the encourage them to conduct cybercrimes:

Category	Definition	Examples
Initial Access Tools	It helps customers to get initial access to targeted system. The goal is to insert malicious code in system so that it can be utilized whenever it is required to perform the launch cyber attack.	Exploit kit (hosted to computers as service) Zero-day vulnerabilities

Category	Definition	Examples
Payload Parts	Goods and services that enables customers to create, package, or enhance payloads to continuous access to targeted system to track its activities and making assessment.	Packers Crypters Binders Obfuscation / evasion
Payloads	Imparts malicious behavior in targeted system for destruction, denial, degradation, deception, disruption and data thefting.	Botnet Spyware RATs
Enabling Services	Customers are helped to locate the desired targets. Enabling services helps to divert traffic to desired websites and hosts to increase or decrease search engines ranking.	Search engine optimization Spam services Pay-per-click, install and affiliates Phishing and spear-phishing services Services to divert traffic Fake website design
Full Services (as-a-service)	Cybercriminals are supplied to customers to work on the behalf of customers. These criminals facilitate full cyber attack life cycle.	Hackers for hire Botnets for rent Doxing DDoS as a service

Category	Definition	Examples
Enabling and Operations Support Products	These services are concerned to be ensured that the initial access tools and hacking services are working properly, are being installed correctly.	Infrastructure Leasing services virtual private network bulletproof hosting compromised sites and hosts Cryptanalytic services Password cracking CAPTCHA breaking
Digital Assets	Digital assets are items that are obtained from target or victims during malicious operation. These attacks carry financial values	Banking, debit card and credit card details. e-commerce, social media account information. e-mail login and passwords Online payment service Accounts Credentials

Category	Definition	Examples
Digital Asset Commerce and Cyber Laundering	Digital asset commerce and cyber laundering facilitates cybercriminals to turn digital assets into cash.	Mule Services Counterfeit goods and services Card cloners and fake ATMs Credit card processor services Forwarding products services

***Table 2.1**: Tools and services offered to novices*

Various service providers offer malicious services such as installing malware into number of desired PCs and then providing access to those compromised PCs, selling subscriptions to malware and ransomeware toolkits to increase the frequency of automate attack. Fake debit and credit cards are prepared to facilitate few withdrawals from ATMs before banks get it noticed. The cybercrime underground black market welcomes new criminals and customers, and protects them from law enforcement agencies.

2.8 Cybercrime underground black market

Market makes the accessibility of products to people; some person produces the products and launch in market to deliver its customers in exchange of money. The hacking world now has been shaped as market in which sellers seek the best prices for their products and customers seek the best products to satisfy their needs. Cybercrime black market is illegal market where cybercriminals buy and sells malicious tools and compromised information required to commit a wide range of cybercrimes.

Cybercrime-as-a-Service is a relatively new phenomenon in which services such as DDoS attacks, spammers to hire and renting a botnet are some common services provided to customers in exchange of reasonable prices. Compromised bank accounts and credit cards details are hot commodities in black market. Cybercriminals are monetizing their wares by leasing access to infrastructure, exploit kits, and hacked accounts to make regular income. The black market is continuously growing in size and complexities as purchasing and selling is accomplished electronically worldwide. It is very difficult to have an idea about its entirety, sophistication and pace because it is geographically distributed, diverse, segmented, invisible and cryptographic in nature. The rapid development of hacker market is posing formidable challenges and severe threats to business, government, financial, and defence institutions.

Increased sophistication, specialization and availability of malicious tools make black market popular among the businessmen and novices. Entrepreneurs and marketers are esteemed customers in black market are using hacking tools and compromised information to lead in business and to defeat their business competitors. Communication among hackers, vendors and customers is being innovative and secure. Encryption is applied over off-the-record messaging to apply privacy mechanism to make it unknown and useless to others. Financial transactions in crypto-currencies hide black market from media coverage and remove the chances of financial downfall. Enormous availability of goods and services, from stolen records and exploit kits to financial services such as compromised credit cards and internet banking details attract customers and individuals to have competitive advantages in business and financial gain.

Panda security details some key products shown in *Table 2.2* are available in this market for sale [22][23][24][29]:

S.N.	Product Name/Services	Price range
1.	Credit Card Details	From $2-$90
2.	Physical Credit Cards	From $190+cost of details
3.	Card Cloners	From $200-$1000
4.	Fake ATMs	Up to $53000
5.	Bank Credentials	From $80-$700 (With guaranteed balance)
6.	Bank Transfer and cashing checks	From 10 to 40% of total
7.	Online store and pay platforms	From $80-$1500 (with guaranteed balance)

S.N.	Product Name/Services	Price range
8.	Purchase and forwarding of products	From $30-$300
9.	SPAM rental	From $15-$45
10.	SMTP rental	From $30-$40 for three months
11.	VPN rental	From $30 for a month
12.	Basic Statistical Crypter	From $10-$30
13.	Stub Crypter with various Add-ons	From $30-$80
14.	Polymorphic Crypter	From $100-$500
15.	Joiner	From $10-$30
16.	DDoS Botnet	From $500-$700
17.	DDoS Botnet updates	From $100-$500 per update
18.	Facebook Account	Form $60-$100
19.	Twitter account	From $70-$120
20.	Gmail account	From $117-$130
21.	Hotmail account	From $107-$117
22.	UK Visa/Mastercard data	$15-20 dollars
23.	UK Fullz data (Full ID package)	$35-$50
24.	Generic Ransomware	$225 - $660
25.	Ranion (Ransomware-as-a-service)	$120 per month
26.	MegacortexRansomware	$1000 or 1000 Euros and 10% of ransom
27.	Unhacked Remote Desk Protocol Servers	$20-$30 per RDP server
28.	Amazon gift card with $1000 balance	From $100-$200
29.	ATM skimmers	From $500 to $1500
30.	DDoS attack	$60-$90 per hour
31.	Money Transfer Services	Average of $120 for a balance of $1200
32.	Changes to credit history	From $130-$260
33.	Unhacked Remote Desk Protocol Servers	$20 per RDP server

S.N.	Product Name/Services	Price range
34.	Hacking web server (vps or hosting)	$120-$140
35.	Hacking personal computer	$80-$90
36.	Web Server security Audit	$150-$160
37.	Spyware development	$180-$200
38.	Device Tracking	$80-$100
39.	US Passport USD Template	$18-$25
40.	Driver License, Passport certificat	$700-$783
41.	Generic ransomware build	$200-$270
42.	Cryptolocker binary	$100-$400
43.	Cryptolocker source code	$3000-$4000
44.	Jigsaw ransomware source code	$3500-$4200
45.	Zeppelin builder	$2000-$2700
46.	Crypter as a service	$120-$180
47.	Phone flooder	$120-$140
48.	SMS bulk sender	$25-$500
49.	RATs	$30-$90
50.	Android-based RAT	$80-$120
51.	Rare Fortnite gaming accounts	$999-$1500
52.	1,000 Facebook likes	$84-$120
53.	Social media bot	$140-$270
54.	1000 Youtube likes	$70-$110
55.	New visitor hits	$5-$10
56.	Deepfake videos	$50-$80
57.	Gambling Bot	$75-$120
58.	Sports Betting	$50-$75

***Table 2.2**: Popular products in underground black market*

2.8.1 Characteristics of black market

The rapid and continues expansion of black market offers a common platform to skilled criminals. Skill is valued in monetary terms and delivered to customers under the control of administrators. The attraction of skilled person towards black market is obvious as it offers to make large amount of money with very low or almost negligible investment. The growth of various communication channels allowed cybercriminals to find each other and connect easily, facilitating access to tools, share technologies, and infrastructure. Criminals feel safe behind the digital shield of anonymity and cheat people freely because of low risk and favourable environment. Current architecture and law suits help cybercriminals to pose as legitimate users and provide enough time to commit crimes and flee away. Black market is not much similar to normal market as it mostly deals with activities rather than the tangible products. Due to lack of tangible evidences, it becomes difficult to guess the size of market and to track the criminals. The black market can be compared with some illicit market such as drugs with difference that black market carries less risk and offers more profit:

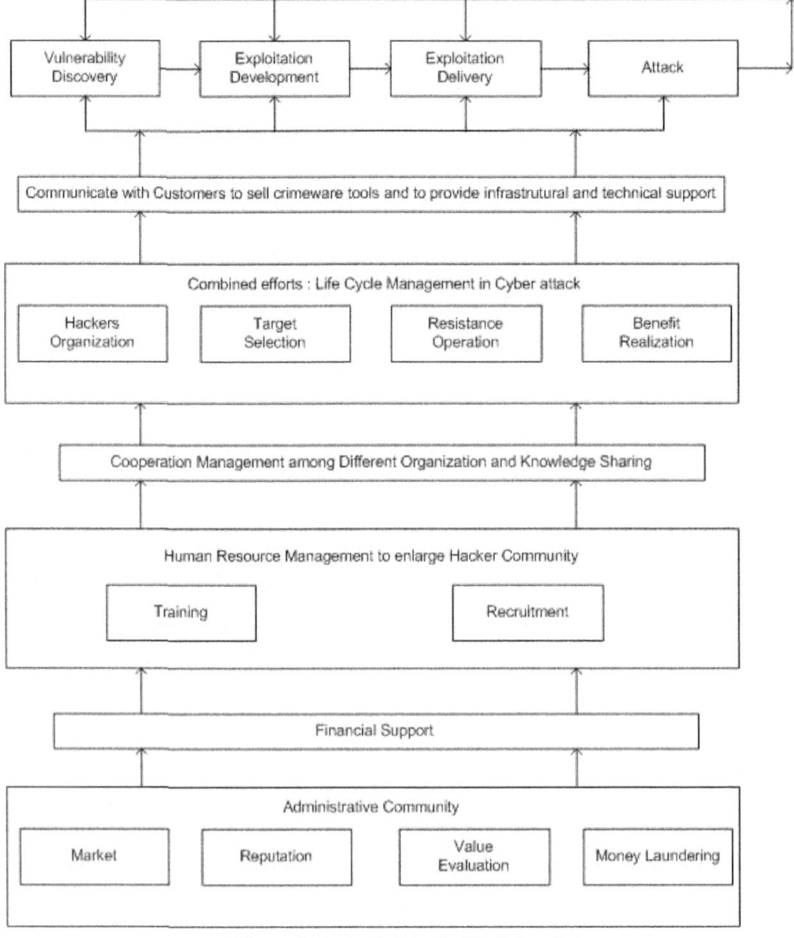

***Figure 2.5**: Activities in black market*

From the preceding *Figure 2.5*, we conclude that number of activities such as financing, recruiting, training, and so on, are required to be performed in underground black market and administrators, toolkit writer, suppliers, vendors, buyers, and panders perform their own role with their level of expertise. The underground black market is almost amorphous, virtual, digital and globally scattered where face-to-face meeting among customers, suppliers and vendors is not essential at all. It is challenging to describe the entirety of black market because it is too vast and containing large number of players with continuously changing behavior.

2.8.1.1 Structure of black market

Sophisticated tools easily available in black market can cause widespread damage to organizations, business and individuals at very little cost. There are various types of criminals available from toolkits writer to sellers on internet. These criminals have their own priorities, specializations and role in black market. The regional, cultural and economic needs of cybercriminals influence their motivations in selecting the targets. Cybercrimes are now more organized, sophisticated, and long-lasting result oriented in which well-equipped cybercriminals get involve with a business vision and earn profits. Professionals with criminal brain write the crimeware tool kits and offer technical services to less skilled criminals, non-professional, and novices to let them earn for survival.

Administrators control the black market and provide financial support to bring skilled hackers to a single virtual platform. Administrators recruit the people with their specialized services and provide them appropriate training to enhance their sophistication. These recruited people work as regional managers and coordinate with other freelance hackers, professionals and students to strengthen hacking and seeking vulnerabilities.

2.8.1.2 Participants of black market

A person carrying soft skills with networking knowledge can participate in black market. Seeking vulnerabilities and system penetration require advance computing skills, crimeware tool kits, and infrastructure. Skilled programmers, toolkits operators and infrastructure owners become the parts of black-market community. Obviously, the person who desires monetary advantages in exchange of doing illegal activities using computers, networking and internet can be a participant in black market.

Nowadays, cybercrimes are continuously getting more complex. The criminals hide their involvement and mask their actions to remove the chances of backtracking. The launching of cyber attack and making it more profitable, a group of cybercriminals, including spammers, developers, cashiers, financers, and so on, is required where each individual has different and crucial role. Most frequently, the attackers do not have all the required skills to launch and control cyber attack so they have to rely on other criminals to make launching successful. The services and tools are shared among criminals and knowledge sharing is done to help each other.

Spammers

The main task of spammers in organized cybercrime is to make the computers vulnerable and to prepare platform to launch cyber attacks. A steady revel that around 50 percent of total e-mails circulating on internet are related to spamming [27]. Spammers attract the internet users through e-mails and advertisements, and get control on their devices and infrastructure secretly[28].

Web developers

Web developers are responsible for creating malicious websites that looks like originals one called **website cloning/website spoofing** through which user's data is collected and used for selling in black market.

Cashiers

These are the person who use compromised financial data and convert it into instant cash.

Financers

To conduct the complex coordinated cyber attacks, ranging from targeting individuals to corporate breaches huge amount of finance is often required. This fund is used to prepare infrastructure and recruiting professionals. The financers supply funds to conduct cybercrimes and ensure their share in resultant profit.

Conclusion

In this chapter, we learnt about the historical development of computer and its transformation in a device that was not only capable to perform calculations but also to participate in communication. We learnt how development of computers and its participation in communication, banking, education, business, innovations, entertainment and defence, provides opportunities to criminals to perform illicit activities to earn profits and other more benefits. We understood that internet is not only a medium to earn profits but also a platform where skilled cybercriminals join hands for organized crimes, shares malicious tools and infrastructure, train novices to convert them in skilled human resource, and develop a parallel illegal economy. In this chapter, the costs of cybercrime have been categorised with its analysing framework to determine consequences other than direct losses. Various forms of cybercrime have been explained with their impacts on individuals and society. Furthermore, we determine the factors due to which internet is safe zone for criminals and are obstacles in global legislation formation against the cybercrimes and prosecution. The enormous structure of cybercrime underground black market has also been explained with popular products list and services that attracts the novices and students towards black market.

The next chapter of this book details the strategies used to detect intrusions and presents the ways to mitigate the impacts of these intrusions with various kinds of intrusion detection systems.

Points to remember

- In 1642, famous mathematician Blaise Pascal constructed first non-electronic and mechanical machine that facilitated addition and subtraction of numbers to its users.
- In 1813, another English mathematician named Charles Babbage designed a mechanical calculator that was capable to perform calculations up to 20 decimal capacities.
- In the middle of 1880s, Herman Hollerith played a crucial role in computer development and introduced mechanical and electrical data processing systems for census in USA.

- The act of breaking telephone network and configuring it illegally to make free long distance calls is known as **Phreaking**.
- In 1961, Leonard Kleinrock at MIT published a paper on packet switching theory, which became baseline for data transmission in the form of packets.
- In 1965, Roberts connected TX-2 computer with Q-32 computer in California with a dial-up connection.
- In 1969, US Defence Department and ARPA-Net came together and installed two nodes for the communication purpose. The first node was configured at University of California, Los Angeles, while other was installed at Stanford research Institute, University of Utah, to communicate each other. On October 29, 1969, at 10:30 PM, the node configured at University of California sent a message to node at Stanford Research Institute.
- Robert Tappan Morris, a student at Cornell, created the first worm and unleashed it on the Internet.
- Cybercrime is the area where risk-to-payoff ratio is leading.
- The anticipation cost refers to expenditure on defensive measures taken for the protection from cybercrimes.
- Consequence Cost: The consequence cost refers to total damage cost occurs immediately as a result of cybercrime.
- Costs used to generate appropriate response after the occurrence of cybercrime is referred as response costs.
- Indirect cost includes reputational damage to organisations and firms, loss of confidence in online transactions by individuals and businesses, reduced revenues and the growth of the underground black-market economy.
- Criminal revenue refers to gross receipts from crime in monetary equivalent.
- Direct losses refer to the value of losses, destructions and damages due to cybercrime.
- Indirect losses refer to the value of the losses and opportunity costs imposed on society because of malicious activities.

- Defence cost refers to monetary equivalent of prevention efforts.
- The totality of direct losses, indirect losses and defence costs is known as costs to society.
- Cyber Stalking is a technology-aided stalking in which assailants harass the people with internet technologies such as e-mails, social media account, instant messaging, chat rooms, and much more.
- Cyber Stalking is an act of threatening people to cause distress, anxiety and fear.
- The Intellectual property refers to unique intangible human creation like innovation, literature, art, model, symbol, formula, logo and image with its commercial value.
- Copyright laws protect books, software, literature, music, paintings, electronic games, movies, and so on.
- A trademark refers to a unique symbol, logo, word and quote that belong to a company or its product.
- Phishing refers to a fraudulent attempt to steal sensitive data and useful information such as banking details, login credentials, financial data and corporate information through e-mails.
- Identity theft occurs when a criminal illegally uses identity of someone else and commits crime with his name.
- Spoofing refers to technique in which criminal acquires a networked computer with its IP and impersonates as it by replacing its originals services and communications with its own.
- Trojan Horse is malicious code, but looks legitimate.
- A denial of service (DoS) attack refers to an attempt that leads to shut down a computer or network and making it inaccessible to its legitimate users.
- Distributed denial-of-service (DDoS) attack uses large number of compromised computers to target a single system, server and whole network to cripple their services with flood of requests.

- Pornography is sexually explicit material in textual, visual and audio-visual form, used to arouse and provide sexual satisfaction to audience.
- A defacement attack is carried out by replacing the original webpage of particular website with its almost similar one, but having some hidden changes without its owner consent.
- Ransomware is a threat that encrypts files and documents, and holds a computer hostage until a ransom money is paid as fee.

MCQ

1. **Who invented mechanical calculator:**
   a. Blaise Pascal
   b. Charles Babbage
   c. Joseph-Marie Jacquard
   d. Herman Hollerith
2. **French textile weaver who produced a machine with punch cards to implement endless loop**:
   a. Charles Babbage
   b. Joseph-Marie Jacquard
   c. Presper Eckert
   d. Stewart Nelso
3. **Which of the following is known first commercially marketed computer?**
   a. ENIAC
   b. UNIVAC
   c. PDP-1
   d. UINIAVC
4. **'Phreaking' is an act to:**
   a. Breach bank account details
   b. Breach credit card data
   c. Break the telephone lines and making free calls
   d. Encrypt files and documents

5. **Costs of Society does not include:**
   a. Direct losses
   b. Indirect losses
   c. Defence costs
   d. Consequence Cost
6. **What is truth about 'Zombie'?**
   a. Compromised computer
   b. A threat
   c. A platform
   d. PRB Virus
7. **ARPA stands for:**
   a. Advanced Research Projects Agency
   b. American Research Projects Agency
   c. American Research and Promotion Agency
   d. American Robotics Projects Agency
8. **Victims distress falls under:**
   a. Consequence Cost
   b. Anticipation Cost
   c. Indirect losses
   d. Direct losses

Answer

1. a
2. b
3. b
4. c
5. d
6. a
7. a
8. d

Questions

1. Describe the historical development of computers and cybercrime.
2. Cybercrime is the area where risk-to-payoff ratio is leading. Explain this statement.
3. Cybercrimes are now profession? Justify the statement.
4. Define cybercrime costs with its major categories in detail.
5. Describe the participants in underground black market with their responsibilities.
6. Explain the following:
    - I. Anticipation Cost
    - II. Consequence Cost
    - III. Response Cost
    - IV. Indirect Cost
7. Draw and explain cybercosts analysing framework in detail.
8. Differentiate the following:
    - I. Virus versus Worm
    - II. DoS versus DDoS
    - III. Cyber-stalking Versus Phishing
    - IV. Copyright Theft Versus Trademark Theft
9. Describe the various activities performed in underground black market.
10. Describe the popular forms of cybercrimes in detail.
11. Describe the major challenges in the field of cybersecurity.
12. What do you mean by Intellectual property? Explain its major types.
13. Explain the Hierarchy of employees in underground black market.

References

[1] Allan G. Bromley, *"Charles Babbage's Analytical Engine 1838"*, IEEE Annals of the history of Computing, Vol. 20, No. 4, 1998.

[2] Alexander Randall, *"From ENIAC to Everyone"*, Published on Kurzweil AI .net, February 23, 2006.

[3] Barry M. Leiner, Vinton G. Cerf, David D. Clark, Robert E. Kahn, Leonard Kleinrock, Daniel C. Lynch, Jon Postel, Larry G. Roberts, Stephen Wolff, *"Brief History of the Internet"*, Internet Society, 1997.

[4] Leonard Kleinrock, *"An early history of the internet"*, and Mischa Schwartz, *"History of Communications"*, IEEE Communications Magazine, August 2010.

[5] Leonard Ted Eisenberg, IDavidGries, Juris Hartmanis, Don Holcomb, M. Stuart Lynn, Thomas Sanioro, "The Cornell Commission: On Morris and the Worm", Communications of the ACM, Vol. 32 No.6, June 1989.

[6] Sara Norden, *"How the Internet has changed the face of crime"*, Master of Science thesis, Florida Gulf Coast University, December 2013.

[7] Gisela Wurm, Stalking, A Report before Committee on Equality and Non-Discrimination, June 2013.

[8] A Report available at **http://searchsecurity.techtarget.com/definition/mail-bomb**.

[9] A Report available at **http://www.businessdictionary.com/definition/e-mail-bomb.html**.

[10] A Report available at **http://www.sse.gov.on.ca/mcs/en/pages/identity_theft.aspx.**

[11] A Report available at **http://www.rcmp-grc.gc.ca/scams-fraudes/id-theft-vol-eng.htm**.

[12]A Report, *"virus and worm"* available at **http://www.webopedia.com/DidYouKnow/Internet/virus.asp**.

[13] A Kpmg International Issues Monitor. *Cyber Crime –A Growing Challenge for Governments*, Volume 08, July 2011.

[14] Eric A. Fischer. *Creating a National Framework for Cyber security: An Analysis of Issues and Options*, CRS Report for Congress, February 2005.

[15] Martin C Libicki, David Senty and Julia Pollak. *An Examination of the Cybersecurity Labor Market*, RAND National Security Research Division.

[16] F. Lipson. *Tracking and Tracing Cyber-Attacks: Technical Challenges and Global Policy Issues*, November 2002.

[17] Rajesh Kumar Goutam, ‚*Challenges in Cyber Security*‛, Bilingual International Conference on Information Technology: Yesterday, Today, and Tomorrow, 19-21 February 2015, PP. 108-113.

[18] A Fifty Second Report. Cyber Crime, Cyber Security and Right to Privacy, Ministry of Communications and Information Technology, Department of Electronics and Information Technology, Govt. of India, February 2014.

[19] A Report form Trend Micro, *"Ransomeware: Past, Present, and Future"*, 2017 available at **https://documents.trendmicro.com/assets/wp/wp-ransomware-past-present-and-future.pdf**.

[20] Steve Morgan, *"2019 Official Annual Cybercrime Report"*, Cybersecurity Ventures, Herjavec Group.

[21] A Report from Mcafee, *"Economic Impact of Cybercrime—No Slowing Down"*, February 2018 available at: **https://www.mcafee.com/enterprise/en-us/assets/reports/restricted/rp-economic-impact-cybercrime.pdf**.

[22] A Research Report from Home Office Science Advisory Council, *"Understanding the costs of cybercrime A report of key findings from the Costs of Cyber Crime Working Group"*, January 2018.

[23] Ross Anderson, Chris Barton, Rainer Böhme, Richard Clayton, Michel J. G.Van Eeten, Michael Levi, Tyler Moore, and Stefan Savage, *"Measuring the Cost of Cybercrime"*, The Economics of Information Security and Privacy, Springer-Verlag Berlin Heidelberg 2013

[24] Ross Anderson, Chris Barton, Rainer ohme, Richard Clayton, Tom Grasso, Michael Levi, Tyler Moore, Marie Vasek, *"Measuring the Changing Cost of Cybercrime"*, The 18th Annual Workshop on the Economics of Information Security, 2019.

[25] A McAfee Summary report on, *"Net Losses: Estimating the Global Cost of Cybercrime: Economic impact of cybercrime II"*, 2014.

[26] Harald Drebing, Josef Bailer, Anne Anders, Henriette Wagner, Christine Gallas, *"Cyberstalking in a Large Sample of Social Network Users: Prevalence, Characteristics, and Impact Upon Victims"*, Cyberpsychology, Behavior and social networking, Volume 17, Number 2, 2014.

[27] A report, *"Cybercrime-as-a-Service: No End in Sight"*, available at: **https://www.darkreading.com/endpoint/cybercrime-as-a-service-no-end-in-sight/a/d-id/1333033**

[28] A report a, "Spam, steganography, and e-mail hacking", available at **https://www.britannica.com/topic/cybercrime/Spam-steganography-and-e-mail-hacking**.

[29] A Report form panda security, "The Cybercrime black market: Uncovered", the cloud security company, 2010.

[30] A report from Gisela Wurm, *"Stalking"*, Committee on Equality and Non-Discrimination, Socialist group, parliamentary assembly, council of Europe, Austria, 2012.

[31] Paul E. Mullen, Michele Pathe, Rosemary Purcell, *"Study of Stalkers"*, American Journal of Psychiatry, 1999.

CHAPTER 3
Information Security and Intrusion Detection System

The race to adopt technologies leads us to share business and personal information over internet. The situations may worsen if the information lands up in wrong hands. We use various security measures, but experiences confirm that most of them are penetrable and breached by skilled criminals. This chapter explains how critical national infrastructure is important for a country and how it is at risk due to security breaches. The Confidentiality-Integrity-Availability Triad is discussed to furnish the basic details of system and data security. Further, the chapter details Intrusion Detection and Prevention Principles and explain the functioning of intrusion detection system with its architecture and vital components.

Structure

In this chapter, we will cover the following topics:

- Critical National Infrastructure
- Confidentiality-Integrity-Availability Triad
- Defensive Lifecycle
- Intrusion Detection System
- Characteristics of IDS

Objective

The objective of this chapter is to explain the importance of Critical National Infrastructure and to elaborate that how it is at risk due to Cybercriminals. With the help of CIA triad and Defensive Life-Cycle, we tried to explain the basics of Information Security to its readers and detailed possible categories of vulnerabilities, frequently exploited to conduct crimes. In this chapter, you shall know the functioning of Intrusion Detection System with its detailed architecture and will have the knowledge about Intrusion Detection and Prevention Principles.

3.1 Critical National Infrastructure

In middle of 1990, the term *Critical Infrastructure* came in literature that refers physical and non-physical assets, cyber resources, and systems that are necessary to offer essential services to citizens, to run government operations, and to maintain the economy of a country [1]. **Critical National Infrastructure** (**CNI**) is a subset of the critical infrastructure that incorporates those elements of critical infrastructure which are recognized from government and are considered to have strategic national importance [2]. The failure and even partial breakdown of these elements can cause enormous consequences on national security. The loss and breach to these elements can leave severe and widespread effect on economy and social well-being too for a nation [3]. The critical national infrastructure includes processes, systems, facilities, technologies, networks, assets and services that are essential for a nation to its financial and social health, safety, security or economic well-being [4]. Critical national infrastructure can be standalone or shared among the nations across the world.

Critical National Infrastructure is like a life support system for services offered to citizens for their survival in a country. Most of the countries are sustaining with highly complex and sophisticated networked infrastructure, and interconnecting institutions for data sharing to deliver rapid and reliable services to their citizens [5]. These life support systems are continuously being updated in order to meet the citizen requirements. Governments are trying to make these systems more productive and efficient, and lots of technological advances are being adopted for citizens and their health, safety, security and economic well-being. The worldwide inter-connectivity and globalization allows remote monitoring, functioning and controlling of critical national infrastructure, which is harmful if the control goes in wrong hands [5]. The heavy reliance and real-time connectivity make them vulnerable to threats and increase the risk of being frequent target. The dependence and interconnectivity among the organizations, institutions and individuals across national boundaries can cause far-reaching consequences of an attack and even single attack can cause disruption and destruction to multiple vital systems and can interrupt their service delivery process [5].

3.2 Confidentiality-Integrity-Availability Triad

A simple but widely used system security model is the CIA triad which explains the importance of three key parameters named confidentiality, integrity, and availability in the field of system and data security [21]. To be ensured about the data and system security, these three parameters should be incorporated in analysis to meet security standards. If one of these three parameters is breached, it can leave serious consequences in the system security. The *Figure 3.1* shows a CIA triad, which is a model used even today to chalk out information security framework and to prepare security guidelines within an organization:

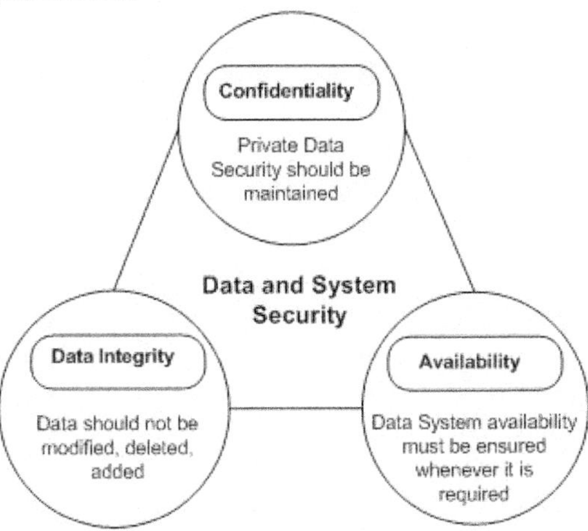

***Figure 3.1**: CIA triad*

Security administrators evaluate threats and vulnerabilities on the basis of their impacts on confidentiality, integrity, and availability of digital assets of any organizations. These are described as follows:

- **Confidentiality**: Confidentiality refers to the ability to hide sensitive data and information from unauthorized people to view it. The most common ways to maintain confidentiality, cryptographic techniques such as **SSL (Secure Socket Layer)** and **TLS (Transport Layer Security)** are used. Access control also helps us in this direction as it grants access only to legitimate users.
- **Data Integrity**: Data integrity refers to the assurance of originality of data. It is the ability to ensure that the available copy of data is accurate and unaltered representation of original data. The most common technique used to maintain data integrity is digital signature and besides these, SSL, TSL, and **Media Access Control (MAC)** are also used to protect original data from tempering.
- **Availability**: It is very essential to ensure that the data and concerned resources are accessible to the legitimate users whenever needed. Authentication mechanisms, access controls and systems are required to function together to ensure availability of data and resources. Availability can be secured with hardware maintenance, software patching and network optimization.

3.3 Defensive Lifecycle

Security threats are now rapidly emerging, causing exposure of data that not only have financial value, but also carry trade secrets. Threats that monitor online activities can leak your personal information to ruin your societal image and permits strangers to snoop you. Defensive lifecycle examines the interconnected digital environment and signals about break-in into systems. It warns the security administrators when confidentiality, integrity and availability of systems, and network are breached. Defensive lifecycle shown in *Figure 3.2* works in four phases, namely, analysis, mitigation, prevention, and maintenance:

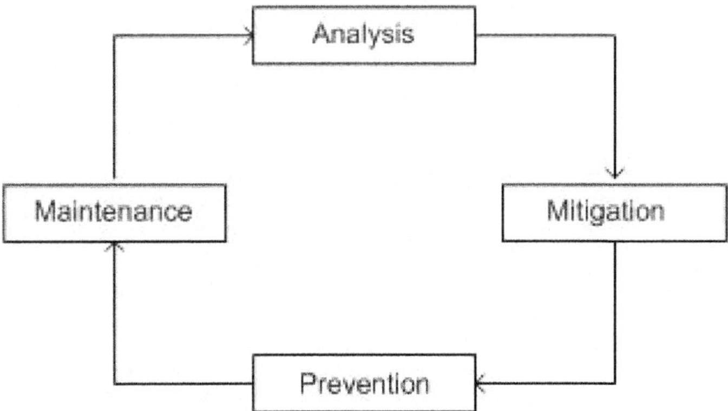

Figure 3.2: *Defensive life-cycle*

In the analysis phase, an auditing is performed to search vulnerabilities and mis-configurations. Integrity of operating system files and data files is assessed, and abnormal activities are detected through statistical analysis to know attacking pattern. Once the occurrence of intrusion is detected, security administrators are notified to protect interconnected digital infrastructure and mitigate its adverse impacts. In the mitigation phase, the intrusion pattern is recognized and categorized, and matched with already recognized attacking patterns to get a quick solution. Mitigation process deals with procedure that diminishes the impacts of intrusions. It also deals with vulnerability patch-up process and prevents malicious traffic transmission across the network. Prevention phase drops malicious packets and re-configures the connections to transmit data to subsequent nodes. Prevention phase respond to suspected threat by blocking it quickly to prevent it transmitting further. The content of malicious packets is changed and reconfiguration of security controls is done to disrupt an attack.

3.4 Intrusion and its types

Intrusion refers to malicious activity within software, nodes, network, and in the IT infrastructure. It is a set of actions that violate security policies, including the integrity and confidentiality of data and the availability of services too, through the use of vulnerabilities in system, network, software and infrastructure as well. The *Figure 3.3* shows various categories of intrusions:

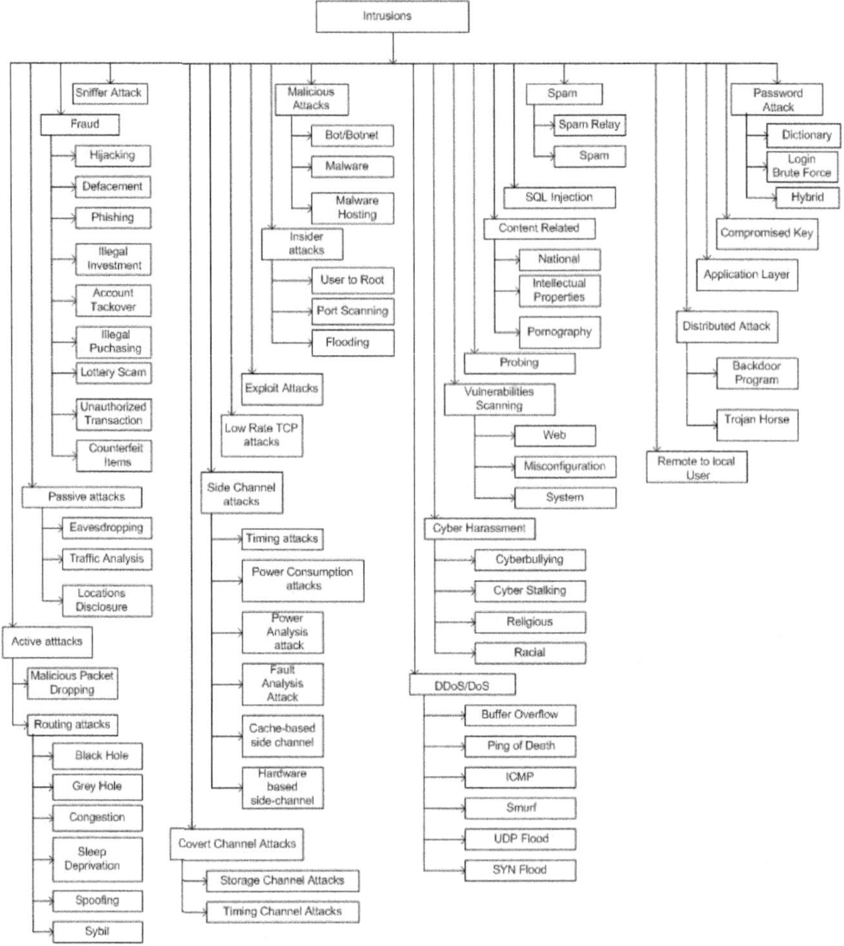

***Figure 3.3**: Intrusion Categories*

Although several defensive mechanisms such as cryptography, firewalls and access control for secure communication have been developed, but all these anti-threat systems have their own limitations. Firewalls mainly protect the front-line system access from threats and attacks. Cryptography facilitates secure communication while access control deals with privileges and authentication purposes. However, these anti-threat mechanisms protect system from external threats, but are inadequate to detect internal threats. The following *Table 3.1* details the different categories of intrusions:

Attack type	Attack Name Category	Category	Description
Active Attacks	Malicious Packet Dropping		Malicious Packets are injected in traffic
	Routing Attacks	Black Hole	Routers delete packets needs to be forwarded.
		Grey Hole	It acts as malicious node to inject malicious traffic and returns back to normal.
		Congestions	It helps to achieve Packets loss and delay.
		Sleep Deprivation	Helps to maximize power consumptions at a particular node.
		Spoofing	A device impersonates another device to receive packets or launch attacks.
		Sybil	A node creates multiple fake identities to receive disproportionately large influence.
Passive Attacks	Eavesdropping		Network traffic is maliciously captured for later analysis.
	Traffic Analysis		Communication patterns are analyzed to launch an attack.
	Location Disclosure		Information regarding locations of nodes and structure of network is captured.
Fraud	Hijacking		Criminals takeover the network and put communication under its own control

Attack type	Attack Name Category	 Category	Description
	Defacement		Attacker penetrates a website and changes its appearance and contents.
	Phishing		It is an attempt to steal personal data such as login credentials and credit card numbers.
	Illegal Investment		Making investment with someone else's account illegally.
	Account takeover		It leads to fraudulent transactions from a compromised bank account.
	Illegal Purchasing		Paying bills with stolen, compromised and fake credit cards and debit cards.
	Lottery Scam		This crime begins with unexpected email informing a person that he has won a large sum of money and he is required to pay advance fee for further details.
	Unauthorized transactions		It deals with paying fees from a hijacked bank account or stolen credit cards.
	Counterfeit Items		It deals with delivery of inferior items in the price of original product.
Sniffer Attacks			Attackers put a close eye on data traffic passing through a channel.

Attack type	Attack Name Category Category	Description
Covert Channel Attack	Storage Channel Attacks	In this attack, the crucial information is given to criminals for their malicious use.
	Timing Channel Attacks	It is related to operations that affect response time.
Side-Channel Attacks	Timing attacks	Timing to execute cryptographic algorithm is manipulated and cryptosystem is breached.
	Power Consumption attacks	It is related to breaching secret information with power consumption and electromagnetic radiation.
	Power Analysis attacks	Power analysis helps to breach cryptographic algorithms.
	Fault Analysis attacks	Used to uncover secrets by introducing faults in computations.
	Cache Based Side Channel	It deals with exploiting shared cache memory to retrieve sensitive information.
	Hardware-based Side Channel	Criminals exploit physical characteristics of hardware such as running time and current flow.
Low rate TCP attacks		The congestion-control mechanism of TCP protocol is breached by sending malicious packets repeatedly in bulk.

Attack type	Attack Name Category Category	Description
Exploit Attacks		Exploit is malicious code that uses vulnerabilities and security flaws to breach system.
Insider Attacks	User to Root	Malicious code interrupts the working of root users and prevents them to access the root directory.
	Port Scanning	Port scanning helps to find exploitable vulnerabilities and flaws in system.
	Flooding	Flooding is used to fill memory buffer of server.
Malicious Attacks	Bot/Botnet	A group of compromised computers works under the control of attacker.
	Malware	Malicious software surreptitiously installed on someone's computer to gain his personal and financial information.
	Malware Hosting	Hosting a malicious website or putting malicious code over legitimate server.
DDoS/DoS	Buffer Overflow	It relies to divert heavy traffic to particular node or server that exceeds than processing capacity.
	Ping to Death	Making request with large number of ICMP packets and overwhelming target server that attempts to process each request.

Attack type	Attack Name Category Category	Description
	Smurf	It is a resource consumption attack that uses all available bandwidth and leaves the system in an inoperable state.
	UDP Flood	Making request with large number of UDP packets and overwhelming target server that attempt to process each request.
	SYN Flood	Making large number of SYN requests that consumes server resources and become nonresponsive for legitimate users.
Cyber Harassment	Cyberbullying	Writing or posting anything online with the intention to hurt, harass, or getting someone else upset.
	Cyber Stalking	It is related to harassment or frightening someone with the use of internet technologies.
	Religious	It is related to criticism about particular religion over internet and promotes communal violence.
	Racial	Person receives negative and abusive comments because of its own race over electronic media
Vulnerabil-ities Report	Web	It refers to attempts to breach resources in the World Wide Web.

Attack type	Attack Name Category	Category	Description
	Misconfiguration		It refers to attempts of disturbing or abusing configuration of resources on the World Wide Web.
	System		It refers to attempting to disturb system configuration.
Probing			Probing refers to searching vulnerabilities across various ports and preparing platform to launch a DoS/DDoS attack.
Content Related	National		Disclosure of confidential information related to national security.
	Intellectual Properties		Disclosure of innovation, new research, method, model and formula that have an economic value.
	Pornography		Dispersion of printed or video material such as books, magazines, photographs and video-clips that contain description or showing sexual organs over internet.
SQL Injection			SQL injections are malicious database queries used to fetch records illegally from a corporate database.
Spam	Spam Relay		Attacker intercepts the communication between two people and breaches the integrity of messages.
	Spam		It refers to receiving massive unsolicited messages on e-mails or mobile phones.

Attack type	Attack Name Category	Category	Description
Remote to Local user			It is concerned with remotely capturing local user's privileges.
Distributed attacks	Backdoor Program		It is a malicious code normally used to bypass authentication procedure to access a system.
	Trojan Horse		It is malicious code that cause damage to system and disrupt stored data.
Application Layer			The attacks interrupt the services of application layers such as HTTP GET and HTTP POST.
Compromised key			Attackers illegally gain access to secure network with stolen digital keys.
Password attacks	Dictionary		It refers to attempts of breaking password by entering each dictionary word.
	Login Brute Force		It refers to successive attempts to guess the password with possible combinations.
	Hybrid		It is an attempt to guess the password by using dictionary and login brute force method in combination.

***Table 3.1**: Intrusion Classification*

To develop effective anti-threat mechanisms, it is important to know the pattern of attack and areas where it leaves adverse impacts in order to breach integrity, availability, and confidentiality of data. For instance, if an attack breaches the integrity of database, then there is need for quick response to secure data integrity while in case of network attack, appropriate response is needed to improve resource availability and network performance.

3.5 Intrusion Detection system

Intrusion takes the benefits of vulnerability and can cause the remarkable damage. The basic motivation behind the intrusion can range from espionage and exploitation to data leaks and network jamming. **Intrusion Detection (ID)** refers to the process of monitoring the events and activities occurring inside the computer system or in network, and analyzing them for the signs of intrusions and seeking possibilities of being compromised [6]. It identifies the attempts to compromise the confidentiality, integrity and availability of computers and network. Attempts to bypass the security mechanisms are also assessed to find out vulnerable routes.

Detecting intrusions need three activities [7]:

- The ability to log security-relevant events.
- There should be a robust procedure to ensure that logs are being monitored regularly.
- Provision to respond an intrusion if once detected.

Security-relevant events incorporate authentication events, audit events, intrusion events and antivirus events, and these events get registered and stored in operating system logs, security logs or database logs [8]. Organizations that are much concerned about their security policies require security events to get monitored and assessed at regular time of intervals to determine vulnerabilities and attempts to breach their inter-connected infrastructure. Information stored in security logs becomes crucial for reconstructing the sequence of events, which is essential to know the routes and timeline of cyberattack. The sequence of events and related activities when correlated, we get the information about impacts of attacks, its nature and launching procedure, which is essential to know to develop its countermeasures.

Intrusion detection system (IDS) refers to software or hardware systems, or a combination of hardware and software that automates the process of monitoring the events taking place inside a computer system or network, analyzing logs to identify the signs of security problems [6]. The hardware and software components of IDS work together to detect unexpected events, which may alarm an attack is about to happen, is happening, or has been happening [9]. The detection process may include different technologies and policies to detect the intrusion that varies from one system to another. Suppose, if our IDS uses signature-based identification technologies, it will immediately find the reason to raise alarm. However, if it uses statistically-based technologies, then intrusion detection may be delayed because of configuration management unit involvement [9].

The goal of intrusion detection system is to detect malicious activities working together with other legitimate system and network activities. A malicious attack is transient activity which harms the system through vulnerabilities. Vulnerability represents exposure and produces the chances to malicious activities to happen. IDS allows the organizations to protect their assets and digital infrastructure from the threats and malicious attacks. In recent scenario, due to heavy reliance on network technologies the chances of malicious activities and cyberattacks have been increased so the question for security professions whether to use IDSs or not is irrelevant.

3.5.1 Functions of Intrusion Detection System

Intrusion Detection System performs the following tasks [10]:

- Intrusion detection system monitors the operations of routers, firewalls, servers to help security controls in order to detecting, preventing and recovering from cyberattack.
- It monitors and records the security-relevant events.
- It helps administrators to organize operating system audit trails.
- It preserves the back-up and highlights the changes in configuration at different checkpoints.
- It provides user friendly interface to ensure system security management.
- It monitors and records human activities to draw the pattern for users' behavior.
- Continuous configuration inspection process is examined to seek possible vulnerabilities and their assessment.

- The unit-wise record keeping is performed with file system management and continuous assessment is done to minimize the risk.
- It stores abnormal system activity patterns and assess them for possible risks.
- Categorize the malicious activities on the basis of their behavior, pattern and frequency.
- Security state of system is continuously evaluated to know the impact of abnormal activities.
- Base-lining the security state of a system to make the tracking and tracing easy.
- Raising alarm and identification of checkpoints is communicated to administrator when security is breached.
- Blocking intruders and source of malicious activities.

3.6 Characteristics of IDS

IDS is a hardware device, software application, or may be a combination of both that examines the network traffic, incorporated systems configuration in order to locate malicious activities, their sources and to respond quickly to counter [11]. An IDS detects policy violations and reports them to security administrators. An IDS should have following characteristics [12, 13], regardless of what mechanism it is based on:

- **Minimum Human Supervision**: IDS do not require human efforts and supervision to get operated.
- **Fault Tolerant**: Good IDS becomes fault tolerant, which means the identification of intrusions does not affect its normal functioning even in an event of system failure.
- **Persistent in nature**: It has capability to run continuously in background without disturbing the system and network configuration setting.
- **Recoverable**: IDS remains unaffected if system crash happens and situation to rebuilt knowledge-base is completely avoided.

- **Resistant to Attacker**: IDS performs periodically assessment of its own to get ensure about its security and non-vulnerabilities.
- **Minimal Overhead**: IDS should comprise limited hardware and software resources to reduce overhead.
- **Self-updateable**: Self-updateability is the desirable feature of IDS in order to reduce human involvement.
- **Accuracy**: High accuracy is always desirable in IDS to generate minimum number of false positives and false negatives alarms.
- **Completeness**: IDS should be able to detect all kinds of malicious patterns and attacks whether from inside or outside the enterprise.
- **Quick-to-action**: IDS should be quick enough to detect the intrusions and respond them appropriately to minimize the damage.

3.6.1 How IDS is important in business organization

Connectivity among the computers and devices, and rapid sharing the information through internet brought people much closer to each other. Networking is now baseline to technology transfer and knowledge sharing. The dark aspect of networking is the threat of intrusions which may cause infiltrations to digital infrastructure that leads to steal data, damage data and disrupt digital life in general. Intrusion detection systems inspect all incoming and outgoing traffic and seek possibilities to intrusion. It raises an alert whenever it finds any vulnerability and malicious activity running across the computers and networks too. Intrusion detection system offers variety of benefits to organizations starting from identification of vulnerabilities to action against the culprits. The Intrusion detection system measures the frequency of attacks to various components of digital infrastructures and analyzes the threats to know their functioning, complexities and even its source too. It highlights drawbacks in existing infrastructure and recommends security measures needs to be implemented in order to have better and effective control. It not only evaluates the existing scenario of threats, but also recognizes their pattern of action and suggests associated future risks.

IDS facilitates a second line of defence that plays a crucial role to enhance security to under-laying digital infrastructure in an enterprise. Although it is difficult to develop a complete and concrete solution to quick response against the malicious activities in order to prevention of attacks, it detects threats and makes appropriate response such as notifying administrators and terminating damaging network connections to minimize the risks.

3.6.2 Components of IDS

There are three main components of IDS named **Data Collection** unit, **Intrusion Detection** unit and **Response** unit. As depicted in *Figure 3.4*, the data collection unit is implemented to network entry point where initial inspection of incoming traffic is matched with log files records where the malicious activities pattern is stored. If the network traffic pattern is matched with log file records, then initially an alert is raised and traffic is blocked. However, if data collection unit remain fail to detect the attack, then intrusion detection unit becomes responsible to neutralize the attack. The Intrusion detection unit is not only to catch intrusion, but also to respond to attack:

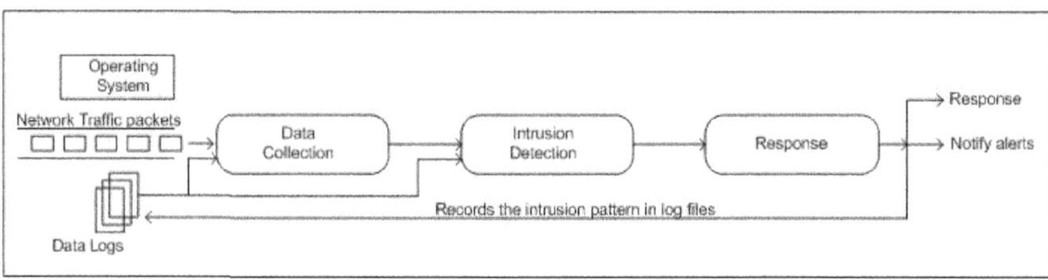

Figure 3.4: *Intrusion Detection System*

Intrusion detection unit deals with inter-organizational and intra-organizational threats and prevent its dispersion across functional units of organization. Response unit notifies the alerts to security administrators and efforts to diminish the impact of attacks. Thereafter, it immediately disconnects the network connections and notifies all the functional units about the occurrence of the malicious pattern.

3.6.3 Architecture of IDS

Intrusion detection systems are designed to detect malicious activities, blocking these activities to reduce the chances of damages and to notify security administrator to register in database as known threat signature. The *Figure 3.5* shows the architecture of IDS:

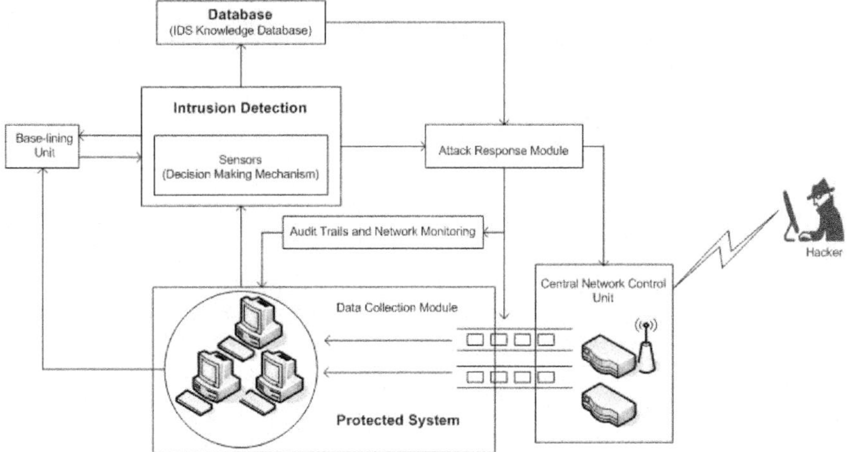

Figure 3.5: *Intrusion Detection System Architecture*

Central Network Control Unit is the central network entry point from where the network distributes across all the functional units of organizations. Intruders target this unit most frequently because each functional unit can be controlled from here as the data is supplied through this unit. This unit acts as a bridge between intruders and enterprise, and becomes beneficial for enterprise on the occurrence of attack to prevent massive damage. This is the unit that talks about the location of intruders and decides whether these are insider or outsider. The attack response module is directly connected to central network control unit that inspects the network traffic pattern carefully. The suspicious network traffic pattern is recognized here.

Data Collection Module is the collection of protected systems that connects with central network control unit and receives the required network traffic to supply their designated place in enterprise digital interconnected infrastructure. The source of network packets is identified and validated here in order to verify authenticity and confidentiality of data packets. The data packets containing malwares, virus and worms are identified and discarded here.

Audit Trails and Network Monitoring unit deals with auditing and helps to fix accountability. Auditing is managed by user logging and their sessional tracking, and to monitor the functioning of other security controls. If the system is not able to verify the individual action, it cannot hold accountable to anyone for their specific action and due to the inability to producing evidences, the culprits cannot be held responsible for their actions. Logging helps to retrace actions and events, provides crucial evidences for prosecution, and helps to re-generate malicious activities paths during the tracking of source of crime. Auditing refers inspection process of logs.It is an inherent functionality of intrusion detection system. Audit trails is the sequence-wise collection of logging incidents, which are recorded in a running file and presented as documentary evidences during the prosecution. Audit trails helps security administrator to know the attempts for security violation, to monitor user activities over time and to identify most vulnerable zones in the interconnected digital infrastructure. Notably, an audit trail is not a protective control, instead it is a record keeping module that maintains the users logging and their activities.

The **IDS Knowledge Database** unit records the information about the previous attempts of intrusions, their methods, patterns, and sources too. It helps intrusion detection unit to recognize the attempts of intrusion and to differentiate the malicious traffic from normal traffic [17]. Whenever a malicious attempt is caught for intrusion, the details like its attacking procedure, route, properties, targeted areas and patterns are recorded in the IDS Knowledge Database unit for future. If a suspicious activity is sensed with intrusion detection unit, its characteristics is matched with previous attempts to verify that the attempt is malicious or not.

The **Intrusion Detection** unit is accountable to detect intrusions and to raise an alarm to the security administrator. It cannot prevent or respond to the malicious attack. The Intrusion detection unit comprises sensor nodes and sinks to detect malicious properties of network traffic and to differentiate it from the normal traffic. Sensors have properties to self-healing and self-organizing due to which their functioning cannot be interrupted and intrusion detection unit remains active during the malicious attacks. The organization of sensors is kept decentralized and distributed in multi-hop intermediate nodes architecture to get quick signals for intrusions across the entire enterprise. The objective of sensors is to collect information about intrusions from their surroundings and to transmit it immediately to sink to raise alarm.

The **Attack Response Module** is a control system that takes immediate action if an intrusion is reported from any functional unit of enterprise. It is an autonomous control system that independently examines the functioning of all units to catch intrusions under its own central control. If the response module diagnoses manipulations in base-line unit and senses hazardous state, then the response module attempts to bring the functioning of all units of intrusion detection systems to its base-line point and restore them at some previous safe state.

Base-line is minimum configuration standards that leaves the intrusion detection system in safe state, means if the configuration standards in base-line unit is found uninterrupted, then it is considered that all functional units are working properly and free from intrusions. The base-line unit meets the minimum configuration standards requirements needs to safety for routers, switches, firewalls and servers working across several units of enterprise.

3.7 Major types of Intrusion Detection System

IDS is a defence mechanism that collects information from system, network and from connected devices too such as routers, bridges, and switches to know the suspicious activities either inside the system or across the network. Information gathered from the mentioned sources is analyzed and used to detect the chances of intrusions and vulnerabilities. This analysis helps security administrator in variety of ways. Initially, it suggests the best solution to administrators to deal with intrusions, vulnerabilities and other malicious activities. Secondly, it encourages them to design a better security framework to tackle such problems for future. Additionally, this analysis lets security administrators to more easily handle the complex problems such as audit-trail management, logging, and monitoring.

3.7.1 Host-Based intrusion detection system

Host-based intrusion detection system (HIDS) monitors the activities running on a specific machine, workstation, server, mobile and devices alike. These activities are examined to detect intrusions and vulnerabilities in a specific host. If intrusions, vulnerabilities and anomalies in system configuration are detected, then it is notified to the security administrator. HIDS acts as an agent that regularly make inspections to ensure the protection of host on which it is installed from insider or outsider threats. The functioning of host-based IDS is dependent on the operating system audit trails and system logs [14]. The operating system audit trail contains security-related chronological records, address of source and destination of records, documentary evidences to justify sequence of activities and their sources. Audit trail sequentially maintains the record of all the activities that affects specific operation, procedure and events [15]. System logs are important resources for computer system management that carry information from various components of computers during their day-to-day operations. The extracted information often becomes relevant to detect the problems in system and helps to security administrator to find anomalies and security breaches [16]. Due to heavy reliance on audit trail and system logs, the protection of audit layer and system logs is highly desirable to remove the chances of misleading information.

After close inspections of the information obtained from audit trails and system logs, HIDS become able to determine attack pattern and abnormal activities across the system. It determines subtle pattern of misuse, subjects accountable for malicious events and affected hardware components and software modules. The HIDS has capability to recover the process that initiated events inside the system and to traceback its source too. Clearly, the processed information can be crucial in stopping future attack and to design a better intrusion detection system [14]. Host-based intrusion system are desirable because it delivers the results in terms of *who accessed what* and trace time-bound irregularities to a specific user ID. In certain circumstances, it is required to judge whether a person working on public accessible computer is part of illicit activities in an enterprise or not. The HIDS decides it well as it keeps track time-bound behavior of individuals with robust evidences [14].

3.7.1.1 Advantages of a host-based system

Host-based intrusion detection systems are in fact much slower than their network counterparts, but the offer several advantages in order to find vulnerabilities and to detect intrusions. These advantages cover stronger forensic analysis, closer inspections of audit trails and low-cost requirement in implementation:

- **Verifies success or failure of an attack**: System logs and audit trails facilitate security administrators to know the malicious activities and their adverse impacts on computers. Host-based IDS uses logs that contain series of time bound events and highlights changes due to external activities. On the inspection of logs and changes to base-line of system, it can be measured whether an attack was successful or not with greater accuracy.

- **Monitors specific system activities**: Host-based IDS not only monitors activities executed by users but also track the changes being done by security administrators. The host-based IDS detects improper changes as soon as these are executed and makes entries at designated places in security related files. To delete these entries, one must have several levels of privileges which is not possible to attain without the co-operation from security administrators. Host-based IDS monitors file access activities such as file access, overwriting, and changes to file permissions and attempts to have a close-eye on added, deleted or modified user accounts.

- **Detects keyboard attack**: Network-based IDS often fails to detect attacks which are triggered suddenly through keyboards. Host-based IDS has ability to detect such attacks.

- **Well-suited for encrypted and switched environments**: Host-based IDS are configured on several hosts across the enterprise and present better solutions to challenges faced with network-based IDS. Network-based IDS are not much effective in switched and encrypted environments as these are not able to detect the malicious activities patterns effectively and let them pass. Switches allow large networks to be managed with many small network segments, having a problem to decide the best location to deploy network-based IDS so that sufficient network coverage can be achieved. In the encrypted and switched environment, Host-based IDS are well suited because intrusions are detected with network traffic monitoring.

- **None additional software and hardware requirement**: Host-based intrusion detection system works on existing network infrastructure containing clients and servers and does not require additional software and hardware to protect systems. As a result, host-based IDS are much cost effective with less maintenance.

3.7.2 Network-based intrusion detection system

Intrusions present several malicious threats enabling the interconnected digital infrastructure surprisingly to be breached. A network-based malicious attack compromises the stability of network and put the security of information stored on several nodes and passing through them in danger. Network-based intrusions cover a wide range of malicious activities, including destabilization of network as whole, gaining unauthorized access to files and privileges, and to disrupt the software installed on. **Network based intrusion detection system (NIDS)** determines the malicious attempts across the network. The information used in detection of malicious attempts and anomalies is collected from the network streams, which refers to transmission of data from one node to another [14]. NIDS examines abnormal behavior of flow of data at ingress and egress points; inspects the contents and header information of all data packets across the network. The availability of wide range of network sensors makes intrusion detection easier as sensors compare the previous malicious attempts patterns with ongoing patterns and discard the similar ones. Advanced sensors are customizable, and are installed as per individual network's needs and usage. Some intrusion detection system facilitates the users to incorporate their own signature with data traffic passing through that allows sensors to identify hostile traffic [14].

3.7.2.1 Advantages of network-based system

Network-based IDS (NIDS) are devices which are strategically positioned over the network to passively inspect network traffic traversing through the network. NIDS are applied to ingress and egress points of data across the network. In some cases, these are also applied to strategic positions and are attached to network devices such as routers, switches, Ethernet, FDDI, and others. NIDS has various advantages are mentioned as follows:

- **Operating system independent**: Network-based IDS are independent to operating systems and function equally for all kinds of operating systems.
- **Detects unsuccessful attacks and malicious intent**: Cyber-attack can be viewed as successful and not successful. In case of successful, malicious attempts achieve their target for which these are launched and their working pattern is not disrupted with any kind of intrusion detection system. On the other hand, the malicious attack which fails due to some detection and prevention system to get control over systems and network is viewed as unsuccessful. To develop a better intrusion detection system, we need to know the working procedure and attacking pattern of malicious attempts, no matter whether it was successful or failure. Successful attack means our strategy to protect the system and network is not adequate and existing vulnerabilities in an interconnected digital infrastructure are making the situations severe. Indeed, in some cases, our system neutralizes malicious attempts but these cannot be ignored completely. Host-based IDS do not detect the unsuccessful malicious attempts effectively, but in case of network-based IDS, these are monitored and detected surprisingly that plays a crucial role in refining security policies.
- **Real-time detection and response**: If we can detect and prevent the malicious activity at its origin point then we can protect our whole infrastructure, but if it goes undetected from origin, then the problem becomes gradually severe as it grows further. Host-based IDS do not have ability to detect the source of a malicious activity as it takes action only when malicious stream come to host. Network-based IDS are capable of restricting the malicious activity at its origin and prevents it to grow further. The network-based IDS performs real-time intrusion detection because it does not require network traffic storage for inspection.
- **Evidence removal is difficult**: Network-based intrusion is detected in real time and data-traffic need not be stored to

get examined for intrusions. Manipulation in data in live network traffic is very difficult and needs highly skilled experts. Security agencies examine evidences rendered with cyber-attacks to locate the origin and to arrest the culprits. To evade the arrest and to hide crime origin, culprits remove the evidences. Evidence removal in live data traffic across the network is much difficult or almost impossible in comparison to host-based intrusion detection. To remove the evidences culprits, we need to manipulate the normal data traffic which is possible only when the data traffic is diverted and people drive into network jams. Network-based IDS uses live network traffic to detect intrusions. Therefore, evidences removal is almost impossible in a network-based system.

3.8 Host-based IDS versus Network-Based IDS

Host based intrusion detection is all about setting up the software on a system, which evaluates the activities running on system. The data which is analyzed to detect intrusions is obtained from system logs and audit trails. Host-based IDS not only monitors suspicious activities, but also evaluates system's internals along with network packets at ingress and egress points to a particular host. Host-based IDS monitors the integrity of system files and evaluate the behavior of system due to integrity violation. Network-based IDS works on different philosophy, it scans network packets at network devices, audits network packets information, maintains special log files to investigate logging records. Network-based IDS is now desirable due to rapid growth of internet and data traffic, and it can scan voluminous amounts of network activities to identify the suspicious network pattern. The *Table 3.2* shows major differences between Host-Based IDS and Network-Based IDS [18]:

Criteria	Host-Based IDS	Network-Based IDS
Deterrence	Strong deterrence within the boundary of organization when the culprits are insiders.	Strong deterrence beyond the boundary of organization when the culprits are outsiders.

Detection	Detect malicious attempts created from the insiders.	Detect malicious attempts created from the outsiders.
Storage	Log Summary and Log Raw Network Data.	Does not require log summary storage.
Notification	Alarm to Console of the system.	Alarm to the security administrator.
Response	Poor real-time response.	Strong real-time response.
Damage Coverage	Damage is limited to the system and the concerned organization.	Damage coverage is unpredictable.
Attack Detection time-period	Comparatively small time-slot is required to detect intrusions.	Large-time slot is required to detect malicious attempts.
False positive and false negative	False-positives and false-negatives are limited in numbers.	False-positives and false-negatives cannot be predicted.
Source Identification	Crime source can be easily identified.	Crime-source identification is difficult and often requires international co-operation.

Table 3.2: *Difference between Host-based IDS and Network-based IDS*

Host-based intrusions are caused due to misuse of system-privileges, while in network-based intrusions, vulnerabilities play a crucial role. Network-based intrusion is difficult process and needs to seek vulnerabilities to enter in the organization personal network, thereafter, privileges of systems are captured. However, in case of a host-based intrusion, insiders do not need to exploit network vulnerabilities because they are already in network and have their own privileges. Once an outsider accesses the organizations private network through network vulnerabilities and gains privileges, then outsiders are considered as insiders.

3.9 Intrusion detection and prevention principles

Intrusion detection is an attempt to identify breach of computer security policies and standard security practices. There are various causes of intrusions such as malware, attackers who are gaining unauthorized access through the internet, and legitimate users who misuse their privileges and doing efforts to get additional privileges for which they are not authorized [6]. An intrusion detection system is software that detects intrusion automatically and alarms the security administrator to patch the security breaches. The **intrusion prevention system (IPS)** performs two tasks: initially, it detects the intrusions thereafter it takes action to neutralize the malicious attempts. IPS is basically extension of IDS in which data traffic with malicious attempts is supplied and threats causing security violations are filtered out. Few researchers [6] describe IPS as **intrusion detection and prevention system (IDPS)**, which facilitates security administrators to disable prevention module to get the functions of intrusion detection.

3.9.1 Functions of IDPS

There are various kinds of IDPS that can be differentiated primarily on the basis of events that they can recognize and the methodologies they use to detect intrusions. In addition to monitoring and recognizing malicious attempts, IDPS also identifies undesirable activities in system and across the network as well. IDPS performs the following functions:

3.9.1.1 Maintaining system log

System logs are important resources that communicate system management details. System logs such as windows Event logs or Linux system logs preserve textual messages containing details about its time-bound operations are extracted from various attached resources. System logs messages highlight problems in systems whether these are trivial or serious; and detect anomalies and security breaches too. Periodic monitoring and maintenance of system logs is vital for better and quick diagnosis [19]. IDPS regularly updates system logs to ensure the security of system.

3.9.1.2 Maintaining audit trail

Auditing and logging are essential components for security of any digital architecture. It is essential for security administrator to know what is being done, where it is being done, when it is being done, and by whom it was done. Logging, activities performed in particular session, and events occurring detail provides a wonderful means to investigate malicious attempts. Audit trail also helps to know the system-resource used during attack and mis-configuration existing in security controls. The IDPS consists a management console that integrates system logs with application logs and records audit trail [20].

3.9.1.3 Recording malicious attempts information

Knowing the pattern of a cyber-attack is essential as it helps to prevent similar attacks in the future. The network traffic is stored and examined to deduce the relevant information even if the traffic is encrypted. Recording malicious attempts information and its close inspection results enable security administrators to know the severity of malicious activities being performed with invading computers and present best possible solutions to protect the individuals' personal data from misuse, digital assets from stealing and the infrastructure from damage. The information about malicious attempts is generally recorded locally, and could be sent to remote centralized logging servers for detailed inspections.

3.9.1.4 Notifying administrators about observed key event

The results of network traffic analysis with highlighted key events are sent to security administrator or network manager to know the motivation behind malicious activity, to determine source and routes, and to know frequency of occurrence. Once the attack is detected and reported to security administrator, the key events are observed to know that how malicious traffic mingles with normal traffic and to determine the areas that seem as targets. Key events help network administrators to locate the vulnerabilities and to patch them, and to reduce the chances of same attack in future.

3.9.1.5 Producing reports

The IDPS report summarizes the events occurring in a computer system or network and highlights the signs of possible incidents that are violating computer security and network security policies. It contains log information of each activity with time slots and is shared with security administrator for immediate response to minimize the risk of damage. All successful breaches are recorded in report with preliminary intention to gain better understanding about the threats and their activation pattern together with frequency. Unsuccessful malicious attempts are also required to analyze as these expose the vulnerabilities in the existing system.

3.9.1.6 Intrusions prevention

An IDPS monitors network traffic and examines it to seek signs of possible attacks. When a malicious activity is detected, it takes appropriate action to stop it and notify the security administrator for permanent solutions. IDPS uses pre-existing database for the recognition of malicious threats and measures the network traffic and behavioral anomalies to know its adverse impacts. Quick response is always expected from IDPS against the suspiciou s activities to prevent them completely from succeeding.

The IDPS perform the following functions to prevent malicious activities [22, 23]:

- Terminating the network connection or user session, in which malicious activity takes place
- Making the target outreached from offending users and related IP address
- Blocking every kind of access to the targeted host
- It makes necessary changes in configuration of network devices such as firewall, router, and switches to block their access from the criminal side
- The removal of malicious portion from network traffic to disable an attack
- Patching up vulnerabilities at target hosts
- Its role as proxy makes it possible to normalize the incoming requests, repackaging the payloads of requests, and discarding header information that leads the discarding of malicious attempts as part of normalization process

3.9.2 Common detection methodologies

IDPS are now integral part of organizations as it protects its digital infrastructure from cybercriminals. It uses multiple numbers of threats detection methodologies which are either performed separately or in an integrated manner, to provide broad and accurate detection. The most common methodologies are signature-based, anomaly-based, and stateful protocol analysis are being used at large scale across the globe.

3.9.2.1 Signature-based detection

The signature-based detection includes a process in which a unique identifier is established corresponding to a known threat [22]. It is the simplest detection method as it compares the arrival procedure of an event or threat with a list of signatures through stings operations. Any activity shows symmetry with available signature or pattern is flagged as threat. The list of signatures can be a database or a list of known malicious threats depicting their breach and activation patterns [24]. The signature-based detection technique is very effective and well-suited for known threats, but remains ineffective against new threats or variants of known threats. It has little overhead as it does not examine every activity across the whole network traffic and seek the symmetry with known signature. The signature-based detection suffers with inability to remember previous requests during processing of newer one. This limitation presents an obstacle for the signature-based detection method to detect an attack comprising multiple events.

3.9.2.2 Anomaly-based detection

Anomaly detection approaches construct models for normal data traffic and sets the baselines profiles. The baseline profile incorporates the behavioral study of users, hosts, network connections, or applications and measures the activities such as sending and receiving messages, successful and failure attempts to gain logins, and processor utilization. The baseline profile refers to an examined normal behavior of the monitored system and is constructed to make a comparison with some suspicious events. This comparison measures the significant deviations from a normal behavior of network traffic and helps to decide whether newly occurring event belongs to normal traffic or showing anomalous behavior. In the anomaly detection methodology, the perturbations against baseline profile suggest induced attacks, faults, defects, and so on [24, 25]. The benefit of anomaly-based approach is its effectiveness in detecting previously unknown threats.

3.9.2.3 Stateful protocol analysis

The intrusion detection systems that use the statistical data to detect the possible intrusions are now more effective as these includes long-term behavior of each user and records it to prepare a profile. This profile is attached to corresponding user and compared with baseline whenever needed. The stateful protocol analysis can be thought as an extension of signature-based detection approach and incorporates protocol analysis to detect the intrusions [24]. It measures how a protocol should behave whenever it is used as a base for the development of IDPS. This detection approach develops a deep understanding about interface and elaborates how the protocols and applications should interact to reduce the impact of intrusions [25]. In the stateful protocol analysis, predetermined profiles of generally accepted definitions of benign protocols are compared against observed events to identify deviations [22]. It believes on universally constructed vendor-developed profiles and sets the specifications for protocols at a certain state. The term *stateful* describes that IDPS has capability to track the state of network, transport, and application protocols with a notation of state [22].

3.9.3 Evaluation of methodologies

Access control and authentication are two basic techniques used to prevent intruders and often fail to prevent sophisticated attacks. Intrusion detection and prevention systems are expected to detect an intrusion as soon as it takes place and to apply countermeasures immediately to reduce the chances of damages. The development of IDPS needs detection methodologies for its proper and effective functioning and security administrators feel problem while choosing one. David Mudzingwa and Rajeev Agrawal evaluated and compared detection methodologies as depicted in *Table 3.3*:

Evaluation parameters	Signature based methodologies	Anomaly-Based Detection	Stateful protocol analysis
Resistance to evasion	Low	Medium	Low
Accuracy rate	Medium	Medium	Medium
Market share	High	Medium	Medium
Scalability	High	Medium	High
Maturity level	High	High	High
Overhead on Monitored system	Low	Medium	Low
Maintenance	Medium	Low	Medium
Performance	High	Medium	High
Configuration	Yes	No	Yes
Ease of use	Low	Medium	Low
Effectiveness against new attacks	Low	High	Medium
False positive	Low	High	Low
False negative	Medium	High	Medium

***Table 3.3**: Evaluation Methodologies comparison*

3.9.4 IDPS technologies

Organizations use IDPS technologies to determine hazards in security polices, preparing database of existing threats and to identify people violating security policies. The IDPS technologies have been categorized in to following four groups on the basis of events they monitor and method with which they are deployed.

3.9.4.1 Network-based IDPS

Network-based intrusion detection and prevention system is applied to ingress point to monitor passing network traffic to particular segments and to associated devices. It examines network traffic as well as application protocols to recognize malicious traffic and to prevent them to cause damages. The pattern and behavior of passing network traffic through entire segment are matched to known attack patterns available in database and decided whether traffic is malicious or normal. The network-based IDPS is constructed with sensors, management servers, multiple interfaces, consoles and database servers, and applied at the common boundary of two networks, routers, **virtual private network** (**VPN**) servers, remoter access servers and wireless networks [22]. Network-based IDPS mainly focuses on the application layer and examines the entire data traffic dedicated to **Hypertext Transfer Protocol** (**HTTP**), **Simple Mail Transfer Protocol** (**SMTP**) and **Domain Name System** (**DNS**). The protocols working with transport layer such as **Transmission Control Protocol** (**TCP**) and **User Datagram Protocol** (**UDP**) are also analyzed to find suspicious activities.

The network-based IDPS can be activated in two modes either in inline or passive. In inline mode, the sensors are deployed to examine real-time network traffic that passes through them, and in passive mode, a copy of the actual traffic is examined for suspicious activities. Passive sensors maintain monitoring of network traffic through spanning port and network tap. The spanning port ensures the monitoring of all network traffic through a switch while network tap establishes a direct connection between as sensor and network itself. The inline network-based IDPS believes in blocking traffic if suspicious activity is detected while passive sensor notifies to security administrators.

The network-based IDPS facilitates a broad range of anomalies detection and includes signature-based, anomaly-based, and stateful protocol analysis together to measure deviations from normal behavior. Its sensors detect unexpected events such as backdoors and vulnerability existence, and sense violations in security policies. Some dedicated sensors examine the established connections in encrypted communications to ensure the appropriateness of configuration.

3.9.4.2 Wireless-based IDPS

Wireless networking facilitates networked devices to communicate remotely and transmitting data without being physically connected to each other. This requires only presence of devices within the stipulated range of wireless network infrastructure. A wireless IDPS examines the wireless network traffic for anomalies and inspect wireless networking for misconfiguration. The **Institute of Electrical and Electronics Engineers** (**IEEE**) 802.11 represents family of **WLAN** (**Wireless Local Area Network**) standards having two fundamental architectural components named a **station** (**STA**) and an **Access Point** (**AP**). A station represents a wireless device and is logically connected to the wired network of an organization through access point. Each access point on WLAN is represented with a name called **service set identifier** (**SSID**) that plays a key role to differentiate one WLAN from another. Wireless sensors work differently due to complexities and use sampling traffic to examine the network traffic. Two frequency bands are used with 2.4 gigahertz and 5 GHz in frequency, and separated into channels.

3.9.4.3 Network behavior analysis (NBA)

A network behavior analysis plays a crucial role to detect intrusions. Network traffic and its related statistics enables security administrator to differentiate malicious traffic from legitimate traffic. The NBA incorporates sensors, consoles, and management servers. The sensors detect the occurrence of unusual traffic and management servers share the traffic loads with the help of console. NBA sensors behave like IDPS sensors as these sniff packets to examine network activity across various segments of network and are arranged to work actively or passively by placing them at network boundaries. The sensors collect the statistics about network flow through routers and other networked devices and compare these statistics with baseline standards to measure deviations. The network flow refers to data transmission between two hosts within a session and uses the IP address of source and destination ends. NBA scans source and destination TCP and UDP ports, and determines the ICMP types to measures deviations and sense intrusions at these ports. The number of packets and bytes being transmitted in a session are analyzed with timestamps to locate the vulnerability existence between two hosts or networked devices.

NBA technologies primarily use anomaly-based detection and stateful protocol analysis techniques to detect unusual traffic and allow customization of filters to detect or stop specific attacks. The NBA sensors primarily facilitate **Denial-of-service (DoS)** attack detection and network port scanning, and completely stop the unexpected application services from activation. These sensors examine malicious events carefully to locate its source and reconstruct reverse chain to determine true origin of attacks. Although NBA technologies are best suited for malicious traffic filtration, it suffers with significant limitations. The delay in intrusion detection is most common and is caused due to hindrance in data sources configurations.

3.9.4.4 Host-Based IDPS

In Host-based IDPS examines each event occurring within host to seek suspicious activities. It monitors network traffic passing through a node, analyses file access privileges preserved on disk, and checks system and network configurations to track illegitimate changes. Host-based IDPS are popularly known as agents and are installed on the concerned host. These agents access the internal architecture of hosts and place a SHIM between existing layers of code. **System Health and Intrusion Monitoring (SHIM)** is used to validate each running process and senses the malicious packets in encrypted interpersonal communications. It is applied at a point from where one code segment is passed to another code of segments and analyzes the network traffic to decide whether to allowed or denied.

The host-based IDPS conducts the code analysis with the specimen of detected malicious code and executes it in the virtual environment or in sandbox to know its adverse impacts over windows repositories, system files, operating systems layers and its internal architecture. The process, due to which the data is preserved on disk and transferred to memory and further to microprocessor, is analyzed to ensure the security of stack and heap buffer. The instructions sequences through which memory portions are assigned to some files and process are validated to ensure its safety from malicious codes. It facilitates integrity checking and generates cryptographic checksum for system file to determine whether its integrity is breached or not. Some host-based IDPS allows file attributes checking to validate files ownerships and permissions.

Conclusion

In this chapter, we have discussed the CIA triad with its key parameters named confidently, integrity and availability, and elaborated Defensive Life-cycle with its four major phases. The detailed categorization of intrusions has been presented for broad understanding about different kinds of cyber-attacks. The intrusion detection system has been defined with its architecture and major components. We have also discussed its characteristics, functions and major types. Furthermore, we have explained Intrusion Detection and Prevention System with its major functions and detailed the methodologies used to detect intrusions. The signature-based detection, Anomaly-Based Detection, and Stateful protocol analysis have been elaborated to detect known threats and unknown data traffic.

In the next chapter, we shall focus on cyber forensic and detail some techniques that are used by criminals to hide their true locations. The major traceback schemes shall be discussed to have a broad overview about trace back system and its utilization to prevent the cybercrimes.

Points to remember

- The critical national infrastructure includes processes, systems, facilities, technologies, networks, assets and services which are essential for a nation to its financial and social health, safety, security or economic well-being.
- Critical national Infrastructure is like a life support system for services offered to citizens for their survival in a country.
- Confidentiality refers to the ability to hide sensitive data and information from unauthorized people to view it.
- Data integrity refers to the assurance of originality of data. It is the ability to ensure that the available copy of data is accurate and unaltered representation of original data.
- Intrusion refers to malicious activity within software, nodes, network, and in the IT infrastructure.
- Intrusion detection system (IDS) refers to software or hardware systems, or combination of hardware and software which automates the process of monitoring the events taking place inside a computer system or network, analyzing logs to identify the signs of security problems.
- A malicious attack is a transient activity that harms the system through vulnerabilities.
- Intrusion detection system monitors the operations of routers, firewalls, servers to help security controls in order to detecting, preventing and recovering from cyber-attack.
- Intrusion detection system (IDS) facilitates a second line of defense that plays a crucial role to enhance security of underplaying digital infrastructure in an enterprise.

- There are three main components of IDS named Data collection unit, Intrusion Detection Unit and Response Unit.
- Intrusion detection unit deals with inter-organizational and intra-organizational threats and prevent its dispersion across functional units of organizations.
- Audit trails is the sequence-wise collection of logging incidents, which are recorded in a running file and presented as documentary evidences during the prosecution.
- Baseline is minimum configuration standards that leaves the intrusion detection system in safe state, means if the configuration standards in base-line unit is found uninterrupted, then it is considered that all functional units are working properly and free from intrusions.
- **Host-based intrusion detection system (HIDS)** monitors the activities running on a specific machine, workstation, server, mobile and devices alike.
- Operating system audit trail contains security related chronological records, address of source and destination of records, documentary evidences to justify sequence of activities and their sources.
- Audit trail sequentially maintains the record of all the activities that affect specific operation, procedure and events.
- System logs and audit trails facilitate security administrators to know the malicious activities and their adverse impacts on computers.
- **Network-based Intrusion detection system (NIDS)** determines the malicious attempts across the network.
- NIDS examines abnormal behavior of flow of data at ingress and egress points; inspects the contents and header information of all data packets across the network.
- Intrusion prevention system (IPS) performs two tasks: initially, it detects the intrusions thereafter it takes action to neutralize the malicious attempts.
- System logs such as windows Event logs or Linux system logs preserve textual messages containing details about the its

time-bound operations are extracted from various attached resources.

- IDPS uses pre-existing database for the recognition of malicious threats and measures the network traffic and behavioral anomalies to know its adverse impacts.
- The signature-based detection includes a process in which a unique identifier is established corresponding to a known threat.
- The signature-based detection technique is very effective and well-suited for known threats but remains ineffective against new threats or variants of known threats.
- Anomaly detection approaches construct models for normal data traffic and set the baselines profile.
- Baseline profile incorporates the behavioral study of users, hosts, network connections, or applications and measures the activities like sending and receiving messages, successful and failure attempts to gain logins, processor utilization, and so on.
- The baseline profile refers to examined normal behavior of the monitored system and is constructed to make a comparison with some occurring suspicious events.
- The benefit of an anomaly-based approach is its effectiveness in detecting previously unknown threats.
- Network-based IDPS mainly focus on application layer and examines entire data traffic dedicated to Hypertext Transfer Protocol (HTTP), Simple Mail Transfer Protocol (SMTP) and Domain Name System (DNS).

MCQ

1. **Which of the following does not belong to CIA triad?**
   a. Confidentiality
   b. Integrity
   c. Availability
   d. Authenticity

2. **TLS stands for?**
    a. Transmission Layer Socket
    b. Transport Layer Security
    c. Transport Layer Secrecy
    d. Transmission Logs Session

3. **Which one of the following does not belong to Defensive life-cycle?**
    a. Analysis
    b. Prevention
    c. Detection
    d. Maintenance

4. **Network-based IDPS mainly focus on ________ layer protocols?**
    a. Data link
    b. Physical
    c. Presentation
    d. Application

5. **Signature-based detection is not suited for:**
    a. Known Threats
    b. Unknown Threats
    c. Known Signature
    d. Known Data Traffic

6. **The benefit of anomaly-based approach includes:**
    a. Its effectiveness to known threats
    b. Its effectiveness to Unknown Data Traffic
    c. Its effectiveness to Known Signature
    d. Its effective ness to Known Data Traffic

7. **SHIM stands for:**
    a. System Health and Intrusion Monitoring
    b. System Health and Intrusion Management

c. Secure Hosting and Internet Monitoring

d. Secure Hosting and Intrusion Management

8. **SSID stands for:**

a. Service Set Identifier

b. Secure Set Identifier

c. Secure Socket Identifier

d. Secure Socket Intrusion Detection

Answer

1. d
2. b
3. c
4. d
5. b
6. b
7. a
8. a

Questions

1. Describe Critical National Infrastructure and its security in detail.
2. Explain Confidentiality-Integrity-Availability Triad in detail.
3. Describe the utility of Defensive Life-Cycle.
4. Define Intrusion Detection System (IDS) and its major responsibilities.
5. Describe the major functions of Intrusion Detection System (IDS) in details.
6. Explain the following:

   I. Confidentiality

   II. Data Integrity

   III. Availability

   IV. System Logs
   V. Audit trails

7. Explain the major characteristics of Intrusion Detection System.
8. What are major components of Intrusion Detection System? Explain.
9. Explain the architecture of Intrusion Detection System in detail.
10. Differentiate the following:
    I. HIDS Versus NIDS
    II. IDS Versus IDPS
    III. System Logs Versus Audit Trails
    IV. Signature-based Detection Versus Anomaly-Based Detection
11. Describe the Host-based Intrusion Detection System with its advantages.
12. Describe the Network-based Intrusion Detection System with its advantages.
13. What do you mean by Intrusion Detection and Prevention System? Elaborate its responsibilities.
14. What are the major functions of Intrusion Detection and Prevention System? Explain in detail.
15. Explain the methodologies used to detect intrusions in Intrusion Detection and Prevention System?

References

[1] **https://www.profolus.com/topics/critical-infrastructure-definition-and-examples/**

[2] A report, *"Glossary: Revision to Emergency Preparedness"*, Civil Contingencies Act Enhancement Programme, Cabinett Office, March 2012.

[3]**https://publicwiki01.fraunhofer.de/CIPedia/index.php/Critical_National_Infrastructure# cite_note-6.**

[4] A Report, *"National Cyber Security Strategy"*, Isle of Man Government, 2018-2022. Available at **https://www.gov.im/media/1363851/national-cyber-security-strategy.pdf**

[5] A Report, *"The protection of critical infrastructures against terrorist attacks: Compendium of good practices"*, office of counter terrorism, United Nations, 2018.

[6] Rebecca Bace and Peter Mell, *"NIST Special Publication on Intrusion Detection Systems"*, Infidel, Inc., Scotts Valley, CA National Institute of Standards and Technology.

[7] **https://www.owasp.org/index.php/Detect_intrusions.**

[8]**http://www.infosectoday.com/Articles/Security_Event_Management/Security_Event_Management.htm**

[9] A report from, *"Intrusion Detection System Buyer's Guide"*, ICSA Lab, available at: **http://www.forum-intrusion.com/Buyers_Guide.pdf**

[10] **https://searchsecurity.techtarget.com/definition/intrusion-detection-system**

[11]**_http://www.ids-sax2.com/articles/IDS(tasks&architecture).htm**

[12] **http://shodhganga.inflibnet.ac.in/bitstream/10603/86847/9/09_chapter%201.pdf**

[13] A Report, *"IDS – Intrusion Detection System"*, CERT-In Indian Computer Emergency Response Team Handling Computer Security Incidents, CERT-In Security Guideline CISG-2003-06, Department of Information Technology, Ministry of Communications and Information Technology, Government of India.

[14] A Report, *"Host- vs. Network-Based Intrusion Detection Systems: Use offence to inform defence. Find flaws before the bad guys do"*, SANS Penetration Testing site, 2000.

[15] **https://en.wikipedia.org/wiki/Audit_trail**

[16] Sivan Sabato, Elad Yom-Tov, Aviad Tsherniak, Saharon Rosset, *"Analyzing System Logs: A New View of What's Important"*,

[17] Leonid Portony, ElezarEskin and Sal Stolfo, *"Intrusion Detection with unlabeled data using Clustering"*, In Proceedings of ACM CSS Workshop on Data Mining Applied to Security, 2001.

[18] Harley Kozushko, *"Intrusion Detection: Host-Based and Network-Based Intrusion Detection Systems"*, Independent study, 2003.

[19] Sivan Sabato, Elad Yom-Tov, Aviad Tsherniak, Saharon Rosset, *"Analyzing System Logs: A New View of What's Important"*, 2007.

[20] **https://www.stigviewer.com/stig/idps_security_requirements_guide_srg/2012-03-08/finding/SRG-NET-000112-IDPS-000072**

[21] Saman Shojae Chaeikar, Mohammadreza Jafari, Hamed Taherdoost and Nakisa Shojae Chaeikar, *"Definitions and Criteria of CIA Security Triangle in Electronic Voting System"*, International Journal of Advanced Computer Science and Information Technology, October 2012.

[22] Karen Scarfone and Peter Mell, *"Guide to Intrusion Detection and Prevention Systems (IDPS)"*, National Institute of standards and technology, US Department of Commerce, February 2007.

[23] A Report, *"Intrusion Detection and Prevention Systems"*, available at **https://tsapps.nist.gov/publication/get_pdf.cfm?pub_id=901146#:~:text=IDPS%20technologies%20use%20many%20methodologies,more%20broad%20and%20accurate%20detection.**

[24] David Mudzingwa and Rajeev Agrawal, *"A study of Methodologies used in Intrusion Detection and Prevention Systems (IDPS)"*, in Proceedings of IEEE Southeastcon, 2012.

[25] Aleksandar Lazarevic, Levent Ertoz, Vipin Kumar, Aysel Ozgur, Jaideep Srivastava, *"A Comparative Study of Anomaly Detection Schemes in Network Intrusion Detection"*, Published in SDM 2003.

CHAPTER 4
Cybercrime Source Identification Techniques

Network-based intrusions are now central concern and are now dangerous to complete digital infrastructure and network in an organization. The existing security mechanisms like Intrusion Detection System and firewall are not much effective as these efforts to protect not to react. The complete prevention of these network-based intrusions requires a mechanism that can trace the complete attack-path, identify the source of malicious packets, and apply counteraction against detected intrusions. This chapter mainly emphasizes on tracing the path along which criminals commit crimes. It also details popular traceback schemes used to deter network-based intrusions and elaborates the techniques used to locate the true source of cybercrime.

Structure

In this chapter, we will cover the following topics:

- Cyber forensic
- Assumptions in traceback
- Classification of traceback schemes

- Evaluation of IP traceback schemes
- Sleepy Watermark Tracing (SWT)

Objective

The main objective of this chapter is to elaborate technologies usually used to reach to the exact origin from where the crime is conducted and to trace the route of malicious transition. It defines Cyber forensic and suggests different actions when an intrusion is detected across digital infrastructure. In this chapter, you shall understand traceback mechanism and its detailed classification to know the basic assumptions of each one. The evaluation of these traceback mechanisms with different parameters will help you choose the most suitable scheme and to know the benefits and drawbacks of each one. The **sleepy watermark tracing** (**SWT**) with its detailed architecture will enable you to understand the benefits of active response whenever intrusion is detected.

4.1 Cyber forensic

In the physical world, it is believed that criminals always leave something at the crime scene and takes away something with them that helps security personnels to reach the criminals [1]. Identifying the origin of cybercrime has always been a difficult task and the field of cyber forensic helps us in this direction. Cyber forensic refers to a scientific process that performs identification, seizure, collection, authentication, analysis, documentation and preservation of digital evidences left during malicious activity [2]. It is basically a science that extracts forensic information from associated hardware and software that can be submitted during legal prosecutions as evidences [2]. Although there is a complementary relationship between cyber forensic and cyber security in general, in order to ensure the security of interconnected digital environment cyber forensic process has a key role. Cyber forensic primarily focuses on collection, preservation, and analysis of digital evidences after the occurrence of cybercrime, while cyber security is a procedure that is usually applied before the occurrence of cybercrime and deals with the maintenance of confidently, integrity, and availability.

4.2 Intrusion activities

Intrusion detection, Intrusion prevention, intrusion tolerance and intrusion response are major activities needed to be performed to effectively deal with network-based intrusion [19]. Intrusion detection systems classify the intrusion activities in four categories as shown in *Figure 4.1* to tackle with intrusions. Intrusion detection means to detect malicious code in network traffic. Intrusion prevention refers to the procedure to ensure the security of particular node or infrastructure from malicious threats. Intrusion tolerance is the ability of the system and infrastructure to bear the intrusions, and at the same time, ensure the availability and integrity of system [19]. Intrusion response means application of countermeasures to fix the cause to prevent future attack. It is the reaction made in response to intrusion to the attacker in order to break the attack path or to patch up the source of malicious packets:

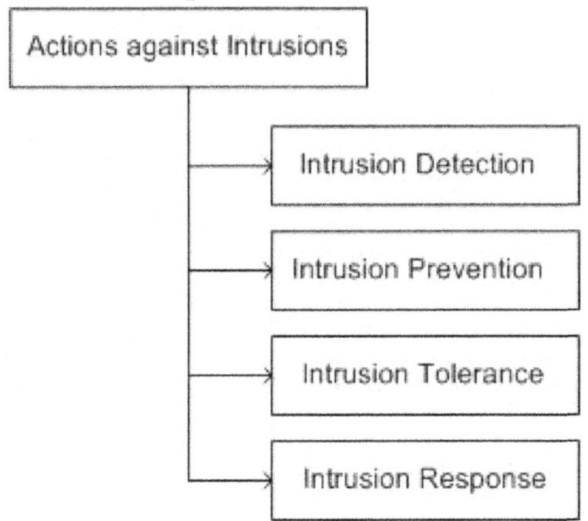

***Figure 4.1**: Intrusion activities*

It is desirable to determine network-based intrusion quickly near its source to protect the slave computers and infrastructure from being compromised. There are several approaches used to deter intrusions across network, but most of them are passive in nature, means these approaches require storage of network traffic for further analysis. The storage of voluminous data traffic limits the practical use of these passive approaches. Active intrusion detection approach dynamically identifies the malicious packets without storing the data traffic. It does not need to compare incoming data traffic with concurrent outgoing data traffic to sense deviation.

4.3 Attribution and traceback

Our interconnected digital environment is now at higher risk and extremely vulnerable to financially and politically motivated criminals. The availability of affordable hacking tools in black markets in the dark web is making the situations more severe. These tools help novices to get converted into cyber criminals without requiring technical and hacking skills. A single well-targeted malicious packet can degrade performance or even disable vital network services too [4]. To fix the accountability of such criminals who are generating malicious, packets must be identified.

Attribution refers to the process of determining the identity or location of cybercriminal. Identity of cybercriminal incorporates geographic location, IP address, account, and ethernet address [3]. Attribution not only deals with origin, but also identify intermediary nodes through which a system is victimized. An ideal attribution process always determines the true source of malicious packets with concrete evidences. Identification of true source of cybercrime is extremely difficult; criminals are using sophisticated tools to hide themselves behind the digital shield of anonymity. They launch attack through a chain of hundreds to thousands compromised computers scattered across different countries. In practice, most of the countries do not show affirmative and immediate cooperation during the investigation and prosecution against the cybercrime. Also, these countries restrict the investigation agencies to investigate the crime scene and its origin due to fear of image disruption on international platform.

If we do not know the true source of malicious packets, we cannot apply the appropriate counter measure at the right place.As a result, the possibilities of future attack remains alive and culprits evade from punishment. Traceback is a method to reach from victim computers to source of attack. It refers to a procedure to know the origin of malicious packets that begins from defending computer and recursively steps backwards across attack path toward the attacking computer [3]. Unfortunately, the anonymity of IP protocol makes it difficult to accurately identify the attacking computer and facilitates criminals to hide themselves.

4.4 Why attribution is difficult?

Ideally, a traceback mechanism should locate the criminal in person who commits the crime, but in reality, the computer with which malicious activity is initiated is identified. Criminals conceal the IP address of their computer to avoid detection and impersonate as another computer. David A. Wheeler et al. [3] details some common approaches used to conceal the IP address of computer through which crime is conducted. These approaches are detailed as follows:

1. Forging and modifying the source IP address is a popular way to hide the actual IP address through which crime is conducted. This forging is known as **spoofing** and is based on the fact that the source of the packet remains unused until it reaches the destinations. The criminals send malicious packets to target computer and forge their IP address to impersonate as another computer as shown in *Figure 4.2*. Whenever the destination hosts responses to the criminal computer, it is found missing:

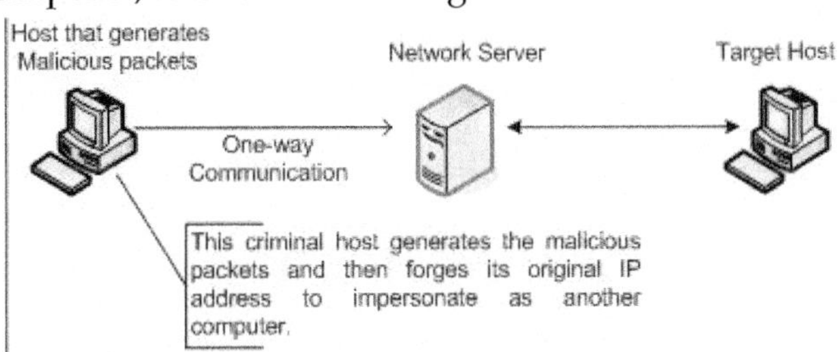

***Figure 4.2**: Forging IP address*

2. The true location of criminal is hidden with the use of reflector host that enables criminals to pass malicious packets through it to target host, but does not permit the victims to communicate with criminals. The reflector host acts a shield that hides the criminals behind it. Whenever the response is generated from the victim hosts for criminals, the reflector hosts communicate with it as the original packet sender host:

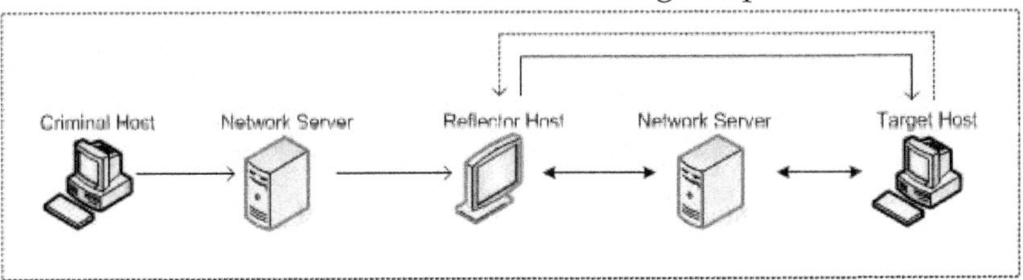

***Figure 4.3:** Reflector host*

The preceding *Figure 4.3* shows that reflector host captures the IP of criminal host and communicates with victim. The communication between reflector host and criminal host becomes unidirectional. Therefore, the reflector host only follows the instructions received from the criminal host.

3. Sometimes **time-to-live** (**TTL**) logic is used to temporarily setup a host for a very short span of time. The malicious packets are delivered with this temporary host and thereafter it is removed.
4. Cybercriminals generate the time-gap between the delivery of malicious packets and their activation. Laundering hosts inject the delay in packets to remain inactive for a specific time-period. Laundering hosts provides the ample opportunities to criminals to make them flee from crime scenes.
5. Criminals are now cleverer; they break the whole malicious program into a number of modules and preserve it on different previously compromised computers existing at different geographical locations under the control of the master computer. The malicious modules are transmitted through different sources and routes, and assembled at the target computer to trigger an attack.

4.5 Assumptions in traceback

Network-based attacks cause huge financial loss and can disrupt vital services across the world. The existing network security mechanism such as IDS and Firewall are not adequate to protect the systems and network infrastructure because they do not block origin of malicious packets, instead these mechanisms protect the systems and personal network infrastructure. Ideally, a traceback system should be capable of identifying the source of any piece of data transmitted over network, whether it is containing malicious code or not. There are several assumptions that should be considered during formation of the traceback system, which are as follows [4]:

- Packets may be addressed to more than one computer
- Duplication of packets is possible across the network
- Routers performance can be below standard
- Attackers are well equipped, clever and know that they are being traced
- Packet size is same across the network channels

- The target and intermediary nodes can be resource constrained
- Traceback is not a frequent operation

4.6 IP address and traceback mechanism

Internet Protocol address uniquely identifies a device on network. It refers to a 32-bit numeric label used to represent source and destination addresses over the computer network. It addresses a computer as well as network and is assigned to a networked computer to make communication over the internet and to facilitate its identification whenever is required [14]. The IPv4 structure of addressing is used for internet protocol addressing. The **Internet Protocol Version 4 (IPv4)** suffers with a limitation as it can support less than 4.3 billion total addresses and growth of internet shows that IPv4 is no more sustainable. The **Internet Protocol Version 6 (IPv6)** resolved the mentioned problem and facilitates 128-bit address space, which is much bigger than IPv4.

IP packet carries source and destination address. The packet is transmitted to its destination from source with the help of destination address. Unfortunately, the IP network routing infrastructure still lacks an effective mechanism to verify the authenticity of the source address. Due to the architecture of internet, none entity can be held responsible for the correctness of source address [5]. This is almost similar to postal service where destination address is important for letter delivery while authentication of source address is often ignored. Consequently, internal architecture of the IP protocol and packet forwarding mechanism make it difficult to locate the source of packets. These few drawbacks invite the cybercriminals to commit a crime and conceal their identity and source [5].

The objective of IP traceback system is to determine the source of packets, not necessarily to be malicious but genuine packets too. Several approaches have been proposed to address this problem that can be categorized into two groups: logging and marking [6]. In the logging scheme, routers record information about particular packet when it passes through that router to ensure whether suspected packets have been forwarded by specific router or not. In the marking scheme, the router marks a packet with its previous path link. All the routers through which a packet is transmitted, record the information about packet. When a packet is forwarded through a router, the previous path link information is added with packet which helps further in reconstruction of malicious packet path. Packet information is attached with packets in two ways. In the first method, the packet information is inserted in the same packet, popularly known as inbound marking. Obviously, inbound marking does not require additional bandwidth. In another method, an additional ICMP packet is attached with packet in which packet detail is preserved, known as **outbound marking**.

There are several challenges that need to get resolved in order to find an efficient and scalable way to locate the source of IP packet and tracing its transmission across the channel. The source of malicious packet can belong to an ingress point of network, inside a host or can be compromised routers. During attack, some routers can be compromised through which malicious packets are transmitted. When the source is located through traceback, the compromised routers evade themselves and mark their absence during an entire course of data transmission. In this way, the actual path of attack gets changed and misleading information is supplied to security administrators to divert their attention from actual paths and incorporated devices.

4.7 Classification of traceback schemes

Zhiqiang Gao and Nirwan Ansari [6] classified traceback schemes into five different categories. They used basic principle, processing mode, function implementation, locations and infrastructural requirement to categorize traceback schemes. The traceback classification shown in the *Figure 4.4* incorporates **Probabilistic Packet Marking (PPM)**, **Internet Control Message Protocol (ICMP)**, popularly known as **iTraceback, Source Path Isolation Engine (SPIE)**, also known hash-based traceback, **Algebraic-based Traceback Approach (ATA)**, and **Deterministic Packet Marking (DPM)** to cover important approaches used to perform traceback:

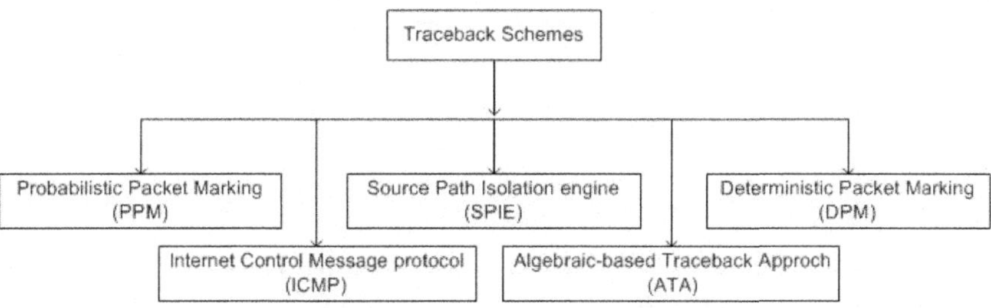

Figure 4.4: *Major traceback schemes*

Basic principle-based classification further classified under marking and logging groups. Packet marking is the most common and significant technique for an IP traceback. Marking uses the field of an IP header to store the audit trail where the field size required for marking varies from scheme to scheme. The routers mark the IP packets with some additional information so that victim can use them to identify the attack path. The approaches proposed in this direction include node append, node sampling, and edge sampling [5, 7]. In the node append mechanism, the address of successive routers through which the packets are transmitted are added to packets in order to re-construct the transmitted path. However, this approach presents additional overhead such as router processing and packet size [5]. These problems are rectified with node sampling approach that works together with probabilistic packet marking. In the edge sampling approach, the edge of network topology is marked through which the packets are transmitted. In all marking approaches, the marking information is put in the Identification field of the IP header. Marking schemes have few disadvantages such as these that affect the format of the IP packets and standardization of the format for IP marking is also an issue [5]. In logging scheme, the information like packet digest, signature and fields of IP header is stored on all routers or few routers through which packets are transmitted [7]. If an attack is detected, the victim queriesthe nearest upstream router about the malicious packets. If the information is available on upstream router, then it is considered a hop in the attack and process is further repeated to reach towards its origin. The major drawback of this scheme is the overhead on network and storage requirement on routers [7].

4.7.1 Probabilistic Packet marking (PPM)

In PPM scheme, the router marks the packet with some probability, let's say *p* for example. p=1/100, which means the router marks a packet received after 99 packets. The marking includes 16 bits' identification field in the header, out of which five bits are reserved for marking hop count that is used for reconstruction of attack path. The remaining bits are utilized by a router to send its information [7]. If the information is large enough, then it is broken into fragments. As a result, the marking identifies multiple packets each one containing partial information about the path [7]. In the PPM scheme, victim needs to receive an adequate number of packets to re-construct the path and will not require prior knowledge about topology. The production of false positives is the major drawback of PPM scheme that disturbs the sequencing and probability of packets. A router is considered as false positive when it exists in reconstructed path, but it is not involved in the real attack path. False negative refers to the situation when a router is not incorporated in the reconstructed path while it participates in the real attack path [8]. As a result, the packets once marked with farthest router might not be marked with the nearest router to attack-source. The traceback schemes based on PPM mechanism use traffic rates of packets to locate the source of attack. In the PPM mechanism, the marking field contains start, end and distance [7]. The start and end fields contain the IP address of the routers existing at two end points across the network and forming an edge in topology. The distance field counts the number of hops between current position of packet and the origin.

4.7.2 Deterministic Packet Marking (DPM)

Deterministic Packet Marking (DPM) was proposed to overcome the problem with probabilistic packet marking approach. In PPM, it was possible to inject a packet with erroneous information and to get it marked successfully through routers. This is popularly known as **mark spoofing**. Andrey Belenky et al. [9] believe that mark spoofing can be controlled through special coding. If every packet that is directed to reach victim is correctly marked, then the need for such complex and processor intensive coding will not arise. In DPM, it is tried to mark all the packets across the network correctly with routers so that if an attacker tries to spoof the mark with a packet, his spoofed mark will be overwritten with correct marking [9]:

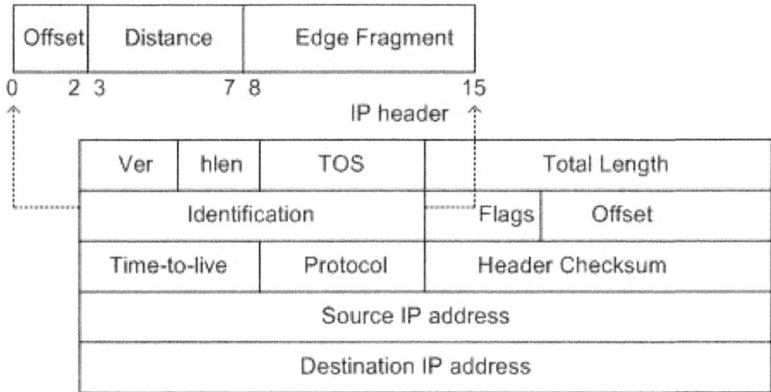

***Figure 4.5**: IP header*

Andrey Belenky et al. [9] observed in an IP datagram that the full path traceback is as good as the address of an ingress point in terms of attack source identification. Conceptually, each packet is individually routed from source to destination and packets can choose different routes even their source and destinations are same. ISPs use both public network and their own developed private network in order to provide services to their customers. In this situation, the full path traceback becomes important. In the DPM, the IP address is divided into two fragments as shown in *Figure 4.5* and each fragment contains 16-bits [11, 16]. Each packet is marked when it makes an entry to network and the packet keeps this mark unchanged until it goes beyond the network. The closest interface near the packet source marks the packet on the edge of ingress router.

In the DPM, 32-bit long IP address is required to pass to victim. The 16-bit ID field and 1-bit reserved flag help to mark the packets as shown in *Figure 4.5* [10, 21, 22]. Clearly, these 17bits are not sufficient to supply whole IP address to victim. Therefore, DPM use two packets to constitute complete IP address. The ID field of each incoming packet can represent either of these parts and then reserved flag bit is set to zero if ID field represent first part; otherwise, it is set to one to represent second part [9].

4.7.3 Algebraic-based traceback Approach (ATA)

An attack may comprise packets transmitted through different slave's computers, which most often come under the control of a remote computer. The transmission of such packets is achieved either explicitly or implicitly. In an explicit manner, the individual computers (slaves) are compromised directly to perform designated tasks, while the reflector is used to send false requests to the slaves in an implicit way. Drew dean et al. [11] believed in packet marking through routers and used the concept of algebraic functions as a foundation to develop the algebraic traceback approach [10]. In ATA, algebraic techniques were used to embed path information through routers into packets and to encode path information as points on polynomials. The basic idea in this approach for any polynomial f(x) of degree d is to recover *f(x)* at *(d+1)* unique points. Consider A_1, A_2,..........,A_n are the 32-bit addresses of the routers on path P [10]. The path function can be represented as $fp(x)=A^1X^{n-1}+^{A2Xn-2}+.........A_n-_1X+A_n$. We add a packet Id x_j with j^{th} packet and then compute $fp(x_j)$ as packet moves across the path. When an adequate number of packets reaches the destination from the same path, the function *fp* is reconstructed through interpolation [10].

4.7.4 ICMP traceback or iTrace method

In this approach, routers generate traceback messages with low probability that is sent along to the destination and back to its source. Traceback messages generated through routers along the path determine the traffic source and path of forged packets [12]. To understand ICMP traceback approach, we need to know some key terms, which are described as follows:

- **Element**: This refers to the basic component of message, which is explicitly identified with type-code and encoded with **Type-Length-Value** (**TLV**) format.
- **Field**: It also refers to message-component, which is identified with its relative position within the message header or in particular element.
- **Generator**: This refers to a router which generates the ICMP traceback messages either by itself or authorizes some other entity on its own behalf [12].

- **Link**: It refers to a logical connection that links generator with some other entity along, which traced packets get transmitted [12].
- **Peer**: It refers to entity at other end of the link, which either receives the traced packet generated through generator or sent the traced packets to generator.
- **Traced packet**: This refers to the packet that contains the subject of an ICMP Traceback message.

The primary objective of ICMP is to diagnose network and report an error. The network diagnostics operations like traceroute and ping use ICMP to detect fault across network. The following *Figure 4.6* shows the format of ICMP message in which the **TYPE** field is responsible to identify control messages. Code field furnish additional contextual details about the messages that ICMP packets carries. The checksum is an error-detection field that holds a numeric value:

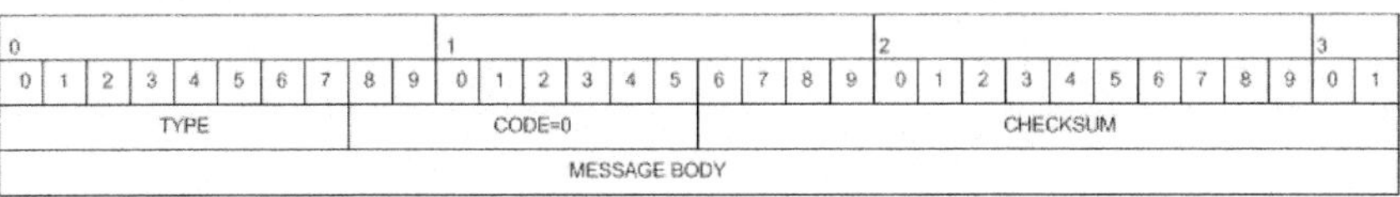

***Figure 4.6**: ICMP Traceback message format*

The body of ICMP message comprises a series of individual elements that are self-identifying in nature. These elements follow **TYPE-LENGTH-VALUE** scheme as shown in *Figure 4.7*:

TYPE	LENGTH	VALUE

***Figure 4.7**: ICMP Type-Length-Value (TLV)*

The message is encapsulated in the ICMP packet with ICMP TYPE of traceback. The **TYPE** field is a single octet containing values assigned by **Internet Assigned Numbers Authority (IANA)** [12]. It ranges from 0x01 to 0x7f for top-level elements and 0x81 to 0xff for sub-elements [12]. Steve Bellovin defines the TOP-level type codes and sub-element type codes in following ways as shown in *Table 4.1* and *Table 4.2* in reference to ICMP traceback:

TYPE	Element Name
0x01	Back Link
0x02	Forward Link
0x03	Timestamp
0x04	Traced Packet Contents
0x05	Probability
0x06	Router ID
0x07	HMAC Authentication Data
0x08	Key Disclosure List

***Table 4.1**: Top-level type codes*

TYPE	Element Name
0x81	Interface Name
0x82	IPv4 Address Pair
0x83	IPv6 Address Pair
0x84	MAC Address Pair
0x85	Operator-Defined Link Identifier
0x86	Key Disclosure
0x87	Disclosure Signature

***Table 4.2**: Sub-element type codes*

The **CODE** field is set to have value zero and ignored by receiver [12]. Checksum contains 16-bit one's complement of the sum of the ICMP message beginning with Type field [12]. The default checksum is set to zero before generating the actual checksum [13].

In the ICMP traceback scheme, the full path of attack is determined by configuring the routers to select a packet statistically and generate an ICMP traceback message in a format as shown in *Figure 4.6*. As the ICMP message contains the address of next node as well as previous node, if we select one packet from each router involved in path, the malicious network traffic path can easily be traced.

4.7.5 Source Path Isolation Engine (SPIE)

The **Source Path Isolation Engine** (**SPIE**) technique uses Bloom filters to trace the source of malicious packets, and to know its destination with time of receipt [15]. Bloom filter is space-efficient data structure used to store packet digests. This technique does not require the storage of whole packets instead it requires its digest. Router stores time-stamped packet digest into digest table and maintains logs for each forwarded packets through it. SPIE reduces vulnerabilities to eavesdropping and cut down memory requirement of up to 0.5% of link bandwidth per unit time [16].

In SPIE, routers maintain a cache to keep the information about each forwarded packets and whenever intrusion detection system detects a packet for its offensive activities, a query is raised to SPIE for packet digest in relevant time period. The results received in response are simulated to locate the source of packet and **reverse-path flooding (RPF)** algorithm is used to reconstruct the reverse attacking path.

4.7.5.1 The SPIE architecture

The packet auditing, query processing, and attack graph generation are the primary activities generally performed with SPIE. Each router in SPIE is equipped with **Data Generation Agent (DGA)** that generates the packet digests of each packet when it leaves the router. DGA is deployed as software agents to present an interface to switching bus or to auxiliary box. The packet digests are mapped into digest table with the help of hash function. The digest tables are refreshed frequently to represent the traffic pattern that passes through router for a particular span of time:

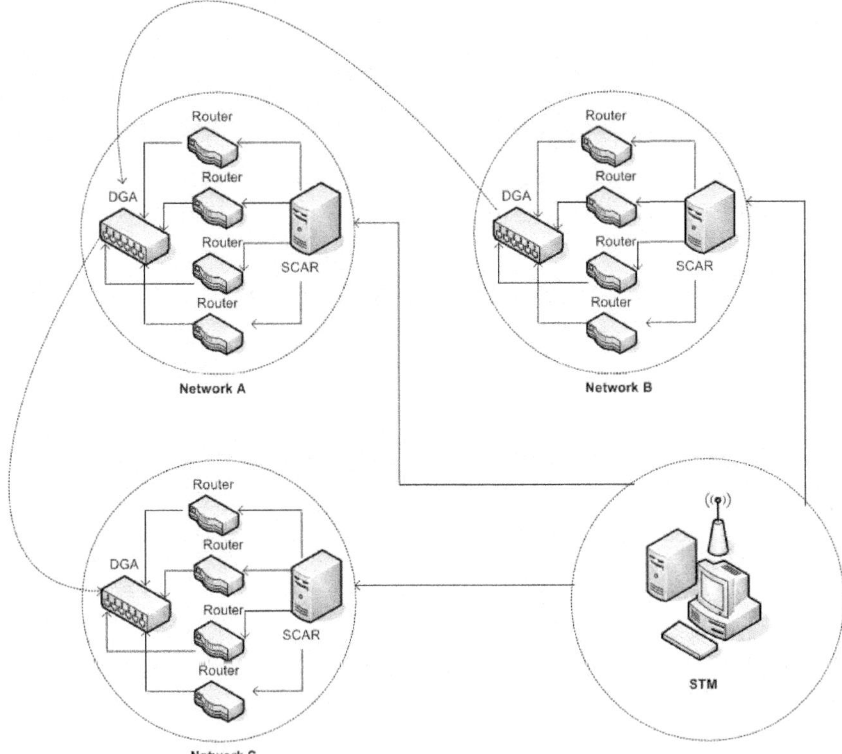

Figure 4.8: *SPIE architecture*

The *Figure 4.8* shows the SPIE architecture in which three network segments named **A**, **B**, and **C** have been taken. These three network segments belong to three different organizations with their own digital infrastructure. DGA maintains its own digest table and delivered to SCAR agent of the same network whenever it is requested with some interest in the data traffic pattern. SCAR represents SPIE Collection and Reduction Agent to store packet digests and digest tables for longer storage and analysis. Each network segment has its own SCAR agent that has control over all routers and their activities. The SCAR examines the topologies used in particular segment, keeps a close watch of packet movements through all the routers, and facilitates traceback of packets across network segment. Due to the enormous shape, a network segment can have multiple SCAR agents to cover all the regions contained in. SCAR agent becomes responsible to prepare attack graph in its own coverage. The complete attack graph is prepared by **SPIE Traceback Manager (STM)** by joining all the attacked graphs received from each SCAR agents across all network segments.

The STM has control over the SPIE system and works as an interface for intrusion detection system that requests for malicious packet trace. When IDS presents queries to STM to know the route of packet transmission across the network segments, STM verifies the request and communicates with corresponding SCARs to collect the information about attack paths to form a complete attack route [15].

4.8 Evaluation of IP Traceback Schemes

IP traceback techniques are not used to stop the cyberattacks instead these are used to locate the true origins from where the malicious activities are being performed [17]. Criminals regularly effort to make it complicated to reach to origins of cybercrimes and to hide the original IP address with spoofing. The literature shows the availability of number of traceback mechanisms and each of these mechanisms claims its superiority in its own way. The evaluation of existing traceback mechanisms is essential as it helps to know the strengths and drawbacks of each one and becomes beneficial in developing better traceback scheme. Vijayalakshmi Murugesan et al. [7] presented a brief survey about traceback mechanisms with evaluation parameters as depicted in *Figure 4.9*. The following section describes the same parameters on which a traceback scheme is measured and evaluated.

4.8.1 Deployability

Deployability means installation of hardware and software on network segments. The traceback scheme may require installation of software and hardware, should support the network environment without making much and unnecessary changes in infrastructure [7]. Most of the existing traceback schemes now need changes in digital infrastructure for activation because marking and logging is not supported with routers.

4.8.2 Scalability

Scalability refers to the number of additional configurations needed to be updated over other devices if a device is added in the traceback scheme. It is the ability of the traceback scheme to adjust itself to function in such increasing size network. More configuration dependability among the devices deteriorates scalability. In an ideal traceback scheme, there should be zero-impact scalability means configuration changes in a device or insertion of new hardware does not need updation in related hardware and software.

4.8.3 Memory requirement

Memory requirement is another important metric to know the effectiveness of traceback scheme. Some traceback schemes reserve their additional storage at routers and dedicated servers, and store the packets for analysis for their malicious activities. An ideal traceback scheme should not require additional storage as it introduces overheads and disrupt network performance. Most of the traceback schemes like marking and logging require storage at routers but iTraceback scheme does not need storage to analyze packets:

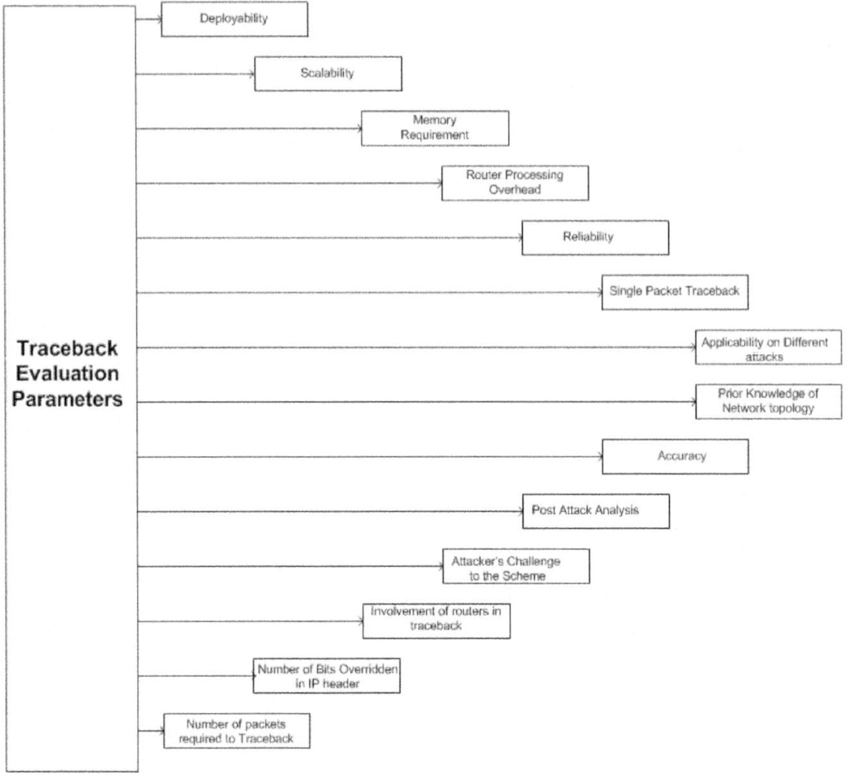

***Figure 4.9**: Traceback schemes evaluation parameters*

4.8.4 Router processing overhead

Transmission of data packets and their routing share same network bandwidth and packets movement engage the routers as each packet necessarily need to pass through them. Router processing overheads are undesirable in traceback schemes as these degrade the network performance and make routers busy due to additional functioning. Ideally, the traceback schemes should have minimal router processing overhead, but practically, it does not seem to be possible as packet movement means creating overheads to routers.

4.8.5 Reliability

Reliability means confidence in results. The small coverage and less involvement of networked devices produce reliable results.

This is because of their frequent monitoring. The traceback schemes require high-level protection as the manipulation in statistics of one networked device can mislead security administrator to assemble the attack path. Protection in traceback schemes means to produce only reliable traces, excluding false positives and false negatives. A traceback scheme that summarizes the statistics from each router has a greater possibility to get failure if one of its router fails to produce results.

4.8.6 Singlepacket traceback

Most of the traceback schemes analyze traffic pattern to detect intrusion. These schemes require multiple packets to analyze to get the complete path of attack. The attackers have now changed the way to attack and trigger attack with a single packet. So, the tracing single malicious packet is now desirable functionality needs to be incorporated in traceback schemes. SPIE scheme has ability to track single malicious packet but remaining require multiple packets and routers to detect intrusions.

4.8.7 Applicability on different attacks

Cyberattacks can be classified into two major categories named flooding attacks and software exploit attacks [7]. In flooding attacks, the criminals make superfluous requests in order to overload system, while in software exploit attack, only few malicious packets are sufficient to take control of the system. Software exploit attacks occur due to vulnerabilities in operating system at victim machines. A traceback scheme should have the capability to deal with flooding attacks as well as software exploit attacks and should be applicable to each subcategory of these attacks.

4.8.8 Prior knowledge of network topology

Some traceback schemes take underlying topology in consideration in advance to function. These schemes work with fixed algorithms and do not adopt instant changes in strategies. The criminals are now cleverer and are well aware of the algorithms being used to traceback; so, it is desirable for traceback schemes to incorporate instant changes for reliable traces. Working with pre-established topologies means inviting criminals to exploit traceback scheme and its functioning.

4.8.9 Accuracy

There should be complete avoidance of false positive and false negative in traceback schemes. False positive means to mark a legitimate node as criminal node, while false negative refers marking a criminal node as legitimate node. As DPM and PPM traceback schemes believe in multiple packets to store IP address, it can cause false positives. SPIE creates packet digest and maintain hash table with bloom filters; so, overwriting in the hash table may generate false positive and false negative.

4.8.10 Post attack analysis

If a cybercriminal succeeds once to achieve his target, then the benefits of cybercrimes shall surely invite him to commit crime again. It means the identification of criminals is essential whether they are committing crime or not. Some traceback schemes need the attack to be alive to function to prepare the attack graph, which is not an ideal situation. The traceback schemes should function and be able to prepare the attack graph even after attack is stopped.

4.8.11 Attacker's challenge to the scheme

The continuous changes in traceback schemes and their functioning are desirable. If the criminal knows working algorithm behind a particular traceback scheme, then he shall also be aware of its strengths and weakness. The weakness can be exploited to avoid detection and to hide location. Suppose an attacker knows that an organization uses flooding based traceback schemes to know the origin of malicious packets, then he shall not use flooding methods to commit crime as he has alternatives to adopt signature-based method to attack.

4.8.12 Involvement of routers in traceback

Routers are the pathway through which the data packets are transmitted to its target. Attackers also send malicious packets with legitimate packets to conduct the crime. Routers record the information about each packet with its source and route. Since routers are responsible to pass malicious packets means routers are accessible to criminals and are configured as per their requirements. The traceback scheme that does not need router to traceback a malicious packet is considered good. The DPM, PPM, and iTraceback schemes trace the attacker through victim end and do not require router support.

4.8.13 Number of bits overridden in IP header

The IP header does not facilitate storage of audit trails. The security administrators utilize the rarely used fields such as identification field to store audit trails. Traceback schemes override the contents of Identification field to write audit trails. Similarly, the fragment offset, TOS, and the flag field are also overridden to accommodate tracing information. The overridden fields affect the fragmented traffic, so the traceback scheme that supports lesser bits to overridden is considered better.

4.8.14 Number of packets required to traceback

The traceback scheme that requires minimum number of packets to trace the origin is considered better. The storage of few packets is easy across the routers and their analysis require less time to extract attacked-path details. The involvement of minimum number of packets reduces the chance for false positives and false negatives.

Vijayalakshmi Murugesan et al. [7] evaluated and compared the popular traceback schemes as shown in following *Table 4.3*:

Evaluation Parameters	**Probabilistic Packet marking (PPM)**	**Determin-istic Packet marking (DPM)**	**Algebra-ic-based traceback Approach (ATA)**	**ICMP Or iTrace Approach**	**Source Path Isolation Engine (SPIE) Or Hash-based IP traceback**
Deployment	Average	Average	Good	Good	Good
Scalability	Poor	Fair	Average	Good	Average
Memory requirement	Not required in network instead victim side required	Medium requirement	Average requirement	Medium require-ment	Limited requirement
Router processing overhead	Medium	Medium	High	Low	Low
Reliability	Good	Good	May gen-erate false positive and false negative	Good	Limited chances for false positive and false negative
Single Packet Traceback	No large number of packets required	Requires less number of packets compared to PPM	Number of packets required to traceback	ICMP messag-es are required and Huge number of packets required to perform traceback	Single packet is need to traceback
Applicability on Different types of attacks	DoS/DDoS flooding attacks	DoS/DDoS flooding attacks	Effective to network based attack	DoS/DDoS-Network layer attacks	Effective to network based attack

Prior Knowledge of Network topology	Not required	Not required	Required	Not required	required
Accuracy	Risk of huge false positive rate in DDoS attack	Good	Average	Good for limited number of attack-ers	Good
Post Attack Analysis	Possible	Possible	Not possible	Possible	Possible
Attacker's Challenge to the Scheme	Poor	Poor	Poor	High	Poor
Involvement of routers in traceback	Not Required	Not Required	Required	Not Required	Required

***Table 4.3**: Traceback schemes evaluation and comparison*

4.9 Active response characteristics

An effective and quick response is preferred to tackle network-based intrusions. Active tracing methods are desirable as these do not need additional storage and inspection of stored network traffic to detect threats. Ideally, an effective and active tracing response should have following characteristics:

1. It should be able to neutralize detected intrusions in real time.
2. It should have the capability to prevent the criminals from attacking further targets.
3. It should help to identify the criminals in real time with legal evidences.
4. It should have the ability to recover compromised computers and servers to bring them in the previous state.
5. It should be able to recognize malicious packets transmission path starting from its source to target in order to have an idea about complete malicious path.
6. It should have the ability to prevent future intrusions that are similar to previously detected ones.

4.10 Sleepy Watermark Tracing (SWT)

The **Sleepy Watermark Tracing** (**SWT**) approach is active tracing approach. It is called *sleepy* because it does not add overheads, while none intrusion is detected [18]. When target senses intrusion, it injects a watermark into backward connection and makes all intermediate routers along the intrusion path active. SWT have number of benefits over existing tracing schemes. These are described as following:

1. SWT differentiates intrusion tracing from intrusion detection and does not need to have intrusion detection abilities in all nodes existing in intrusion path, except the target node [18].
2. It does not work in a similar manner as thumb printing, timing-based and deviation-based approaches work and does not need storage of all incoming and outgoing connections to compute correlations to detect intrusions [19].
3. SWT does not need clock synchronization.
4. SWT is robust against retransmission variation.
5. It traces intrusions and malicious packets whenever it is needed.
6. In the SWT approach, the attacker need not be active all the time during intrusion detection activity instead a single keystroke from the attacker is sufficient to trace intrusion connection-chain back to its origin [18].
7. It does not add considerable overheads to routers.
8. It needs few network server applications at target host to inject watermarks.

4.10.1 SWT concepts

In order to have a close view to network-based intrusions to hosts, it is desirable to observe hosts to its nearest router or gateways. The nearest router or gateway to a host is known as **Guardian Gateway** for that host. The **Incoming Guardian Gateway** to a host **H** is defined as its nearest router that forwards the network traffic to it. The nearest router that forwards network traffic from a host H to further is known as **Outgoing Guardian Gateway**. A host in network can have multiple Incoming Guardian Gateway and Outgoing Guardian Gateway:

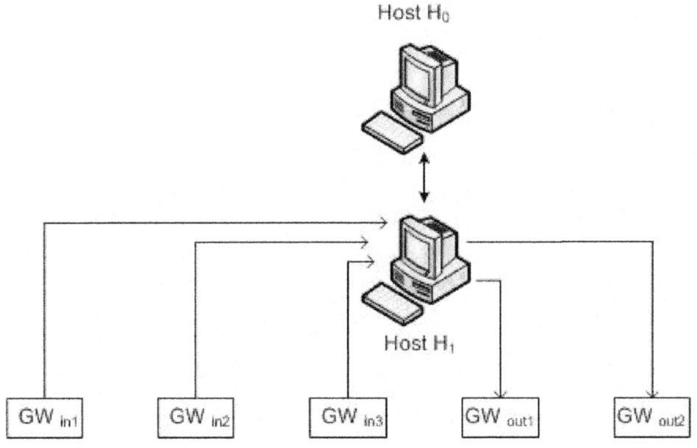

Figure 4.10: *Guardian gateway set*

The union of **Incoming Guardian Gateway** and **Outgoing Guardian Gateway** is known as **Guardian Gateway Set**. The set {GW_{in1}, GW_{in2}, GW_{in3},GW_{out1},GW_{out2}} of routers in *Figure 4.10* is known as **Guardian Gateway Set**. Suppose **G** is a guardian gateway set and the hosts in **G** are known as **Guarded hosts** whose guardian gateway set is subset of G [18, 19]. Xinyuan Wang et al. [18, 19] define **leap** as one connection step between hosts within a connection chain. The networked-connection from host H1 to host H2is called a **leap in tracing model** shown in *Figure 4.11*:

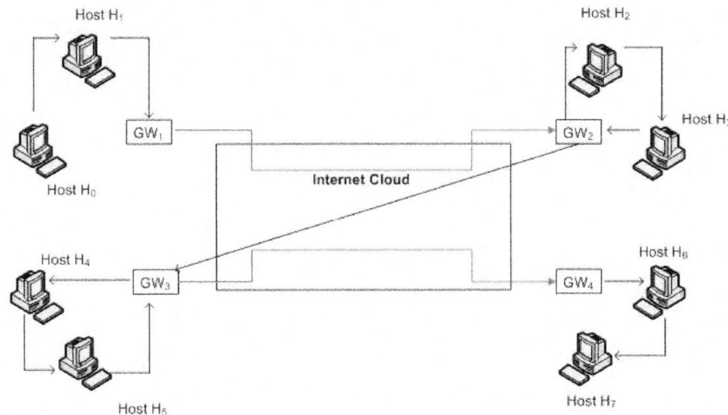

Figure 4.11: *Tracing model*

One leap can have multiple hops and will have two guardian gateways for two end hosts. A leap is specified with 5-tuple with following fields:

1. Protocol number
2. Source IP address

3. Destination IP address
4. Source Port Number
5. Destination Port Number

4.10.2 Basic SWT assumptions

Xinyuan Wang et al. [18, 19] constructed the sleepy watermark tracing framework with the following assumptions:

1. Intrusions become interactive and bidirectional
2. Routers are assumed to be trustworthy while hosts are not
3. Each host has at least single SWT guardian gateway
4. None encryption exists among links to connections

The first assumption is related to the nature of intrusions. The intrusion in SWT refers to an attack with the objective of having an unauthorised access rather than flooding. Xinyuan Wang et al. [18, 19] believed in CERT security incidents studies and concluded that most of the unauthorized access incidents take place at hosts rather than routers incorporated. Therefore, hosts have been considered more vulnerable than routers in the second assumption. To simplify the elaboration of SWT architecture, it is considered that each host has at least one guardian gateway, but in reality, it can have multiple guardian hosts. Xinyuan Wang et al. [18, 19] perceived the lack of link-to-link encryptions in connections and correlated the network traffic across incoming and outgoing connections to detect intrusions. This is the reason to ignore encryption of network traffic across connections in fourth assumption.

4.10.3 The SWT architecture

The Sleepy Watermark Tracing architecture includes two important components named SWT guarded host and SWT guardian gateway. SWT guarded host requires protection from SWT and SWT guardian gateway helps in SWT functioning to achieve protection form guarded hosts. Xinyuan Wang et al. [18, 19] used a unique SWT guardian gateway for each SWT guarded host in his SWT architecture as shown in *Figure 4.12*. A SWT guardian gateway may protect one or more SWT guarded hosts. A list of SWT guarded hosts is prepared with corresponding SWT guarded gateways that protect them for better controlling:

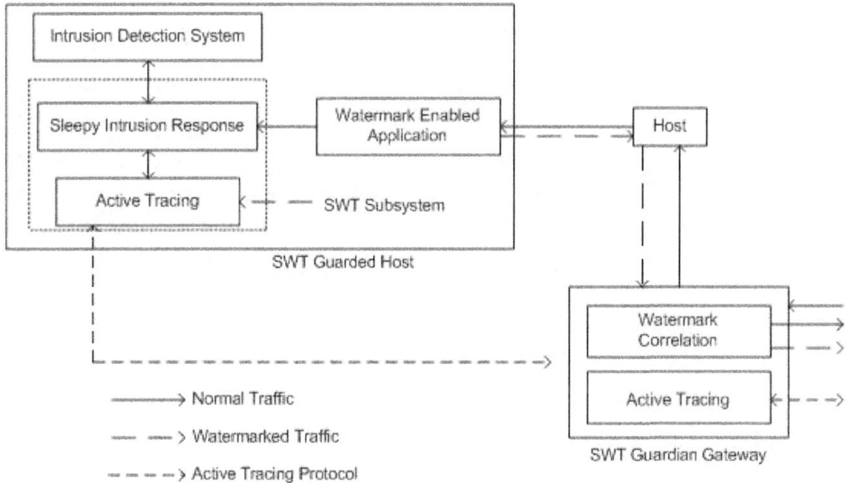

***Figure 4.12**: SWT architecture*

The SWT guarded host includes **Intrusion Detection System** and **Watermark Enabled Application** as supporting components. Intrusion detection system in the SWT guarded host has an interface to connect with external IDS. This interface is responsible for SWT tracing. The intrusion detection system communicates with SWT subsystem once it detects intrusion within guarded host and triggers active watermark tracing to trace the malicious packets. Watermark enabled applications refers to network service applications such as telnetd and rlogind can be modified to inject watermarks upon request.

Xinyuan Wang et al. [18, 19] mainly emphasized on three interacting components named **Sleepy Intrusion Response** (**SIR**), **Watermark correlation** (**WM**) and **Active Tracing** (**AT**) in his SWT architecture and details how malicious activities are detected and traced to protect infrastructure from damage. **Sleepy Intrusion Response** (**SIR**) receives tracing request from intrusion detection system and coordinates with active tracing component to keep a close watch on intrusion. The **Watermark correlation** (**WM**) unit at SWT guardian gateway correlates incoming and outgoing connections with watermarks. The active tracing is responsible to communicate with all other components in architecture and collaboratively to trace the complete path of malicious packets and to detect their source.

4.10.4 Sleepy Intrusion Response

Sleepy Intrusion Response (**SIR**) unit has a crucial role in SWT tracing. It belongs to SWT guarded host and communicates with intrusion detection system and watermarked-enabled applications in the same host to trace the intrusion. To avoid the overheads and increase the efficiency, SIR introduces 'Sleepiness' in SWT architecture. Sleepiness means inactivity of tracing system until the intrusion occurs and detected by intrusion detection system. By default, SWT system remains in the inactive mode and is activated when IDS detects intrusion and notifies to an active tracing unit through SIR. Sleepy Intrusion Response initially logs intrusion connection as in the active mode and triggers its active tracing unit on its guardian gateway. SIR also notifies to watermark-enabled application to disconnect the intrusion connection and to inject watermarking to enable tracing backwards to reach the source. SIR manages the tracing information received from SWT guardian gateway about intrusions and provides these details to intrusion detection system whenever it is requested from IDS. Sleepy Intrusion Response unit goes in sleeping mode if none information or notification is received from SWT guardian gateway about intrusions within stipulated timeout period.

4.10.5 Watermark –Enabled application

Watermark refers to a small piece of information that is injected in network to uniquely identify a connection chain. Ideally, a watermark represents almost negligible code that is easy to inject with network traffic and have capability to be invisible to normal users and evade itself to avoid detection from network applications software. Watermark is expected to remain invariant as this is used to measure correlations between incoming and outgoing network traffic across multiple connections. The major challenge with watermark is to make it invisible to end users. In text-based network applications such as telnet and rlogin, it is similar to cryptography used to hide data in text. Xinyuan Wang et al. [18, 19] prefer open space method to hide data in text by manipulating white spaces. In an open space method, the hiding bits of confidential information is achieved by adding additional white-spaces in the text. These white-spaces are added at the end of line and can be put at the end of paragraph [20]. For more clarification, suppose a string that is showed across network application may not be essentially same as it displayed. This can be understood with the following example:

Suppose, the following string

"Computer Network\b\b\b\b\b" transmitted to telnet or rlogin, is displayed as following:

"Computer Network"

Here **\b** represents a blank space.

Xinyuan Wang et al. [18, 19] defined the virtual null string for network application as a string that looks as a null to end users. In the preceding string, "\b\b\b\b\b" is a virtual null string for telnet and rlogin. So, the virtual null sting is a convenient way to make watermark invisible to network applications.

Watermark becomes application specific and requires to be inserted into backward traffic by application itself [18]. Watermark-enabled application refers to server-side network application that can be modified to inject watermark into its response traffic whenever it is requested [19]. As shown in the *Figure 4.12*, the watermark-enabled application needs to process two requests received from the SIR unit. The first request is WM-Start that notifies Watermark-enabled application to start injecting watermark into network traffic for stipulated time-period. The second request is WM-End, which indicates to Watermark-enabled application to stop injecting of watermark in network traffic.

4.10.6 Watermark correlation

To traceback intrusions across a connection chain, we need a mechanism to compare incoming network traffic with outgoing network traffic to match adjacent connections that reside on same connection chain. The connections matching mechanism is defined as **correlation**. The SWT approach does not believe in hosts instead it considers router as trustworthy. Therefore, SWT compares and correlates network traffic across SWT guardian gateways. In reference to guarded hosts, the network traffic passing through a SWT guardian gateway can be broadly classified in two classes named **guarded** and **bypassing** as shown in *Figure 4.13*. The guarded traffic refers to network traffic that either terminates at or initiates from a guarded host belonging to SWT guardian gateway. The correlations between incoming leap and outgoing leap is also computed to know the degree of matching at SWT guardian gateway:

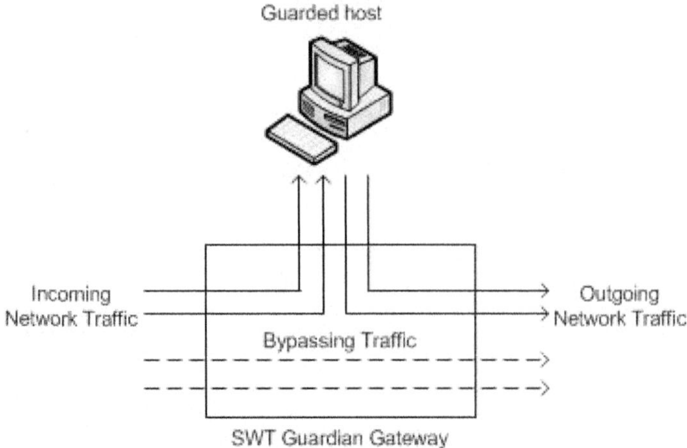

***Figure 4.13**: Network traffic transmission*

The major challenge with guardian gateway is to compute correlations when there are multiple incoming and outgoing leaps at single guardian gateway. Xinyuan Wang et al. [18, 19] considered m incoming leaps and *n* outgoing leaps in their single SWT guarded host model and measure *mxn* possible combinations of correlations to match the traffic across guarded host.

Conclusion

In this chapter, we argued that only detection of intrusions is not sufficient to reduce the adverse impacts of cybercrimes, instead we also need to trace attacking-path along which malicious traffic is transmitted to know the true origin of cybercrime. We have defined cyber forensic and shown the classification of intrusion activities to know their role in cybercrime prevention. We detailed how criminals achieve anonymity in networked-infrastructure to avoid detection and commit crime with someone else's name. This chapter classifies the traceback schemes and details their implementation in order to find the route through which malicious packets are transmitted. We have explained parameters on the basis of which traceback schemes are judged and evaluated popular traceback schemes to know their merits and limitations. Finally, the Sleepy Watermark Traceback framework has been elaborated with its architecture to find the complete path of cyberattack.

The next chapter of this book details the problem of accountability across the internet and shows the role of stepping-stones to complicate the criminal identification process. Intrusion response systems are categorized and the activities of each one are elaborated to know their suitability in interconnected digital environment.

Points to remember

- Cyber forensic refers to a scientific process that performs identification, seizure, collection, authentication, analysis, documentation and preservation of digital evidences left during malicious activity.
- Cyber forensic is basically a science that extracts forensic information from associated hardware and software that can be submitted during legal prosecutions as evidences.
- Intrusion detection means to detect malicious code in network traffic.
- Intrusion prevention refers to the procedure to ensure the security of particular node or infrastructure from malicious threats.
- Intrusion tolerance is the ability of system and infrastructure to bear the intrusions and at the same time ensuring the availability and integrity of system.
- Intrusion response means application of countermeasures to fix the cause to prevent future attack.
- Attribution refers to process of determining the identity or location of cybercriminal.
- Identity of cybercriminal incorporates geographic location, IP address, account and Ethernet address.
- Forging and modifying the source IP address is popular way to hide the actual IP address through which crime is conducted. This forging is known as 'spoofing'.
- Time-to-live (TTL) logic is used to temporarily setup a host for a very short span of time to trigger cyberattacks.
- Laundering hosts inject the delay in packets to remain inactive for specific time-period.
- Internet Protocol address uniquely identifies a device on network.

- In the logging scheme, routers record information about particular packet when it passes through that router to ensure whether suspected packets have been forwarded by specific router or not.
- In marking scheme, router marks a packet with its previous path link.
- When a packet is forwarded through a router, previous path link information is added with packet which helps further in reconstruction of malicious packet path.
- Inbound marking does not require additional bandwidth.
- An additional ICMP packet is attached with packet in which packet detail is preserved, known as outbound marking.
- In logging scheme, the information like packet digest, signature and fields of IP header is stored on all routers or few routers through which packets are transmitted.
- In the Probabilistic Packet marking (PPM) scheme, router marks the packet with some probability.
- The production of false positives is the major drawback of PPM scheme that disturb the sequencing and probability of packets.
- False negative refers to the situation when a router is not incorporated in the reconstructed path while it participates in real attack path.
- In PPM, it was possible to inject a packet with erroneous information and to get it marked successfully through routers. This is popularly known as 'mark spoofing'.
- In the Deterministic Packet Marking (DPM), the IP address is divided into two fragments each containing 16 bits. Each packet is marked when it makes an entry to the network and the packet keeps this mark unchanged until it goes beyond the network.
- In an Algebraic-based traceback approch (ATA), algebraic techniques were used to embed path information through routers into packets and to encode path information as points on polynomials.
- In the ICMP traceback scheme, the full path of attack is determined by configuring the routers to select a packet statistically.

- Bloom filter is space-efficient data structure used to store packet digests.
- Scalability refers to the number of additional configurations need to be updated over other devices if a device is added in traceback scheme.
- The nearest router or gateway to a host is known as 'Guardian Gateway' for that host.
- The 'Incoming Guardian Gateway' to a host H is defined as its nearest router that forwards the network traffic to it.
- The nearest router that forwards network traffic from a host H to further is known as 'Outgoing Guardian Gateway'.
- The union of 'Incoming Guardian Gateway' and 'Outgoing Guardian Gateway' is known as 'Guardian Gateway Set'.
- Watermark refers to a small piece of information that is injected in network to uniquely identify a connection chain.
- The traceback scheme that requires minimum number of packets to trace the origin is considered better.

MCQ

1. **Which one of the following is not an action against intrusions?**
   a. Intrusion collection
   b. Intrusion detection
   c. Intrusion prevention
   d. Intrusion response

2. **The function of Reflector host is:**
   a. To inject watermark
   b. To hide the criminals
   c. To detect intrusion
   d. Pump delay in malicious packets

3. **The function of Laundering host is:**
   a. To inject watermark
   b. To hide criminals behind a digital shield of anonymity.

c. To inject the delay in packets
d. To collect the information from SIR unit.

4. **The Internet Protocol Version 6 (IPv6) facilitates:**
   a. 16-bit address space
   b. 32-bit address space
   c. 64-bit address space
   d. 128-bit address space

5. **Which one of the following schemes supports marking?**
   a. PPM
   b. ATA
   c. ICMP
   d. SPIE

6. **SPIE stands for:**
   a. Search Path Isolation Engine
   b. Source Path Isolation Engine
   c. Shortest Path Isolation Engine
   d. Suitable Path Isolation Engine

7. **Which one of the following is not an evaluation parameter for traceback schemes?**
   a. Deployment
   b. Scalability
   c. Usability
   d. Reliability

8. **SWT stands for:**
   a. Source Watermark Techniques
   b. Sleepy Watermark Techniques
   c. Source Watermark Tracing
   d. Sleepy Watermark Tracing

Answer

1. a

2. b
3. c
4. d
5. a
6. b
7. c
8. d

Questions

1. Describe Cyber forensic in detail.
2. Define Intrusion and explain the categorization of intrusion activities in detail.
3. Describe the various tactics used by criminals to hide their locations.
4. What do you mean by traceback? Elaborate various assumptions that are considered during development of effective tracing mechanism.
5. Describe the utility of IP address in traceback mechanism.
6. Explain the following:
   I. Reflector Host
   II. Laundering hosts
   III. Guardian Gateway
   IV. Sleepy Intrusion Response
   V. Watermark
7. Explain the classification of Traceback Schemes in detail.
8. Differentiate the following:
   I. PPM versus DPM
   II. Incoming Guardian Gateway versus Outgoing Guardian Gateway
   III. IDS versus SIR
   IV. Guarded Host versus Guarded Traffic
9. Define Source Path Isolation Engine with its architecture.
10. Why do we evaluate traceback schemes? Describe the parameters that are used to evaluate the traceback schemes.

11. What are the major characteristics of Active Response?
12. Describe Sleepy watermark tracing approach with its architecture in detail.
13. What are basic assumptions in a Sleepy watermark tracing approach?

References

[1] Susan C. Lee and Clay Shields, *"Technical, Legal and Societal Challenges to Automated Attack Traceback"*, IT Pro, 2002.

[2] A report, *"Cyber forensics"*, available at: **www.cyberforensics.in/**.

[3] David A Wheeler, Gregory N. Larsen, Task Leader, *"Techniques for Cyber Attack Attribution"*, Institute for Defense analyses, October 2003.

[4] Alex C. Snoeren, Craig Partridge, Luis A Sanchez, Christine E. Jones, Fabrice Tchakountio, Beverly Schwartz, Stephen T. Kent and W. Timothy Strayer, *"Single-Packet IP Traceback"*, ACM SIGCOMM' 01 in San Diego, CA, August 2001.

[5] Henry C. J Lee, Vrizlynn L.L. Thing, Yi Xu, and Miao Ma, *"ICMP Traceback with Cumulative Path, An efficient solution for IP Traceback"*, In proceeding of 5th International Conference on Information and Communications Security, ICICS 2003, Huhehaote, China, October 10-13, 2003, pp. 124-135.

[6] Zhiqiang Gao and Nirwan Ansari, *"Tracing Cyber Attacks from the Practical Perspective"*, IEEE Communication Magazine, may 2005.

[7] Vijayalakshmi Murugesan, Mercy Shalinie, Nithya Neethimani, *"A Brief Survey of IP Traceback Methodologies"*, Acta Poltechnica Hungarica, Vol. 11, No.09, 2014.

[8] Dong Wei, *"Implementing IP Traceback in the Internet: An ISP Perspective"*, in proceedings of workshop on Information Assurance, United States Military Academy, West Point, NY, June 2002.

[9] Andrey Belenky and Nirwan Ansari, *"IP traceback with Deterministic Packet Marking"*, IEEE communication letters, Vol.7, No.4, April 2003.

[10] Stefan Savage, David Wetherall, Anna Karlin and Tom Anderson, *Practical Network Support for IP Traceback,* SIGCOMM'00, 2000, Stockholm, Sweden.

[11] Drew Dean, Matt Franklin and Adam Stubblefield, "*An Algebraic Approach to IP Traceback*", ACM Transactions on Information and System Security, December 2000.

[12] Steve Bellovin, *ICMP Traceback Messages*, AT & T Labs Research, Marcus Leech, Tom Taylor, Nortel Networks, February 2003.

[13] A Report, "*Internet Control Message Protocol*", available at: **http://www.networksorcery.com/enp/protocol/icmp.htm**

[14] George Thomas, "*Introduction to the internet protocol: How does IP impact control networks?*", Introduction to Industrial Ethernet, Part 2, Volume 1, Issue 4, Winter 1999.

[15] Alex C. Snoeren, Craig Partridge, Luis A. Sanchez, Christine E. Jones, Fabrice Tchakountio, Stephen T. Kent, and W. Timothy Strayer, "Hash-Based IP Traceback", Published at SIGCOMM'01, August 27-31, 2001, San Diego, California, USA.

[16] Alex C. Snoeren, Luis A. Sanchez, Christine E. Jones, Fabrice Tchakountio, Stephen T. Kent, and W. Timothy Strayer, "*Single-Packet IP Traceb*ack",ACM Transactions on Networking, Volume: 10, Issue: 6 , Dec 2002.

[17] Vahid Aghaei-Foroushani and A. Nur Zincir-Heywood, "On Evaluating IP Traceback Schemes: A Practical Perspective", IEEE Security and Privacy Workshops, 2013.

[18] Xinyuan Wang, Douglas S. Reeves, S. Felix Wu, Jim Yuill, "Sleepy Watermark Tracing: An active Network-Based Intrusion Response Framework", IFIP International Information Security Conference, 2001, pp-369-384.

[19] Xinyuan Wang, Douglas S. Reeves, S. Felix Wu, "*Tracing Based Active Intrusion Response*".

[20] Sangita Roy and Manini Manasmita, "*A Novel Approach to Format Based Text Steganography*", In Proceedings International Conference on Communication, Computing & Security, ICCCS 2011, Odisha, India, February 12-14, 2011.

[21] Vijayalakshmi Murugesan and Mercy Shalinie, "*Single Packet ICMP Traceback Technique using Router Interface*", Journal of Information Science and Engineering, Vol. 31, No.05, 2015.

[22] Dong Wei and Nirwan Ansari, "*Implementing IP Traceback in the Internet— An ISP Perspective*", Workshop on Information Assurance, United States Military Academy, West Point, NY June 2002.

CHAPTER 5

Stepping Stone Detection and Tracing System

We preserve and share our confidential information and emotions on the internet and unknowingly invite criminals to enter our levies to cause financial loss, hazards, anxiety and defamation. Criminals steal, disrupt, manipulate, destroy and deny access to our sensitive digital information and data, and damage infrastructure. Interestingly, they hide themselves with sophisticated technologies and evade from detection and legal prosecution. In this chapter, we mainly focuson series of computers technically known as connection-chain and determine the computers that help criminals to trigger the attack. We will discuss Stepping stone detection methods and explain the role of jitter and chaff in network traffic manipulation.

Structure

In this chapter, we will cover the following topics:

- The problem of accountability
- Stepping stones
- Timing-based stepping stone detection approach
- Brute force content-based algorithm

- Simple content-based algorithm
- Anomaly detection techniques

Objective

This chapter is to introduce you to the problem of accountability across internet and to explain stepping stones that add complexities to detect true origin of crime. After reading this chapter, you would know about the intrusion response system and its classification, and will have the knowledge about possible actions taken at the event of intrusion detection. This chapter details stepping stone detection algorithms that will help you to decide whether a particular computer is a part of connection-chain and involved in crime or it is incorporated to mislead thetraceback process. You will also understand how anomalies are caused with jitter and chaff in network traffic and learn about different anomaly detection techniques to remove anomalies.

5.1 The problem of accountability

The internet has global coverage and its associated peripherals are scattered across the world. As a user accesses the remote computers to retrieve the desired information and to make communication, the evidences needed to be held responsible to someone for their activities on internet are also distributed over the network. The collection of these evidences from different geographical continents, their access serialization and accusing someone on the basis of these evidences for crime is a difficult task. Authentication and auditing functionality of the operating system manages the accountability on the local system [5]. In such systems, authentication mechanism verifies users with its associated password and the auditing mechanism records the activities performed by the authenticated users. Unfortunately, accountability disappears when the user crosses its local system's operating system and accesses other system on network through logging. Although the user can be authenticated with a new password on new computer in some cases,the accounting of user's activities is distributed in the form of audit trails across multiple computers.

5.1.1 Network identifier

Intrusion detection systems (**IDS**) are designed to maintain accountability over the network of heterogeneous systems. To achieve accountability, a **network identifier** (**NID**) is assigned tothe user when he logs in for the first time to the network. All the activities performed by a user over the computers in network are mapped to assigned NID to know what action has been performed and on which computer too. To account the user for their activities, IDS maintainthe auditing mechanism for each system and establish a link between the user's UID for a session and the assigned NID [5]. For instance, If a user A with computer (*COM1*) access another computer (*COM2*) via remote login over the network as user B, then IDS tracks *A@COM1*to *B@COM2* and the activities performed over COM2 by user is mapped to same NID where the activities over A have been mapped. Similarly, if the user subsequently performs a second remote login from computer (*COM2*) to Computer (*COM3*) as a user, C. L.T Heberlein et al. [5] summarize these action as follows:

NID(C@COM3)= NID(B@COM2)...................(1)

NID(B@COM2)= NID(A@COM1)...................(2)

Equation (1) and equation (2) concludes that the NID for *C@COM3* is same as the NID for *A@COM2*.

The tracking between users and computers is achieved through network connection. A network connection is a shared resource over network, which helps to bind the session's activities to the related user and further connects to NID. For example, if a user **A** on **COM1** creates a remote login session (Called session 2) on **COM2** as shown in *Figure 5.1*, IDS initially determines computer-to-computer connection (net-rsrc). In our case, it is COM1-to-COM2. IDS initially identifies network connections through which COM1 communicates with COM2; thereafter, it binds the activities performed over COM2 as user **B** to its original user **A**. The network connection connecting COM1 to COM2 and managing the session over COM2 is represented as *<net-rsrc, session2@host2>*:

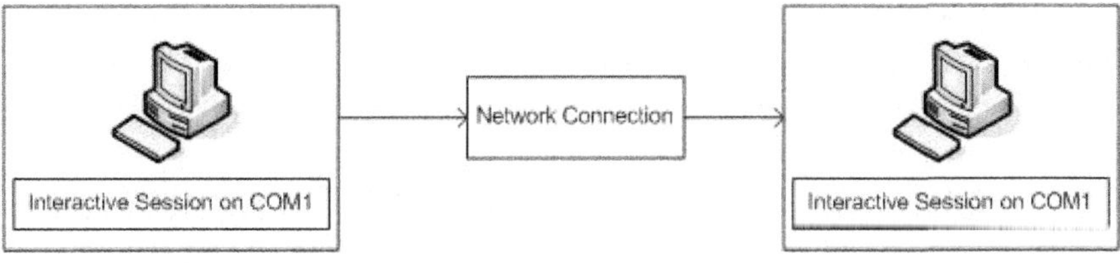

***Figure 5.1**: Session management*

The intrusion detection system locates a particular session and determines the NID to which this session is attached; thereafter, the investigation about the NID is performed to know original system and user for which it was generated.

As we know, the internet is a huge network that encompasses large number of small networks. Unfortunately, computers existing on different networks do not support host monitors and make the situation worse to fix accountability across the internet. Host monitor carries information about users' activities in particular session and on different computers too across the network which helps security administrator to track users.

Unfortunately, in many environments, not all computers on the network support a host monitor, which provides either the accountability for that particular host or the information required to track users across the network. In such environments, security and accountability can be increased by using a network monitor such as the **Network Security Monitor** (**NSM**).

5.1.2 Temporal thumbprint

Suppose a situation in which client (Host 1) communicates with server (Host 2) within a particular session. The send request from the client is observed with its acknowledgement received from the server together with the 'Echo' packet. Jianhua Yang et al.[16] elaborate Temporal Thumbprint with a sequence of packets $<p_1, p_2, \ldots, p_{n+1}>$ sent from Host 1 to Host 2 with corresponding time-stamps $<t_1, t_2, \ldots, t_{n+1}>$. The temporal thumbprint refers to the sequence$<t_2-t_1, t_3-t_2, t_4-t_3, \ldots, t_{n+1}-t_n>$ in which each element represents a time gap between two consecutivetransmitted packets [16]. The length of temporal thumbprint depends on the number of packets received at the server end whenever these are transmitted from client [16]. Thumbprint can be divided into subsequence's with the help of time unit like 1-minute interval, 2-minute interval, or 3-minute interval. Temporal thumbprint can be defined for incoming connection as well as outgoing connection. These are generally represented as iT-thumbprint and oT-thumbprint, respectively. The computation of iT-thumbprint and oT-thumbprint is crucial in tracing criminals across connections. We compute correlation between iT-thumbprint and oT-thumbprint to determine the involvement of jitter and chaff in cyberattack [16].

5.2 Stepping stones

The anonymous nature of internet facilitates cyber-criminals to hide their identity and commit crimes on behalf of someone else's identity. As a result, the chances of their detections and arrests are almost negligible. The cyber-criminals continuously effort to attain anonymities and manipulate the attacking paths to evade themselves from being detection. One widely used method to attain anonymity is the utilization of stepping stones, which are already compromised intermediary computers through which attack is launched to its final target. David A. Wheeler et al. [19] defines stepping stones as laundering hosts that allow data to be passed immediately without inspection and processing. Initially, intruders identify the compromised computers in network and prepare a chain of these computers in order to control a system from its previous one. A computer is controlled through log-in at its previous system and is accessed to release resources and to get control over its next system. Since stepping stones are heterogeneous, worldwide scattered and are diversely-administrated computers, it is very difficult to traceback the true origin of crime. Stepping stones detection has following benefits:

1. To flag suspicious activity
2. To determine the culprits behind the cybercrime, whether it belongs to its own organization or outsiders
3. To identify the vulnerable areas of your interconnected-digital-infrastructure
4. To ensure that a particular system in network is not participating in cybercrime
5. To break the suspicious connection chain

There is one major issue in intrusion detection, prevention, and tolerance. If an intrusion is detected, the last system through which the attack has been launched is held responsible for the malicious activity, while the actual culprits even remain unidentified. Staniford-Chen and Heberlein [3] initially addressed the problem of stepping stones and explained how their existence can make the network vulnerable.

When a person logs into one computer and control another computer, and by logging to this second computer, he operates the third computer and remaining computers are controlled in same way, makes a sequence of logins and this sequence of logins is known as **connection chain** [4]. The complexity of stepping stone detection process depends upon the length of connection chain. A connection chain containing thousands of computers, scattered across different countries and being governed under different legislations makes the traceback process difficult and impractical too. An intermediate host which belongs to connection chain is called **Stepping Stone**. A pair of network connections is known as **Stepping Stone Connection Pair** if both network connections are part of the same connection chain [4]. The flow of data on connection chain can be unidirectional and bidirectional. The bidirectional connection chain consists of two unidirectional flows, both in opposite direction of each other [4]. To understand the concept stepping stone and connection chain, we need to know the following notations:

- $h_1 \leftrightarrow h_2$: Represents bidirectional network connection between host h_1 and h_2.
- $h_1 \rightarrow h_2$: Denotes unidirectional data flow from host h_1 and h_2.
- C_1, C_2,.....,C_n:Denotes network connections.
- $C_1 \equiv stepping C_2$: represents a stepping stone connection pair between C_1 and C_2.

The general approach normally used to detect stepping stones is network traffic characteristics that remain invariant or highly correlated across stepping stone connection pairs [4]. Some parameters on the basis of which the network traffic across the two connection pairs is compared are connection content, inter-packet spacing, ON/OFF patterns of traffic flow, traffic volume or rate, or possible combination of these.

5.2.1 Direct and indirect stepping stones

Suppose h_1, h_2, h_3, h_4 is a continuous connection chain. If we observe the network traffic in h1↔h2and h2↔h3, almost same network packets are found in both connection pairs. As shown in *Figure 5.2*, all the intermediate hosts (h_2, h_3) excluding attacker and target, are known as **direct stepping stones**:

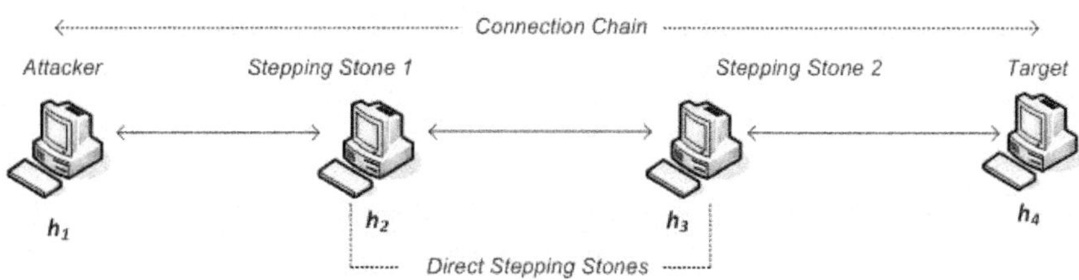

Figure 5.2: *Direct stepping stones*

The two connection pairs $h_1 \leftrightarrow h_2$ and $h_2 \leftrightarrow h_3$ are disjoint and cannot be compared to examine the similarity in connection content, inter-packet spacing and the ON/OFF pattern:

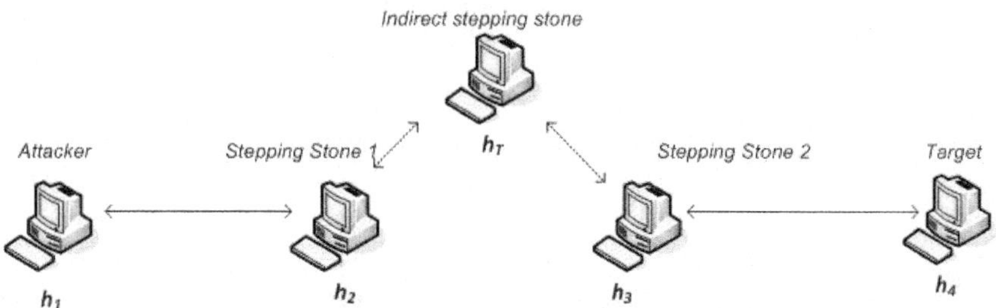

Figure 5.3: *Indirect stepping stones*

To deal this situation, both connection pairs are connected through a temporary host hr as shown in *Figure 5.3* and compared to know the variations in network traffic characteristics. This temporary host is known as **indirect stepping stones**.

5.2.2 Stepping stone detection algorithm consideration

Intrusion detection system (IDS) normally identifies the attack much after its occurrence that leads the damage of infrastructure, stealing of data, financial loss, and privacy breach too. The occurrence of such kinds of frequent attack and the delay in their prosecution not only destroy the morale and confidence of victims, but also provide ample chance to criminals to flee off. Identification of attacks after overall possible damages is almost meaningless. The IDS must be able to detect the threats before their activation in order to avoid the possible damages. In such conditions, real time threats detection becomes crucial. It means to identify of threats as soon as these are launched in web environment. Real-time threat detection does not need to store data for entire network traffic as it becomes voluminous.

In this section, we shall detail the basic essential assumptions that are required to devise a stepping stone detection algorithm. The stepping stone connection pair is differentiated from randomly picked connection pair on the basis of some correlated network traffic characteristics. Stepping stone connection pair means a part of connection chain in which at least two stepping stone computers exist in consecutive positions while in randomly picked connection-pair, the pri or idea about the existence of consecutive stepping stones over the connection chain remains uncertain. The approach that is considered to detect stepping stone utilizes network traffic characteristics that remain invariant or at least highly correlated across two or more consecutive stepping stone computers. In case of arbitrary pairs of connection, these network traffic characteristics may vary. Major network traffic characteristics, which are computed to compare network traffic across the connection pairs are connection contents, inter-packet spacing, ON/OFF activities patterns, traffic volume and traffic rate [4].

5.2.3 Active and passive monitoring

There are two approaches named active network monitoring and passive network monitoring, are used to examine network traffic in real-time for threats and to measure network performance. The active monitoring evaluates the users' behavior over network and detects the hosts which are acting as stepping stones [6]. Test-data set are injected between a connection pair to examine network performance over different evaluative parameters as discussed in *Chapter 4, Cybercrime Source Identification Techniques*. If there is significant variations are examined across network connections, the possibility to exist stepping stones in the connection-pair increases. The major benefits of active monitoring are the ability to quick detection of threats and to maintain complete visibility across the network too [6]. The dark aspect of active monitoring includes the generation of additional network traffic and test-data set packets can disturb the normal operation of network. The passive network monitoring collects the live data (real-time) and analyzes it over a regular interval to identify the behavioral changes of intruders over network from normal users. The passive network monitoring believes in statistics to identify the irregularities in network flow and does not inject test-data to predict loopholes across the network. It measures the network flow to and from a specific device on your network and compares it to find the differences. Minimum difference is desired to avoid the presence of intruders.

5.2.4 Single and multiple measurement points

The ability to detect intrusions and providing protection against malicious attempts to systems and underlying hardware, depends on the information, collected from underlying software and networked devices. For the development of robust security mechanism against the intrusions, it is essential to collect real-time and accurate data from various networked devices and software like operating systems and protocol interfaces, and it is possible if networked devices retain detailed and non-modified information about their utilization and about the network-traffic passing through them. To diagnose malicious attempts and vulnerabilities, the security administrator needs continuous monitoring and timely inspection of data-traffic passing through each underlying network devices, computers and servers, and must aware about the changes in configuration that result diversion and distribution of the network traffic.

Network traffic measurement refers to the close inspection of ongoing data transfer that furnishes the detail about lost and corrupted data packets, delivery of packets, delay in reaching and ordering as well. Network traffic measurement is also performed to know the locations across the network from where disturbance in packet delivery is created, fluctuations and interception in normal traffic flow is also being carried out to perform malicious activities. Traffic measurement plays a crucial role in order to prepare a detailed view of network and facilitates security administrator to detect congestion across the network based on periodic summaries of traffic load and packet loss on each measurement point.

Fixing the position of measurement points across the network is as important as choosing the performance indicators to compare network performance at ingress points and egress points of a particular network that includes network devices such as routers, bridges and switches, and so on:

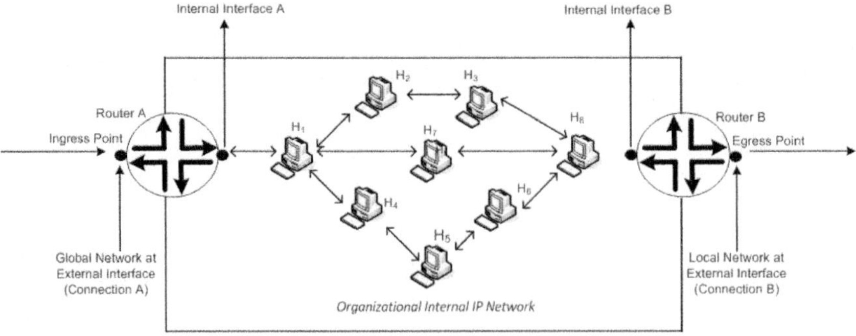

Figure 5.4: *Intrusion detection measurement locations*

Performance indicators are parameters on the basis of which network traffic is compared and desired to be almost correlated at ingress and egress points. Yin Zhang and Vern Paxson [4] compared the network traffic with connection contents, inter-packet spacing, ON/OFF patterns of activities, traffic volume, and traffic rate. The multiple measurement points across the network are always preferable either inside or outside the organization because it increases the chances to catch malicious activities immediately as these propagate from any host. The single measurement point is applied over router as shown in the *Figure 5.4*. If security mechanism is applied over ingress point (Router A) and egress point (Router B), the malicious activities emerging from any intermediate host < H_1, H_2, H_3, H_4.......,H_7, H_8> can affect its leading systems. However, if we apply multiple measurement points, each one for every host at its ingress and egress points, then malicious code can be identified easily and seized to prevent further damage.

5.2.5 Filtering

Network traffic includes several types of data packets and are classified on various parameters such as port number from where these are delivered and to which these are directed, protocols to which these belong and services these offer. Suspecting each packet and processing it to identify its malicious nature is useless as some packets becomes the part of network. Processing each packet adds complexity and requires more time. Ideally, stepping stone detection activity needs to identify only those packets that carry malicious code and can cause damages. The malicious packets that cause anomalies and inject jitter are separated from non-malicious packets, and is achieved through a separate block of code. Jitter refers to variations in time interval, detected to reach the packets from source to destination host. Identifying malicious packets is a difficult activity as single malicious program is carried with different packets and the packets containing partial information cannot be easily marked as malicious. Filtering the packets increases the chances to lose accompanying context and helps to mask intended packets. In *Figure 5.5*, the criminal uses two network segments named **A** and **B** to transmit multiple malicious packets:

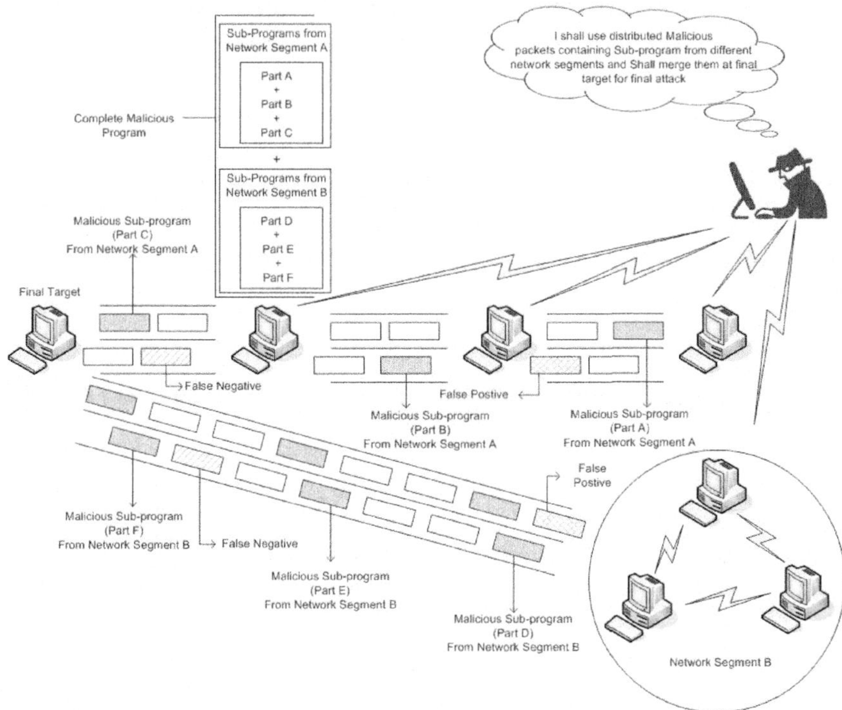

***Figure 5.5**: Traffic filtration*

The criminal does not transmit the whole malicious program in once because of the risk of detection. Criminal divides the malicious program in parts and transmits these parts as different packets through different network segments. As shown in the preceding *Figure 5.5*, complete malicious program is divided into six packets named **Part A, Part B, Part C, Part D, Part E, Part F** and are transmitted through two different network segments. **Part A, Part B** and **Part C** are transmitted through network segment **A** while **Part D, Part E** and **Part F** are transmitted through network segment B. These malicious packets are assembled and arranged to form original and complete malicious program to launch attack at the target. In addition, the predefined criteria for filtering, cautions criminals to evade detection and indirectly help them to plan strategy accordingly. Thus, filtering techniques should be regularly updated and we should not follow the same pattern and level longer. False positives and false negatives mislead the security administrator and change the direction of inspection and investigation in order to find malicious packets. A false positive is an indication, signal or message that shows a positive result for a test where as it is negative in reality. In case of stepping stone detection, it is non-stepping stone connections that are erroneously or intentionally flagged as stepping stones. There is another similar concept, popularly known as false negative, in which negative result is achieved, whereas it is positive. A stepping stone connection is represented as non-stepping stone connection in order to evade its detection.

5.2.6 Minimizing state for connection pairs

There can be large number of active stepping stones in a connection chain, so performing close inspection of each connection pair is often considered infeasible due to N^2 memory requirement [4]. N is the number of stepping stones in a connection-chain. The *Figure 5.2* comprises six connection pairs, three in forward direction and rest in reverse direction as network traffic is bidirectional. The forward direction connection pairs are $C_1 \equiv steppingC_2$, $C_2 \equiv steppingC_3$ and $C_3 \equiv steppingC_4$ where C_1, C_2, C_3, and C_4 are connections with host h_1, h_2, h_3, h_4, respectively. Similarly, reverse connection pairs are $C_4 \equiv steppingC_3$, $C_3 \equiv steppingC_2$ and $C_2 \equiv steppingC_1$. It is very important to know that what a host adds in traffic, when it is part of connection chain. In *Figure 5.2*, we need to compare all six connection pairs in order to measure variations in network traffic, if we perform first three comparisons in forward direction and find almost negligible difference in network traffic at host h_1 and h_4, then it is assumed that this connection chain did not suffer intrusions. As we know, to trigger an attack, we need few lines of malicious code and these lines cannot be easily typed in such a short span of time. Therefore, this code is injected from outside to connection chain that results variations in network traffic across the hosts incorporated in connection chain. Indeed, to evade detection, intruders distribute their malicious code in several hosts and execute them in such a manner that the output of sub-program becomes the input of subsequent sub-program. If we find the network traffic invariant from host h_1 and h_4 in *Figure 5.2*, then we can replace three comparisons between host $h_1 \leftrightarrow h_2$, $h_2 \leftrightarrow h_3$, $h_3 \leftrightarrow h_4$ with only single comparison that is $h_1 \leftrightarrow h_4$.

5.2.7 Traffic patterns

Network traffic analysis is an activity that records, reviews and examines network traffic and its pattern in order to measure performance, ensure security and management of operations like time-bound delivery and recipient of data packets. Network flow data is accompanied with packet header data to make communication between a source and a destination. The flow of communication is differentiated through protocol-level information contained in header and proximity in timing in packets flow. Network flow contains header information for all individual packets and each packet uses same protocol settings within a designated time window. The detailed network traffic pattern report is summarized to record the details of whole communication for a period from months to years. This report is analyzed to draw out malicious communication pattern and to discard it form communication, and to block it at its origin. Network traffic pattern contains sufficient indicative information to assist security administrators to seek threats with their origins, to find out the method of threats activation and to search the method to reduce adverse impacts. Traffic patterns help defenders to understand the complete view of network flow at any selected particular event and to have an idea about past and future flow. The detailed traffic pattern report is analyzed to determine the future hazards and to develop security mechanism accordingly to patch up future vulnerabilities and to nullify further attacks.

The network traffic from web server to client computer becomes quick with high byte volume and relatively with modest number of data packets. In normal case, all these three participants (timing, byte volume and packets) constitute base-lining. If traffic from server to client is detected as voluminous in packets in base-line timing, then it can be questioned and marked as abnormal. The disturbance in baselining, raises security alarms and examines the abnormal flow occurrence in network flow to identify suspicions activities.

5.2.7.1 Path, traffic and demand matrices

Network traffic flow representation is necessary to perform control actions like route changing, traffic classification, filtering and capacity planning [7]. To the best of knowledge, three canonical spatial representations of traffic are used, named path matrix, traffic matrix and demand matrix. These representations furnish the information about current state of network and the traffic flow through it in a descriptive manner and enable us to make predictions about the state of network after performing hypothetical control actions. To understand these representations, consider how a network engineer would manage the network traffic if he has full control over end-to-end connections. There are two common representations that would help to network engineer to examine, detect and diagnose problems and to make evaluation of security controls across the network. The first representation is path matrix as shown in *Figure 5.6* that measures the data volume V (P) between source to destination across the path P:

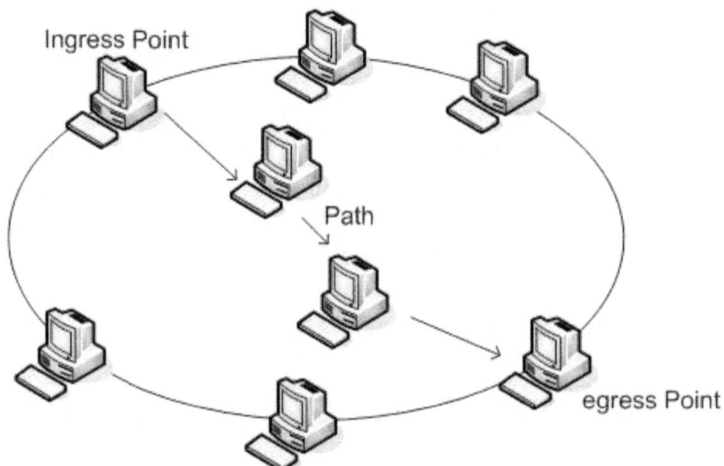

***Figure 5.6**: Path matrix*

The path matrix represents the current state and behavior of network with detailed description about the traffic flow through it [7]. The traffic matrix as depicted in *Figure 5.7* represents the data volume

V(S, D) per source-destination pair and specifies the offered load over the network:

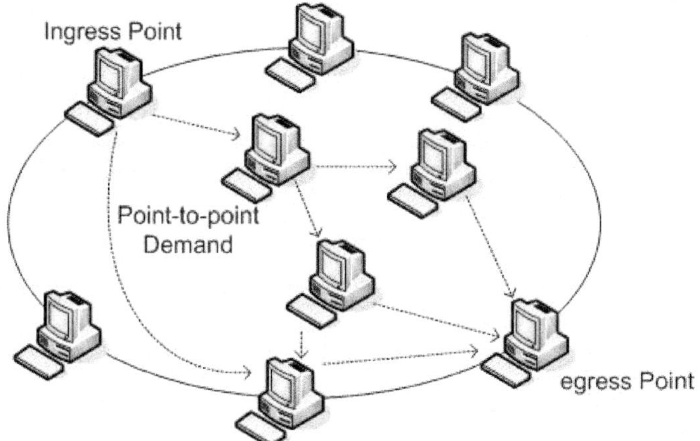

Figure 5.7: *Traffic matrix*

Traffic matrix is an abstract model to represent traffic volume flowing between different sets of source and destination pairs [8]. Each element in the traffic matrix represents the amount of network traffic between source and destination pair. Here, the term amount is measured in number of bytes or packets [8]. Traffic matrices are utilized to achieve various engineering objectives such as prediction of future traffic needs, network optimization, protocol design and anomaly detection, and are also helpful to detect sudden shifts in traffic due to anomalies and malicious activities [8]. The traffic matrix assumes that the offered load remains unchanged to the state and behavior of network [7]. The network service operator has limited controls over small portion of network or to small autonomous system (AS) of a particular organization.

Capturing the network traffic and examining it for attempts which have been made to interrupt the normal traffic flow to perform malicious activities is easier in the **autonomous system (AS)** environment. The path matrix covers the different paths inside AS while the traffic matrix is specified between ingress to egress points. The path matrix and traffic matrix representations are adequate in situations where interdomain and intradomain routing becomes completely decoupled, which means the local control actions do not leave impacts on ingress and egress points [7]. Managing a single AS, means construction of internet like structure for specific purpose on smaller scale [7]. A closely related topic to the traffic matrix is the demand matrix as shown in *Figure 5.8* that deals with the carried load, while the previous one represents offered load [8]:

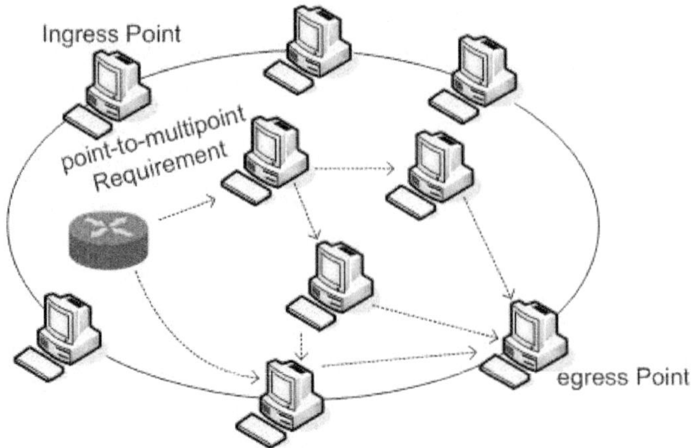

***Figure 5.8:** Demand matrix*

The traffic matrix and demand matrix may have the same element if there is no congestion in network and carried load is not limited in a traffic stream [8].

5.2.7.2 Responsiveness

Responsiveness is yet another parameter, which needs adequate attention during the design of stepping stone detection algorithm. It deals with time duration in which it detects the intrusion and response to related threats even before the possible damages. Clearly, it is desirable to sense jeopardy before it goes in action; it gives us an ample chance to perform additional security actions such as recording network traffic for analysis, shutting down the connections and backing up of devices. Another consideration is the resources that are seized to use for other resources during detection and response. Algorithm must care to not to engage more resources for longer.

In this digital era, information technology-based systems are at higher risk, may be compromised to breach the privacy of individuals and to ruin the financial health and goodwill of organizations and even institutions too. The rapid growth in malicious activities, frauds and cheating made it to feel the organizations that only protection from threats is not the only solution to tackle with cyberattacks instead they would require a proper response system that shall have advanced sense unit against threats and will take action in order to nullify the adverse impacts of threats. Network devices, computers and data are unsecured because of their connectivity to external networks and devices while attacks are now more sophisticated and automated, breach the protection easily, and present severe security-related challenges before an organization. The following *Figure 5.9* shows the classification of an intrusion response system:

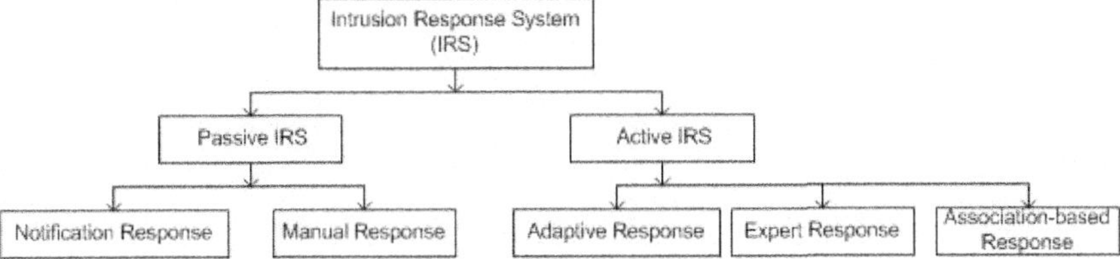

***Figure 5.9**: IRS classification*

Active response mechanism immediately responds to intrusions to protect data assets and networked devices without any human intervention. Passive response mechanisms are not self-activated and requires human efforts in order protect the digital interconnected infrastructure against the malicious activities. The major disadvantage of passive response system is the confidentiality breach of data sets during investigation and the unnecessary delay in traffic flow as traffic events are blocked and are marked as malicious events if negative response is received. *Figure 5.10* shows the possible actions performed by active IRS and passive IRS when an intrusion is detected. The most common operations that are performed by response mechanism include suspending IP addresses, blocking IP addresses, blocking ports, injecting TCP resets to terminate connections, changing access control lists, reconfiguring routers and firewalls [9]. An **intrusion response system (IRS)** is categorized into three parts: notification, manual, and automatic. In the notification system, response is generated in the form of alert and report is generated and sent through an e-mail. In a manual response system, few predefined responses exist in advance and selected well-suited response and triggered by a security manager after detection of an intrusion. In automatic response system, the human intervention between the detection unit and response unit is completely neglected. In the notification and manual response system, a substantial gap is found in detection and generating response, which gives an ample chance to attackers to perform malicious activities without fear of being arrest:

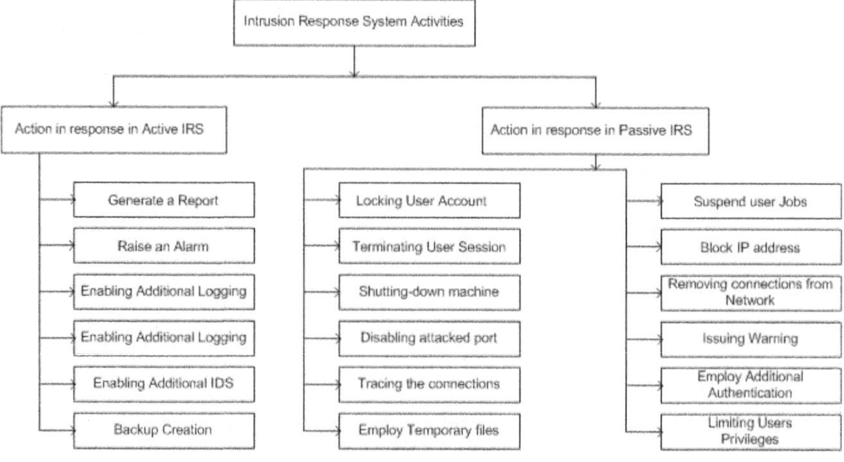

***Figure 5.10**: IRS actions*

Automatic intrusion response system is further classified into three types: adaptive, expert, and association-based. In the adaptive response system uses the hybrid approach that combines the functionalities of active and passive response mechanisms and generates dynamic response as per the nature of attack in the form of pop-up, notification and reports [9]. A feedback loop is encountered to generate the better response on the basis of previous one. Expert systems follow well-defined rules and perform a series of if-then statements to generate the most appropriate and modified response. It uses the signature and anomaly-based approach to detect intrusions and response to security manager. Expert system suffers with a serious problem as it requires excessive initial training and extraordinary care during the lifetime to update various decision-making cases. In associative-based IRS, a predefined response is activated, which is specifically generated in advance and associated to that attack. Associative-based IRS is static in nature, which means that its validation cases are formulated only once and cannot be modified further if upgradation is noticed in associated vulnerabilities and attack [9].

5.2.7.3 Evasive attackers

IDSs are widely being used to enhance the security of digital assets, interconnected infrastructure and network against malicious threats. The IDS function in the same fashion as burglar alarm does in the physical world. Like all alarms, IDSs to have weak points and flaws that help attackers to breach security provisions and hide them during the entire episode of intrusion and attack. We believe that only construction of a robust IDS is not important instead its maintenance and advancement is equally important too. Attackers regularly attempt to gain access and breach security without caring how secure the system is. Attackers adopt various techniques to pass malicious traffic through IDS and present this traffic as legitimate traffic in order to avoid detection. Obfuscation, fragmentation, Denial of Service, and application hijacking are some popular techniques often used to get succeed in intrusions.

5.2.7.4 IDS signature and base-lining

A knowledge-based intrusion detection system, which is also popularly known as a signature-based intrusion detection system, manages a database of previously occurred attacks. These systems evaluate attacking pattern, recognize affected areas and determine system vulnerabilities to maintain the complete records to prevent future attacks. The IDS signature means recorded evidences like attacking pattern, time interval, frequency of activation. Indeed, each surreptitious access leaves some footprints like nature of data packets, failed attempts to activate applications, failed logins, system files and folders deletion and renaming them collectively furnish valuable information about the attacks and in many cases their sources too. These footprints are termed as signatures and are used prevent the repetition of similar kinds of attacks in future. The knowledge-based IDS can be bypassed with new malicious code as its details are not recorded in concerned database. Due to this, the signature-based IDS are required to be continuously updated to maintain signature database. Behavior-based intrusion detection systems, which are also known as Anomaly-based intrusion detection systems works in a different fashion. These systems maintain baseline or learned patterns of system normal activities to identify malicious access. The deviations from baseline or pattern are measured to raise a security alarm.

5.2.7.5 Obfuscation

Obfuscation refers to the process in which the data traffic is manipulated in such a way that the IDS signature could not match with malicious packets. In other words, obfuscation evades malicious traffic from IDS signatures in order to avoid detection and helps attackers for surreptitious access. Corbin Carlo [10] explained the obfuscation in following ways:

Let us consider following string:

"../../c:\winnt\system32\xevent.exe"

Would not be recognized by IDS in the same way as in the case of the following string:

"%5d%5de%2d%2e%2e%2f%2e%2e%2fc:\winnt\system32\xevent.exe"

A web server recognizes these two strings as same with the help of interpretation rules of the Hyper Text Transfer Protocol (HTTP) [10].

5.3 Timing-based stepping stone detection approach

In this section, we will explain timing-based stepping stone detection algorithm. Yin Zhang et al. [4] analyzed the network traffic and inspected the behavior among the different ends of chained connections. The network traffic of a node is correlated with the network traffic of its previous node and the variations are measured in order to find a suspected source of crime. In a connection chain of *N* nodes requires at least *N* correlations. Network traffic or data traffic refers to the amount of data transmitted through the network at a given instant of time [11]. There is slight difference between a flow and data traffic, flow contains the data traffic. Flow basically refers to the data of different protocols through which the two nodes are connected and become able to communicate. The network traffic represents the World Wide Web data, users' individual data or intranet data of some organization. Flow is a continuous process, while the network traffic is discrete.

Yin Zhang and Vern Paxson [4] devised the timing-based stepping stone detection algorithm. For the better understanding of this algorithm, we should know the ON and OFF periods. If there is no network traffic is detected on flow for T_{idle}seconds, then it said to be OFF period for that connection chain; otherwise, it is considered ON period [4]. During the ON period, the packets in network traffic contain new data in their TCP payloads. The term new data represents non-retransmitted and non-keepalive data in the TCP payloads of network packets. The network traffic ends with an OFF period, while begins with the ON period, which lasts till new data is found across the connection pair for T_{idle} seconds [4]. Giovanni Di Crescenzo et al. [14, 18] showed how a correlation is computed with ON and OFF periods across two network connections with following *Figure 5.11*:

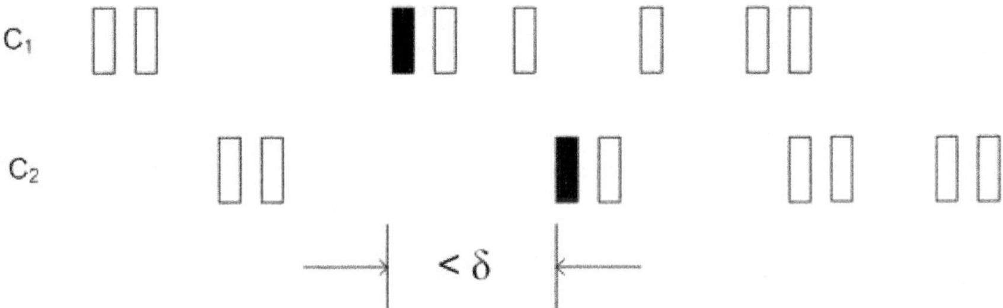

Figure 5.11*: Correlation of packets for connections C1 and C2 based on timing*

Yin Zhang et al. [4] tried to differentiate interactive traffic from non-interactive traffic and used the time interval among the keystrokes to justify whether these are machine driven or belongs to human action. V. Paxson et al. [4, 12] inspected the internet traffic and described the importance of time interval among the keywords with the help of Pareto distribution. In both studies, it has been concluded that the large interval between two consecutive keystrokes are uncommon and about 25% keywords are found with separation of 500 msec. About 15% keywords hold the separation of one second, while 1.6 percent keywords showed their presence with 10 sec or more apart.

5.3.1 Timing correlation when OFF periods end

In timing-based stepping stone detection algorithm, we correlate the connections based on coincidences across the connection either on the ending of OFF periods or in the beginning of ON periods [4, 12]. Suppose two connections C_1 and C_2, are the part of same connection chain and forming stepping stone connection pair C_1≡steppingC_2, Conceptually, C_1 and C_2 shall leave OFF periods on similar times. In other words, if a user presses a keystroke and is made pass initially through C_1 and thereafter from C_2, the OFF periods for keyword across both connections coincide. The inverse becomes also true, that is, if a keyword initially passed through C_2 and thereafter from C_1, then the OFF periods of connection pair C_1≡steppingC_2 shall coincide with C_2≡steppingC_1. This concept is utilized to measure correlations.

It is assumed that two OFF periods correlated if their ending times differ by ≤ δ, the δ depicts to control parameter.

For two connections C_1 and C_2, the OFF_1 and OFF_2 represent the number of OFF periods in each respectively and OFF_1, 2 represents the number of OFF periods which are correlated. Yin Zhang and Vern Paxson [4, 14] derived the following relation:

$$\frac{OFF_{1,2}}{Min(OFF_1, OFF_2)} \geq \gamma$$

Where γ represent control parameter and fixed with 0.3.

The benefit of this approach is the necessity to compute the correlation with significant idle period only [4]. For busy and non-idle connections, we do not compute correlations among connection pairs as it can be ignored if connections are active or idle. We need only a small number of possible connections pairs at any given point of time. We are required to identify the connection pairs that have been transitioned from idle to active and this does not happen frequently because it requires connection to be inactive for significant period of time initially [4]. We compute correlations across connections when ON periods begin. Suppose two connections C_1≡steppingC_2, if throughput capacity of $C_1$is smaller than C_2, then ON period of C_2 ends earlier than C_1. Otherwise, the start time shall be almost similar in time duration. The above approach is adopted because of its simplicity and some refinements to this algorithm can improve its accuracy. In the improvement, timing causality plays an important role [13]. Suppose there are two flows F_1 and F_2 existing on the same flow chain, then their timing correlation is required to be consistent in ordering. In other words, if F_1 ends with the OFF period, prior to F_2, then this ordering should always continue in future. To enhance the accuracy of this algorithm, we compute the number of consecutive coincidences to deter frequency of coincidences and to differentiate true stepping stones from accidentally coinciding connections. Yin Zhang et al. [4, 12, 14] derived the following relations for two connections C_1 and C_2 if both constitute a connection pair:

$$OFF^{*}_{1,2} \geq min_{csc}$$

and

$$\frac{OFF^{*}_{1,2}}{Min(OFF_1, OFF_2)} \geq \gamma'$$

Where $OFF^{*}_{1,2}$ represents a number of consecutive coincidences and mincsc and γ' are the control parameters.

5.3.1.1 Evasion Using Jitter

Packets are delivered from sending end in a continuous manner with a fixed time-gap between the packets. At the receiving end this time-gap between packets can vary due to network congestions and improper trafficking. **Jitter** refers to variation in timing when packets are received at destination end [17]. Attackers intentionally inject delays to disrupt the correlations between the flows across the connection chain with hope to avoid detection. Giovanni Di Crescenzo et al. [14] analyzed Timing-based stepping stone detection algorithm and recognized jitter as a medium that evades the malicious packets from detection from security measures. The timing-based stepping stone detection algorithm is vulnerable to jitter and if an attacker injects jitter with delay more than δ msec with network traffic in one of the connections, then attacker will not be detected [14]. The attacker remains undetected as OFF periods are considered correlated only in situations when their ending times difference becomes less than δ [14].

5.3.1.2 Evasion using chaff

Chaff refers to meaningless padding packets, inserted to data traffic with intention to generate delay at receiving end [15, 17]. Criminal injects chaff packets in connections to reduce the ratio of correlated OFF periods to total OFF periods [14]. Whenever sufficient chaff packets are injected, the mentioned ratio falls down to γ, and situations becomes favourable to criminals to evade them from detection.

5.4 Brute Force Content-based Algorithm

Brute Force Content-based algorithm is based on the concept that for stepping stones, text typed by the user is copied word-to-word across two-connections if there is no encryption mechanism used. Therefore, matching the text in common similar connections are identified with same contents. Yin Zhang et al. [4] suggested that some manual inspections need to be analyzed to identify stepping stones to derive Brute Force Content-based Algorithm. This algorithm incorporates the results of these inspections and works in the following way:

1. The output from Telnet and Rlogin from all occurring sessions used in trace are extracted and aggregated in a separate file [4].
2. The frequency of occurrence is counted for each different line in the output.
3. Ignorance of all lines except those having their replica as another line. These lines are considered good candidates for stepping stones.
4. Identification of connections containing these lines, are listed in a file. This file records each unique line in every connection and preserved in a database. The join operation is performed between these unique lines and the lines remaining in a file created in the first step. Any line that does not have its own replica is ignored [4].
5. Connection pairs are identified with the Unix join utility containing lines appeared twice in both connections of a pair.
6. Connection pairs having five or more such lines those have replica are now considered as candidates to be stepping stones.
7. Connection pairs are again analyzed for their directions and discarded those having the same direction [4].
8. The remaining connection pairs are further inspected visually to confirm that these are playing as stepping stones.

Brute force content-based algorithm [4] details a good baseline assessment methodology to identify stepping-stones. As it incorporates five or more lines to measure duplicity, means it reduces the number of connection pairs which are required to be visually inspected. This algorithm performs better with a limited number of connection pairs, but fails in case of encrypted traffic.

5.5 Simple content-based algorithm

Yin Zhang and Vern Paxson [4] devised two content-based algorithms to detect stepping stones. These algorithms are based on the concepts of text similarity among the logins. Suppose L_1 and L_2 are two consecutive logins and if the text seen in L_1 is further detected in L_2, then these logins are considered correlated [4]. These algorithms are emphasized to search such instances of unique text. Clearly, all the login sessions become unique and different in various ways with difficulty to have evidences to know how these are different [4].

The first algorithm believes in the fact that few Telnet clients transmit X-Windows DISPLAY variable with the aim to locate the user's X display server with remote X-commands. In this algorithm, the value of DISPLAY remains unique as it globally recognizes a particular instance of hardware.Yin Zhang et al. [4] used the Bro, an open source, Unix-based **Network Intrusion Detection System (NIDS)** to examine network traffic passively and to detect malicious activities. During the implementation of this algorithm, the Bro is modified to link with each telnet session and the value of DISPLAY variable is attached to values to flag a session [4].

Inthe second algorithm, when a new interactive session starts, the login dialog incorporates a status line. The possible combinations of different timestamps and previously-accessed hosts make the status line unique in the traceback process [4]. This algorithm suffers with false positives and whenever two or more interactive sessions point to the same user, the computers responsible to sessions are considered as stepping stones [4].

5.6 Anomaly detection techniques

Criminals inject jitter and chaff to network traffic to evade detection. Giovanni Di Crescenzo et al. [14, 18] devised the following three algorithms to detect jitter and chaff-based anomalies in the network traffic:

A. Response-time based algorithm

B. Edit-distance based algorithm

C. Causality-based algorithm

An attacker who is unknown to the presence of traceback mechanism is easily caught with timing-based stepping stone detection algorithm, but if he injects jitter and chaff, then it becomes difficult to detect him. The response-time algorithm is used to detect jitter, and edit-distance based and causality-based algorithms both are used to detect chaff in network traffic [14, 18].

5.6.1 Response-time based algorithm

The Response-time based anomaly detection algorithm believes in response received from server when a request is sent in an interactive session within a certain time-slot. Suppose **C** is an interactive connection between client and server. $\mathbf{C}_{12}$ represents the flow of packets from client side to the server, while $\mathbf{C}_{21}$ represents backward response from the server side to the client. This algorithm assumes that whenever a request is sent from a client to the server, the client immediately receives a response from the server side in the Echo form [14]. Packets involved in request $\mathbf{C}_{12}$ are split into ON and OFF periods by using a parameter T_{idle}. Splitting the request into ON and OFF periods significantly reduces the quantity of packets processing without leaving the impacts on results [18]:

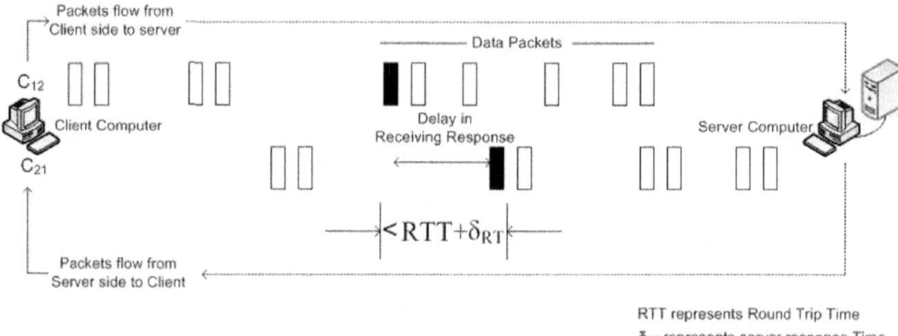

***Figure 5.12**: Response-time based anomaly detection*

Giovanni Di Crescenzo et al. [14] tested this algorithm with different values ranging from 300 to 500 msec for T_{idle} and concluded that results of this algorithm are not affected due to change in T_{idle} parameter. Suppose the packet transmitted across connection C_{12} gets start with an ON period and if its response packet is not received on connection C_{21} in RTT+δ_{RT} time, then this ON period is marked as anomalous as shown in *Figure 5.12*. The RTT stands for round trip time, while δ_{RT} is considered as a fixed time slot (50 msec) that represents response time from server [17]. The ratio of anomalous

ON periods to total ON periods is computed and if found greater than γ_{RT}, then the connection is treated as anomalous. Giovanni Di Crescenzo et al. [14] set 0.67 to γ_{RT} and concluded that very small value for γ_{RT} leads to many false positives, while large value denotes many false negatives. This algorithm generates false positives whenever server is extremely loaded with client-side queries and takes more than δ_{RT} time. It suffers with false negatives if the criminals generate queries at very fast speed and all related packets on connection C_{12} are transmitted within Ti_{dle} time and are not partitioned into ON and OFF periods. If jitter is injected in a time period less than δ_{RT}, then it is also not detected.

5.6.2 Edit-distance based algorithm

The edit-distance based algorithm believes in the fact that for normal interactive connections, the sequence of time durations in both directions (C_{12} and C_{21}) for associated ON and OFF intervals remains either identical or at least very similar [14, 18]. For identical time sequences, the edit-distance is considered to be zero and for almost similar connections the edit-distance is set to close to zero [14]. If the chaff is injected in connections, the time sequences become dissimilar and a positive edit-distance is measured between ON and OFF intervals. This positive edit-distance increases proportionally as the amount of chaff is injected [18].

Giovanni Di Crescenzo et al. [14] devised this algorithm with transmitting sequences of packets across the connections C_{12} and C_{21}. In this algorithm, the packets are partitioned into ON and OFF periods with keeping T_{idle} 300 msec. The time difference between two consecutives ON periods is measured and used to construct a sequence of intervals for C_{12} and C_{21} connections. The transmitted sequences are partitioned into several subsequences and local edit distance for each subsequence is computed. Edit-distance β is permitted for a subsequence to be legitimate. If cumulative edit distance for subsequences becomes greater than β times of number of incorporated subsequences, the connection is marked as abnormal and suspicious [14, 18].

5.6.3 Causality-based algorithm

This anomaly detection method is used to detect the availability of chaff in a network traffic. Giovanni Di Crescenzo et al. [14] analyzed the behavior of criminals before partitioning the packets into ON and OFF periods and it was observed that criminals wait for output when they execute malicious program to trigger attack [14]. If criminal succeeds in his attempt, then he try for next malicious code. This typing and waiting mechanism is considered the baseline for this algorithm [14]. The development of causality-based anomaly detection method takes following two assumptions in consideration:

- For a pair of successive ON periods on connection C_{12}, one ON period is counted on connection C_{21}.
- Similarly, a pair of successive ON periods on connection C_{21}, one ON period is counted on connection C_{12}.

An ON period on connection $\mathbf{C_{12}}$ is flagged as abnormal and anomalous if either zero or more than one ON periods are observed on connection $\mathbf{C_{21}}$ before the occurrence of another ON period on connection $\mathbf{C_{12}}$. The *Figure 5.13* shows causality-based anomaly detection with successive ON periods on Connection $\mathbf{C_{12}}$ and $\mathbf{C_{21}}$:

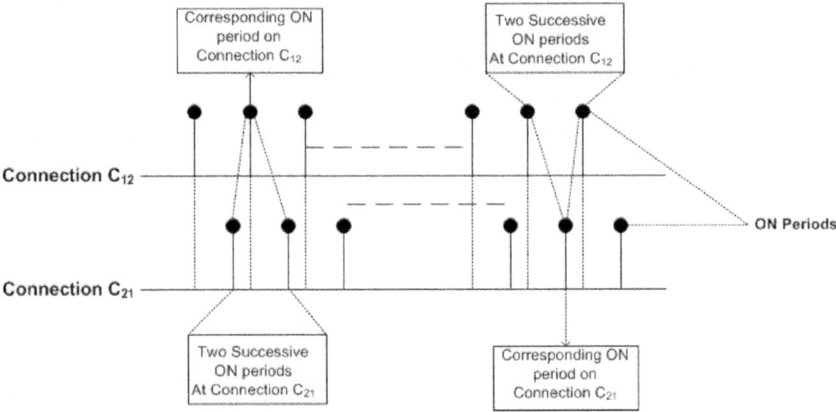

***Figure 5.13**: Causality based anomaly detection*

Giovanni Di Crescenzo et al. [14] computed $\gamma_{\mathbf{forward}}$ that is defined as ratio of anomalous ON periods to the total ON periods on connection $\mathbf{C_{12}}$. Similarly, $\gamma_{reverse}$ is computed for connection $\mathbf{C_{21}}$. The numerical value of both $\gamma_{forward}$ and $\gamma_{reverse}$ becomes low in case of normal connections, but if the value of these measures are greater than 0.67, the connection is considered as anomalous and it is believed that penetration is made through chaff.

Causality-based anomaly detection method suffers with false positive as interactive connections are utilized for bulk file transfer or to deal with commands that have large outputs. It also suffers with false negatives if the criminals use chaff in greater rate than T_{idle}. This greater rate of chaff incorporation is achieved due to involvement of custom server.

Conclusion

The main problem with the internet is lack of an effective technology that binds users' identities with their corresponding activities performed over the internet. We explained network identifier to resolve this issue and presented that how network identifier can be helpful to identify which activity is performed by whom. The utility of thumbprints has been elaborated in correlation computing and to decide the level of symmetry in two network connection chains. Further, we have explained stepping stones and their surreptitious utilization in avoiding criminal detection. The main attraction of this chapter is the Timing-Based stepping stone detection approach that utilizes ON and OFF pattern of the network traffic across a connection chain to determine intermediary compromised and breached computers. As criminals use jitter and chaff to manipulate the network traffic and to generate variations in ON and OFF periods, we explained Brute Force Content-based Algorithm and Simple Content-based Algorithm to detect jitter and chaff in network traffic. Finally, we have elaborated Response-time based algorithm, Edit-distance based algorithm and Causality-based algorithm to determine the anomalies in network traffic and to fix them to remove variations in ON and OFF patterns.

In the next chapter, we will learn about methodologies that are used to detect spoofed packets across network-connection chain and shall also discuss some advance techniques normally used to prevent spoofed packet-based attacks.

Points to remember

- The major barrier in construction of effective network countermeasures is the lack of crime-source identification.
- A user access the remote computers to retrieve the desired information and to make communication, the evidences

needed to held responsible to someone for their activities on internet are distributed over the network.

- Authentication mechanism verifies user with its associated password, while auditing mechanism records the activities performed by authenticated users.
- A network identifier (NID) is assigned to user when he logged in to network for the first time.
- The temporal thumbprint refers to the sequence $<t_2-t_1, t_3-t_2, t_4-t_3, \ldots, t_{n+1}-t_n>$ in which each element represents a time gap between two consecutive transmitted packets.
- Criminals achieve anonymity with stepping stones.
- Stepping stones are previously compromised and breached intermediary computers through which malicious code is transmitted to trigger final attack.
- When a person logs into one computer and control another computer, and by logging to this second computer, he operates the third computer and remaining computers are controlled in same way, makes a sequence of logins and this sequence of logins is known as connection chain.
- An intermediate host which belongs to connection chain is called Stepping stone.
- A pair of network connections is known as Stepping stone Connection Pair if both network connections are part of the same connection chain.
- The flow of data on connection chain can be unidirectional and bidirectional.
- The bidirectional connection chain consists of two unidirectional flows, both in opposite direction of each other.
- Major network traffic characteristicsthat are computed to compare network traffic across the connection pairs are connection contents, inter-packet spacing, ON/OFF activities patterns, traffic volume and traffic rate.
- The major benefits of active monitoring are the ability to quick detection of threats and to maintain complete visibility across the network.

- The passive network monitoring believes in statistics to identify the irregularities in network flow and does not inject Test-data to predict loopholes across the network.
- Network traffic measurement refers to the close inspection of ongoing data transfer that furnishes the detail on lost and corrupted data packets, delivery of packets, delay in reaching and ordering as well.
- A false positive is an indication, signal or message that shows a positive result for a test whereas it is negative in reality.
- A false negative is an indication, signal or message that shows a negative result where as it is positive.
- Network flow contains header information for all individual packets and each packet uses same protocol settings within a designated time window.
- Network traffic pattern contains sufficient indicative information to assist security administrators to seek threats with their origins, to find out the method of threats activation and to search the method to reduce adverse impacts.
- Detailed traffic pattern report is analyzed to determine the future hazards and to develop security mechanism accordingly to patch up future vulnerabilities and to nullify further attacks.
- Path matrix is used to know data volume between the source to the destination across the path.
- Traffic matrix is used to know the amount of network traffic between source and destination pair.
- Demand matrix deals with the carried load.
- The most common operations that are performed by response mechanism include suspending IP addresses, blocking IP addresses, blocking ports, injecting TCP resets to terminate connections, changing access control lists, reconfiguring routers and firewalls.
- Obfuscation refers to the process in which data traffic is manipulated in such a way that the IDS signature could not match with malicious packets.

- If there is no network traffic is detected on flow for T_{idle} seconds, then it said to be OFF period for that connection chain; otherwise, it is considered ON period.
- Jitter refers to variation in timing when packets are received at the destination end.
- Chaff refers to meaningless padding packets, inserted to data traffic with intention to generate delay at receiving end.

MCQ

1. **NSM stands for:**
   a. Network Security Monitor
   b. Network Security Management
   c. Network Security Manipulation
   d. National Security Management
2. **Select the truth about stepping stones:**
   a. These represent computers from where criminal directly launch attack
   b. These represent intermediary compromised and breached computer
   c. These represent target systems
   d. These systems are not part of connection chain
3. **What are temporal thumbprint?**
   a. Sequence of packets
   b. Sequence of time-stamps
   c. Sequence of elements in which each element represents time-gap between packets
   d. Collection of dummy packets with time-stamps
4. **RTT stands for:**
   a. Reverse Trip Time
   b. Reverse Time Time-stamps
   c. Reverse Trip Time-stamps
   d. Round Trip Time

5. **Which of the following does not participate in base-lining?**
   a. Jitter
   b. Timing
   c. Byte volume
   d. Packets
6. **Demand matrix deals with the:**
   a. Offered load
   b. Carried load
   c. Data Volume
   d. Jitter and Chaff
7. **Obfuscation refers to:**
   a. A technique to measure offered load
   b. A technique to measure carried load
   c. A technique to evade malicious code from IDS signature
   d. A technique to measure data volume
8. **Which one of the following is not an Anomaly Detection Technique?**
   a. Response-time based algorithm
   b. Edit-distance based algorithm
   c. Causality based algorithm
   d. Time-stamp based algorithm

Answer

1. a
2. b
3. c
4. d
5. a
6. b
7. c
8. d

Questions

1. What do you mean by problem of accountability in the internet infrastructure?
2. Discuss the role of network identifier in fixing accountability of user?
3. What do you mean by temporal thumbprint? Discuss its utility in detail.
4. Define stepping stones with major types. Elaborate the benefits of stepping stone detection?
5. How will you minimize the states for connection pairs? Explain.
6. Explain the following:
   - I. Session management with network identifier
   - II. Network measurement points
   - III. Traffic filtering
   - IV. Traffic patterns with its utility
7. Define path matrix, traffic matrix and demand matrix in detail.
8. Differentiate the following:
   - I. Direct stepping stones versus indirect stepping stones
   - II. Active monitoring versus passive monitoring
   - III. IDS signature versus base-lining
   - IV. Jitter versus chaff
9. Classify intrusion response system activities in active IRS as well as passive IRS.
10. Describe timing-based stepping stone detection approach in detail.
11. Elaborate Brute force content-based algorithm in detail.
12. Explain simple content-based algorithm and its utility in detail.
13. Explain the following anomaly detection techniques in detail:
    - I. Response-time based algorithm

II. Edit-distance based algorithm

III. Causality-based algorithm

References

[1] A pwc report, *"Securing the nation's cyberspace"*, ASSOCHAM India, August 2017.

[2] Rekha Pahuja, *"Impact of Social Networking on Cyber crimes: A Study"*, Epitome: International Journal of Multidisciplinary Research, vol. 4, Issue 4, April 2018.

[3] S. Staniford-Chen and L.T. Heberlein, *"Holding Intruders Accountable on the Internet"*, Proceeding of IEEE Symposium on Security and Privacy, Oakland, CA, 1995, pp. 39-49.

[4] Yin Zhang and Vern Paxson, *"Detecting stepping Stones"*,In Proceedings of the 9th conference on USENIX Security Symposium - Volume 9, August 2000.

[5] L.T Heberlein, B. Mukherjee, K.N Levitt, *"Internet security Monitor: An Intrusion-Detection system for large-scale network"*, In Proceeding of 15th National Computer Security Conference, pp. 262-271, October 1992.

[6] A Report on *"Active and Passive monitoring"*, available at **https://solutionsreview.com/network-monitoring/active-monitoring-and-passive-monitoring-whats-the-difference/**

[7] Matthias Grossglauser, Jennifer Rexford, *"Passive Traffic Measurement for IP Operations"*, in The Internet as a Large-Scale Complex System, pp. 91-120, Oxford University Press, 2005.

[8] Paul Tune and Matthew Roughan, *"Internet Traffic Matrices: A Primer"*, in H. Haddadi, O. Bonaventure (Eds.), Recent Advances in Networking, 2013. Available at**http://sigcomm.org/education/ebook/SIGCOMMeBook2013v1_chapter3.pdf**.

[9] Shahid Anwar, Jasni Mohamad Zain, Mohamad Fadli Zolkipli, Zakira Inayat, Suleman Khan, Bokolo Anthony and Victor Chang, *"From Intrusion Detection to an Intrusion Response System: Fundamentals, Requirements and Future Directions"*, In Algorithms 10(2): 39, 2017.

[10] Corbin Carlo, *"Intrusion detection evasion: How Attackers get past the burglar alarm"*, A Report from SANS Institute, Information Security Reading room, 2020.

[11]Patrice abry, Richard Baraniuk, Patrick Flandrin, Rudolf Riedi, Darryl Veitch, "*The Multiscale Nature of Network Traffic: Discovery, Analysis and Modelling*", IEEE Signal Processing Magazine, March 2002.

[12] V. Paxson and S. Floyd, "*Wide-Area Traffic: The Failure of Poisson Modeling,*" IEEE/ACM Transactions on Networking, 3(3), pp. 226-244, June 1995.

[13] Sheng Wen, Di Wu, Ping Li, Yang Xiang, Wanlei Zhou and Guiyi Wei, "*Detecting stepping stones by abnormal causality probability*", Security and Communication Network, Security Comm. Networks 2015.

[14] Giovanni Di Crescenzo, Abhrajit Ghosh, Abhinay Kampasi, Rajesh Talpade, Yin Zhang, "*Detecting Anomalies in Active Insider Stepping Stone Attacks*", Journal of Wireless Mobile Networks, Ubiquitous Computing and Dependable Application, Vol. 02, Number 01, pp. 103-120, February 2011.

[15] Pai Peng, Peng Ning, Douglas S. Reeves, Xinyuan Wang, "*Active Timing-Based Correlation of Perturbed Traffic Flows with Chaff Packets*", In 25th IEEE International Conference on Distributed Computing Systems Workshops, June 2005.

[16] Jianhua Yang, Shou-Hsuan Stephen Huang, "*Correlating Temporal Thumbprints for Tracing Intruders*", Journal on Systemics, Cybernetics and Informatics, 2006.

[17] Robert Shullich, JieChu, PingJi, Weifeng Chen, "*A survey of research in stepping stone detection*", International Journal of Electronic Commerce Studies. Vol.2, No.2, pp.103-126, 2011.

[18] Abhinay Kampasi, Yin Zhang, Giovanni Di Crescenzo Abhrajit Ghosh and Rajesh Talpade, "*Improving Stepping Stone Detection Algorithms using Anomaly Detection Techniques*", available at **http://citeseerx.ist.psu.edu/viewdoc/download?doi=10.1.1.63.2034&rep=rep1&type=pdf**.

[19] David A. Wheeler, Gregory N. Larsen, Task Leader, "*Techniques for Cyber Attack Attribution*", Institute for defence analysis, October 2003.

CHAPTER 6

Infrastructural Vulnerabilities and DDoS Flooding Attacks

In this digital era, countries are developing and using new technologies to achieve automation. Technologies bring greater benefits for societies, but also pose new challenges before people. The field of information technology is not exceptional, the development of internet and cyberspace brought people closer without considering physical boundaries and meet their information and communication-related needs in a very short span of time. Criminals also use the infrastructural flaws to achieve their financial and political goals. This chapter details the infrastructural shortfalls in the Internet structure that help criminals to conduct cybercrimes and to achieve anonymity. DDoS flooding attacks are described to present the risks associated with internet.

Structure

In this chapter, we will cover the following topics:

- COTS software and internet security
- Vulnerability life cycle
- Shortfalls in the internet structure

- Cooperative intrusion traceback and response architecture (CITRA)
- DDoS flooding attacks

Objective

This chapter will explain how COTS software are dangerous to digital infrastructure and provides vulnerabilities at large scale to conduct crimes. It describes vulnerability life cycle and introduces you to various shortfalls in Internet Structure that make it favourable to criminals for their malicious activities. With the CITRA architecture, it is detailed how intrusion analysis can be performed without human intervention. Furthermore, DDoS flooding attacks are explained to its readers with complete taxonomy to develop better understanding of its different forms and to know the impacts of these attacks on OSI layers.

6.1 COTS software and internet security

The COTS software means Commercial-off-the-shelf software. These refer to readymade software products that are available in market for commercial use without any modification [1]. These software's neither require technical expertise for installation nor need customization to avail services. Howard F. Lipson [2] believes that each system connected to internet need protection to ensure security of cyberspace. As COTS are easy to accessible and become useful in features, these are installed on a large number of computers across the world. Unfortunately, if vulnerability is detected in COTS, then vulnerability converts into opportunity for criminals. As COTS are installed on millions of computers so each system contains vulnerability and invite criminals for exploitation and conducting crimes. Thus, millions of entry points remain open for criminals.

6.2 Vulnerability Life Cycle

The vulnerability life cycle represents the state of vulnerabilities in its life time. The term life cycle shows definite and linear progression, and transition from one phase to another. However, in case of system and software vulnerabilities, such a pattern is not followed. In case of vulnerabilities, the progression variance depends on a number of interactions between the vulnerable systems and intruder's malicious programs that exploit vulnerabilities. William A. Arbaugh et al. [3] described the distinct states of vulnerabilities named Birth, Discovery, Disclosure, the release of a fix, Publication, and automation of the exploitation. The pictorial representation of these vulnerability states and their occurrence over timeline has been shown in following *Figure 6.1*:

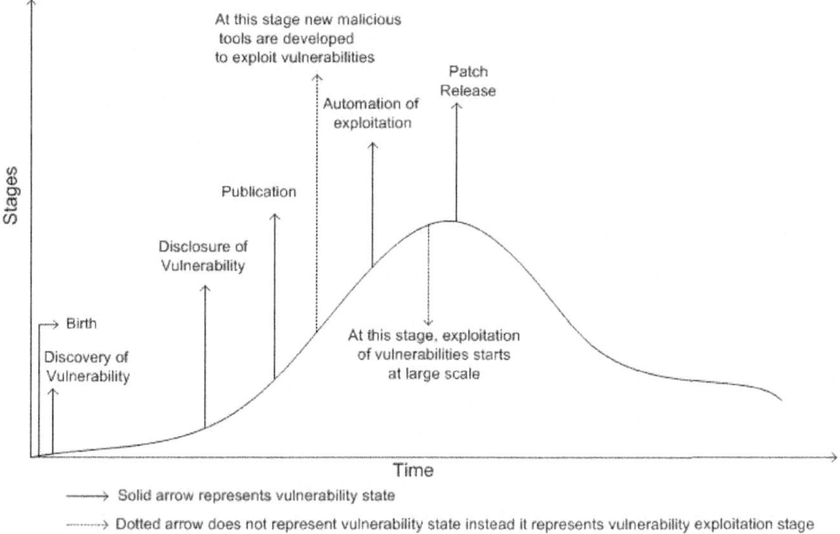

***Figure 6.1**: Vulnerability states*

Vulnerability appears to transition from birth state and continues until its fix is released:

Birth: This refers to time-instant, at which some flaw is created in software. This flaw is created unintentionally during the development of large project.

Discovery: It refers to the first-time detection of security and survivability flaws. The term zero-day vulnerability represents software flaw that is usually discovered by its vendors not from its users. These vulnerabilities do not have patches to fix flaws [23].

Disclosure: It is an event at which discoverer reveals details of vulnerability existence to a wider range of audience publicly.

Publication: When the disclosure goes out of control, people criticize the vulnerability in public reports. This activity becomes harmful as criminals get entry points to launch attacks.

Automation of the exploitation: If vulnerability is exposed in public. The criminals automatically start to exploit vulnerability across the world to launch.

Release of Fix: Whenever the developer knows about the vulnerabilities, he releases modification and configuration change code, popularly known as **patches** to tackle with underlying flaws and corrects them.

6.3 Shortfalls in internet structure

More interactions with internet enable criminals to expose its structure and breach to its key components. Aging and outdated internet infrastructure increases the risks of our exposure to malicious threats and becomes cause to digital catastrophe and cyberattacks. Howard F. Lipson [2] described following shortfalls of internet structure:

6.3.1 The internet structure does not facilitate tracking and tracing user behavior

Internet was basically constructed to form a group of people with common interests and to develop a cooperative and collaborative worldwide platform for the community of researchers for technology transfer and knowledge sharing. It is not just like a telephone system that facilitates communicating parties tracking and billing capability and bill needs to be charged on a per call basis from participating parties. The structure of internet never envisioned to charge on a host-to-host communication basis, so tracking and tracing of participating hosts was never facilitated.

6.3.2 Internet infrastructure does not resist highly untrustworthy users

Internet provides equal opportunities to all kinds of its users. The highly qualified and skilled criminals also avail its services to get monetary profits and political advantages. The major consideration behind the internet infrastructure design was to keep it surviving even during external physical attack or accident that causes considerable damage to its routing infrastructure. In current situations, the billions of hop-to-hop connections with attached networked devices provide millions of alternatives routes to transmit network traffic to directed hosts, if some portion of network infrastructure gets damaged. The structure of internet still lacks technology that can recognize criminals by their appearance and action so criminals get its access with all privileges. As internet infrastructure works properly, even after damage so it becomes difficult to know that a user is either trustworthy or criminal. Another reason due to which we fail to identify and restrict criminals is the internet lacks the technology to link the activities performed by its users.

6.3.3 Malicious packet source address remains vague that severely hinders tracking and tracing

Criminals conduct crime with malicious packets, hide the source from where these packets are delivered and refer to another source as the original source of malicious packets. These activities severely hinder tracking and tracking process and present unclear picture about the true origin of crime. The idea behind the internet protocol design was to form a community of benign and trustworthy users; therefore, it lacks the provision for cryptographic authentication of information resides in IP packets. Therefore, a skilled criminal can manipulate any information contained in the IP packet and modifies the source address to forge it. In one-way communication, the criminal needs to simply insert a false address in source field to forge source address. In two-way communication, reflectors are used to mislead tracing mechanism. Packet laundering is also effective to thwart the traceback process, but it requires time-delay between criminal activities.

6.3.4 Better coordination and collaboration between the criminals and cyber-skilled professionals

As we discussed earlier, the internet was fundamentally developed to serve researchers and educators, not to serve criminals so security mechanisms such as password protection, and so on, seem to be sufficient to prevent users with inappropriate behavior. In our opinion, the current shape and expansion of internet and its incorporation in every aspect of our lives and inclusion of e-commerce, transportation, communication, banking and defence was never assumed during its construction. Therefore, the robust security mechanisms were not developed. The financial transactions on the internet attracted criminals to intercept in its functioning to gain profits so that they perform individually and also do teamwork to conduct crimes. The criminals and cyber-skilled professionals corporate and collaborate to breach internet's infrastructure, its security provisions and develop new methods to conduct cybercrimes with rapid pace. On the other hand, the security mechanisms for internet security are not being invented and implemented to overcome this pace so criminals often achieve success to breach internet security.

6.3.5 Lack of central security mechanism

In the beginning, there were few systems connected to the network and each of these systems was administrated through a central security policies and single mechanism, so breach to these systems was difficult. If due to any reason, the breach occurs, it was promptly tackled to prevent damages. As internet allowed individuals to join and access without verifying person, the central security mechanism became dysfunctional. The rapid addition of new devices to internet infrastructure without having security provisions making the situations severe as the users of these systems neither protect their own devices nor deny the entry of criminals through their own devices to enter in internet infrastructure. These unskilled users are being dangerous for internet infrastructure as the devices in their possession act as stepping stones and are used in cybercrimes.

6.3.6 Cybersecurity suffers with cross-multiple administrative, jurisdictional and national boundaries

In the beginning, networked systems, associated devices, cabling and protocol design were implemented and functional under full central administrative control. Hardware, system software, application software, add-ons and software patches were installed and controlled under single administrative domain due to which vulnerabilities exploitation was not possible. Moreover, the users of these networked computers were the member of single central administrative panel so these members were expert to deal with these systems and inter-connected infrastructure. These members were capable to do quick identification of vulnerabilities and to release immediate and appropriate patches and solutions. Now, the internet is world's common and biggest information resource and incorporates billions of computers and networked devices, cabling and networked infrastructure scattered across the world. The whole infrastructure is now not under the control of single administrative body instead it is now controlled through millions of service providers working on different geographical areas across the several countries. Since multiple countries do not have common legislations for cybercrime prevention, the legislations and jurisdiction are obstacles to proper implementation of the internet infrastructure.

6.3.7 High-speed network traffic prevents tracking

Heavy data access is now essential as a large portion of population is using internet for their variety of needs. High speed internet is desirable now to watch videos, to enjoy live games, or to play online games. Research Institutions also need high bandwidth to meet their high computing needs. Internet with high-speed bandwidth requires a quick movement of data packets among the possible routes. The middleware routers need to pass data packets as quick as possible so routers often ignore processing of packets and as a result malicious packets are evaded. The analysing and processing data packets and determining them for their malicious properties slows down the network speed, which is not desirable in case of fast internet.

During the fast internet service, the packet information that often helps to track and trace it during transmission, and to know its source, are not stored for a longer period in routers' tables due to its limited storage capacity.

6.3.8 Tunnels present barriers in tracking and tracing

'Tunneling' basically refers to a protocol that facilitates secure transmission of data from one network to another network. It allows private network packets to be transmitted over public network such as internet with better protection. Encapsulation plays a crucial role here and encapsulates the private network communications packets inside various outer packets. Thus, wrapping of private network data packets inside outer packets is generally known as **encapsulation** that allows private network packets to be transmitted through public network as these are considered as public network packets [3, 22]. Encapsulated packets protect malicious packets and help them to pass to their target while tracing mechanism only registers the details of public network packets.

6.3.9 Annihilation of logs and audit data

Log refers to a detailed record of events occurring inside an internet enabled device [4]. Information attained from logs and audit data becomes valuable to know the nature of attack, pattern of attack, targeted areas, motivations, frequencies and even its route can be traced and source can be determined with this information. To evade from detection, criminals often destroy logs and audit data, perform meticulous clean-up of antivirus logs and security logs. The protection of log information is critical and essential as compromised logs mislead security investigations and protect criminals from legal actions [4].

6.4 Cooperative intrusion traceback and Response Architecture (CITRA)

The **Cooperative Intrusion Traceback and Response Architecture** (**CITRA**) is an agent-based system that facilitates better coordination among its components such as routers, firewalls security management unit, and sensors. This architecture uses network boundaries to detect intrusions, steps back through neighbouring nodes to the source of intrusions, and communicates these details to centralized security management unit [5]. Dan Schnackenberg et al. [6] introduced the CITRA architecture to perform following tasks:

The CITRA is used to perform following tasks:

1. It identifies the network boundaries and detects intrusions across these boundaries.
2. Quick reporting of intrusions to the centralized security management unit.
3. It helps to prevent or diminish subsequent damages due to intrusions across network boundaries.
4. It tries to establish better coordination among intrusion detection system's components.

The main objective behind the design of CITRA architecture was to automate intrusion analysis and respond without human intervention. This automation requires information from distinct devices to be collected with a central controller and also need dynamic controlling of extent to prevent intruders to its access. The CITRA architecture incorporates two levels of organizations. The first level contains CITRA communities, which are administrative domains under the control of Discovery coordinator. The second level contains interconnected neighbourhoods that represent a collection of adjacent CITRA devices as shown in following *Figure 6.2*:

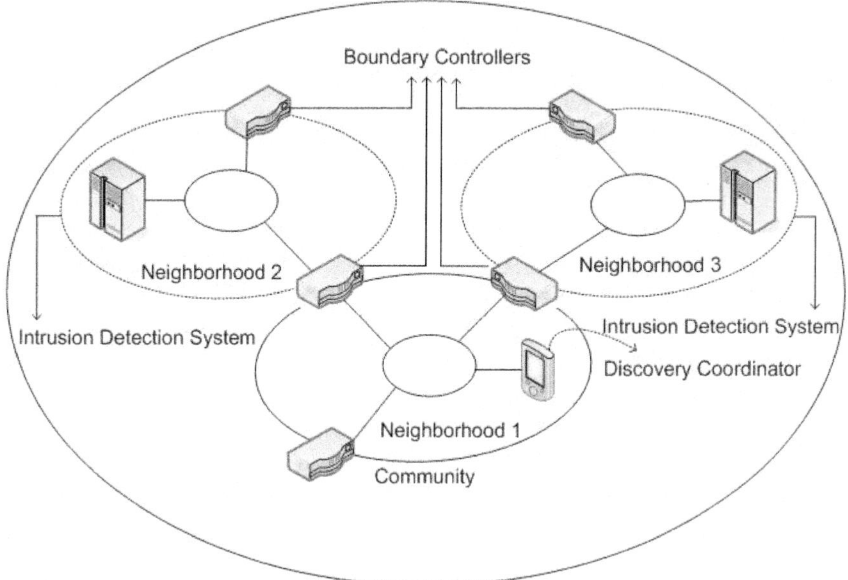

***Figure 6.2**: CITRAArchitecture*

In the CITRA Architecture, neighbourhood 2 and neighbourhood 3 as shown in *Figure 6.2* are used to trace and respond to intrusions. CITRA uses **Intrusion Detection and Isolation Protocol** (**IDIP**) for quick and centralized reporting of malicious intrusion events and to generate immediate effective response to these intrusions [10]. The CITRA architecture facilitates traceback with the help of the IDIP protocol by auditing networks traffic across its various devices. If an intrusion is detected, CITRA examines audit trail to track malicious packets and respond to them appropriately near their source. The traceback mechanism is performed in the following three steps:

In the first step, the CITRA enabled detector device detects intrusions.

In second step, the detector device generates warning signals to all incorporated devices and issues a traceback message to each surrounding CITRA neighbors.

In the third step, the incorporated boundary controllers use their corresponding local network audit trails to determine whether they have passed malicious packets. If a boundary controller finds its own involvement in forwarding malicious packets, then this boundary controller informs its succeeding boundary controllers and hosts. This step is repeated until the source of malicious packet is detected:

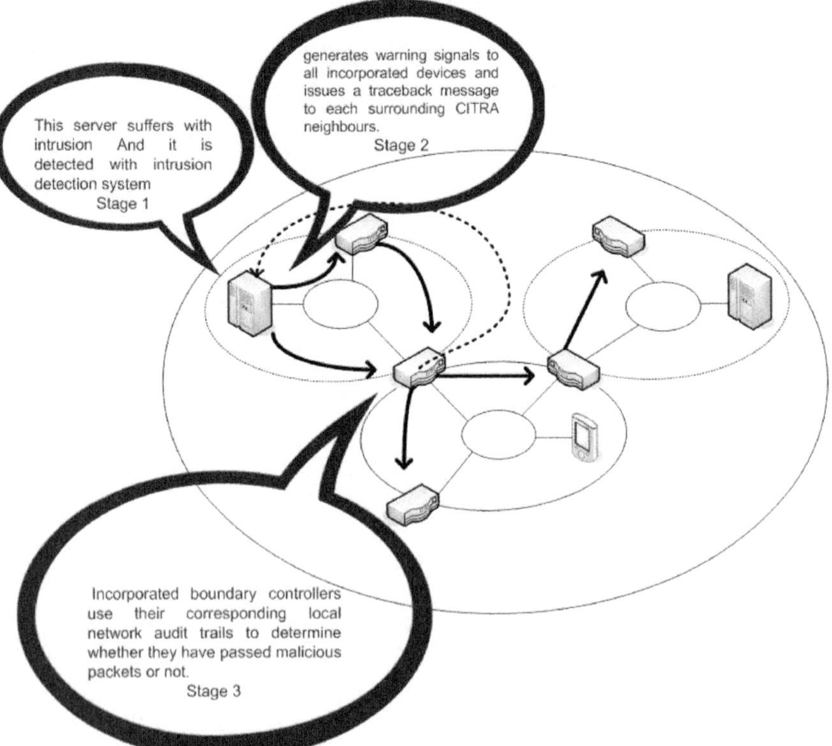

***Figure 6.3**: IDIP Intrusion Detection and Response Mechanism*

The CITRA is implemented with narrowest network response to stop active attacks. The response mechanism uses filtering rules to filter out malicious packets from the network traffic. The Intrusion Detection System prepares a detailed report and sends it to Discovery Coordinator. Each neighbourhood is protected by its own intrusion detection system. Therefore, the CITRA architecture comprises the same number of intrusion detection systems as the number of neighbourhoods exist in the architecture. Each neighbourhood unit notifies its intrusion report to Discovery Coordinator to form a global picture of intrusions across the whole architecture. With the help of this global picture of intrusions and architecture topology, the Discovery Coordinator determines the complete path of attack and generates optimal system response. CITRA facilitates community-wide aggregation and correlation of attacks that helps Discovery Coordinator to have a complete view of security state of system. **INFOCON** stands for **Information Operations Condition** that represents the updated cyber situations and efforts to evaluate the risk of attack on stored information and to digital infrastructure. The most interesting feature of CITRA is the quick adaptation of INFOCON changes. The CITRA uses additional hardware to broadcast INFOCON changes to all available nodes under CITRA community and prepares nodes to adopt changes.

The boundary controllers facilitate boundary defence to organizations and provide primary mechanism for automated traceback. These are capable to block particular network traffic near its source if it contains malicious packets. CITRA auditing mechanism uses intermediate boundary controllers to track criminals back to their sources. The following *figure 6.4* represents CITRA response architecture for performing scans:

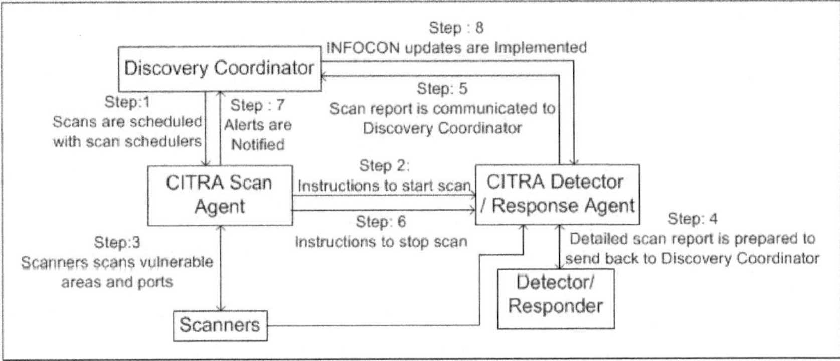

***Figure 6.4**: CITRA response architecture*

This architecture requires eight steps for response intrusions, which are discussed as follows:

1. **Discovery Coordinator** identifies the vulnerable areas on the basis of neighbourhoods' reports and schedules scans for intrusions detection with the help of CITRA Scan agents.
2. **CITRA Scan Agent** notifies to the CITRA detector to have a close watch at port scanning process and to send a message to the detector to prepare a detailed report about intrusion.
3. The CITRA Scan agent enables a scanner to scan the vulnerable areas and various ports for malicious threats and report to the CITRA detector.
4. Each functional area of the CITRA architecture has its own detector and this detector sends detailed report through central CITRA detector Discovery Coordinator.
5. The Central CITRA detector collects the intrusions reports from all sub-detectors and prepares a detailed combined report for Discovery Coordinator.
6. After completing the scanning task, scanners communicate to CITRA scan agent about the status and communicate to the CITRA detector through the CITRA scan agent to stop the scanning.
7. The CITRA scan agent directly notifies Discovery Coordinator about the intrusions detected through scanners.
8. If INFOCON suggests some updates or patches, it directly communicates with Discovery Coordinator that helps to implement these suggestions across the whole architecture with the help of CITRA detector.

6.4.1 CITRA correlation tools

Correlation tools are used to determine and reduce false positives. With the help of correlation tools, the file system management is achieved at discovery coordinator. The correlation tools are applied at discovery coordinator to remove duplicity of reports and to reduce processing time. The IDIP protocol at discovery coordinator ensures the receiving of intrusion reports from all intrusion detection units in the CITRA architecture. In this architecture, various kinds of correlators are integrated to know the symmetry of files and to perform various correlation related tasks with following components:

- **Merger**: As scanners are responsible to scan ports to find vulnerabilities and intrusions in all incorporated neighbourhoods, sometimes, the same entries are recorded into intrusion reports of multiple neighbourhoods. These duplications of records add processing overheads and complexities in preparing a single detailed intrusion report at discovery coordinators. Mergers uniquely identify records from all files and record in to a single file at the discovery coordinator.
- **Graph-based Intrusion Detection System (GrIDS)**: S. Staniford-Chen et al. [7] represented the graphical view of network traffic assigned to different activities running inside computers. This graphical view helps to determine the malicious activities and to aggregate applied traffic to them. The main attraction of GrIDS is the capability to analyse network activities on the TCP/IP network comprising up to thousands of computers [7]. In the CITRA architecture, GrIDS helps to remove redundancy and to prepare detailed reports at discovery coordinator with unique records.
- **Filters**: Silicon defence Perl-based filters are used to remove false positives from all neighbourhoods as well as from the discovery coordinator.
- **Event processor**: The CITRA architecture works like a distributed system as it comprises multiple neighbourhoods to report intrusions to the discovery coordinator. The main function of event processor is to analyze the events occurring inside a neighbourhood to find intrusions [8].
- **EMERALD**: The term "EMERALD" stands for Event Monitoring Enabling Responses to Anomalous Live Disturbances. It is a distributed scalable tool suite to identify malicious activities, to track the path of malicious packets transmission and to locate the source of malicious traffic [9, 22]. The neighbourhoods use the EMERALD tool to detect intrusions.

6.5 DDoS flooding attacks

The distributed nature of DDoS adds complexities to traceback to true origin. Attackers normally forge their source addresses to hide their identities and to make tracking process complicated [11]. To develop a defence mechanism against DDoS attacks, we need to understand the various aspects of DDoS flooding attacks and their classification. On the basis of protocol levels, Saman Taghavi Zargar et al. [11] classified DDoS flooding attacks into two categories as shown in following *Figure 6.5*.

6.5.1 Network/Transport-level DDoS flooding attack

These DDoS attacks are triggered to overwhelm the victim system by requiring more bandwidth than available. The goals of these attacks include overtaxing website's bandwidth, reduction in processing speed of server and slowing down CPU operations. These DDoS flooding attack suse the existing flaws in TCP, UDP, and ICMP protocols and overwhelm the network routes and devices to slow down a request and delivery process:

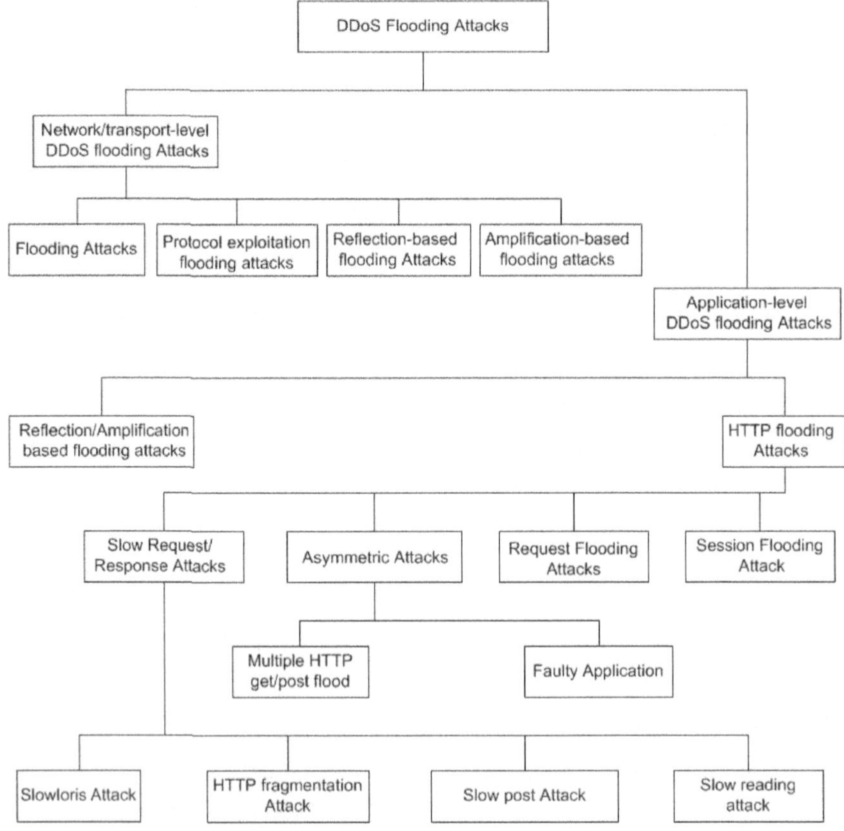

***Figure 6.5**: DDoS Flooding attacks taxonomy*

6.5.1.1 Flooding attack

Flooding attack is a way to evade detection of malicious network traffic. The attacker transmits a large volume of traffic over the communication channel. The intrusion detection mechanism fails to examine such a large amount of data in a limited time constraint and passes the traffic to target without examination. With flooding attack, the attackers attempt to disrupt legitimate users' network connections by exhausting with heavy traffic load. Saman Taghavi Zargar et al. [11] listed some common examples of flooding attacks that are as follows:

- Spoofed and Non-spoofed UDP Flood
- ICMP flood
- DNS flood
- VoIP (Voice over IP) Flood

6.5.1.2 Protocol exploitation flooding attack

Protocols and interface enable legitimate users to connect with devices through connections. Intensive changes in the interface and protocols can restrict legitimate users from accessing networks and resources. Attackers alter the codes of protocols and interfaces to exploit specific features and add malicious codes to engage victims' resources to overwhelm. Saman Taghavi Zargar et al. [11] suggested few examples of protocol exploitation flooding attack, which are as follows [11]:

- TCP SYN flood
- TCP SYN-ACK flood
- ACK and PUSH ACK flood
- RST/FIN flood

6.5.1.3 Reflection-based flooding attack

Attackers hide themselves and achieve anonymity through the use of reflectors. The attackers work behind the reflectors and receive the responses from victims while victims communicate with reflectors by assuming it to be legitimate users. The ICMP echo request, Smurf attacks and Fraggle attacks are some examples of reflection-based flooding attacks [11].

6.5.1.4 Amplification-based flooding attack

Criminals exploit services by generating multiple copies of same message in response to a single received query. The generation of these duplicate copies of response message is known as **amplification** in flooding attacks. The amplification of response message is achieved with botnet that refers to a series of compromised and remotely controlled computers generally used to exhaust network channels and target to disrupt services. The most common examples of amplification-based flooding attacks are as follows [12]:

- Synonymous IP flooding
- Excessive VERB
- Media data flooding
- Ping flooding

6.5.2 Application-level DDoS flooding attacks

If we think that criminals are always outsiders, it is completely wrong as employees of an organization also trigger attacks for their personal benefits. In case of insiders, the criminal is detected as legitimate user and access to applications is granted to criminal [13]. Application-level attacks particularly make servers unresponsive by overwhelming server resources such as sockets, CPU, main memory, disk storage, I/O bandwidth, database [11]. In application level-flooding attacks, the characteristics of some crucial applications like HTTP, DNS and **SIP** (**Session Initiation Protocol**) become on target and disrupted to make them unavailable to process request and to deliver services [11].

6.5.2.1 Reflection/Amplification based flooding attack

In amplification-based flooding attacks, the criminals send malicious codes to botnet. With the help of this code, each computer involved in botnet instructs the routers to pass all IP addresses within the broadcast address circle range. Further, the malicious traffic received from criminal at the botnet computers is amplified with the help of routers, and transmitted to all IP address. This amplification process is performed by each computer involved in botnet. In reflection or amplification-based flooding attacks, the role of a reflector becomes crucial as it sends network packets back. Reflectors refer to intermediary nodes with the capability to launch amplification attacks to increase the traffic load at channels and to consume victim bandwidth [11]. Thus, Web servers, DNS servers and routers act like reflectors as these devices use SYN, ACK and RST signals to response TCP queries [14].

6.5.2.2 HTTP flooding attack

A HTTP flood attack is a special kind of attack in which a server becomes unresponsive when high volume network traffic is diverted in the form of countless queries. The attacker attempts to crash a server or application by sending access requests from multiple computers from different locations at the same time. HTTP flooding attacks are launched with GET and POST requests. The GET request is used to receive static contents like images and text from server, while with the POST request we receive dynamic contents like database records [15]:

- **Session flooding attack**: When session connection requests rate from attacker becomes higher than the rate of legitimate users, the session flood attack occurs. The HTTP GET/POST flooding attack falls in this category and exhausts server resources to response [11].
- **Request flooding attack**: When sessions contain bulk amount of requests and exceeds the normal capacity of queries, then this attack occurs. The excessive VERB is most popular request flooding attack.
- **Asymmetric flooding attack**: In this attack, the same resources are requested from botnet-delivered queries to exhaust the server to meet the requirements of all queries. The Regex parsing in ReDoS and connection pool in Slowloris are major vulnerable areas for such kind of attacks [16]. Faulty application attacks under asymmetric flooding attack use the poor design structure of websites and improper database design to disrupt the server. SQL injections can be applied to faulty applications to lock database access [11]. Multiple HTTP get/post flood allows to encapsulate multiple HTTP requests in single packet in single session that lead complexities in transmitting such packets; as a result, the server does not response to all encapsulated queries [11].

- **Slow Request/Response attack**: The request to server is slowly transmitted by creating congestions in communication channels with forge packets as a result large number of requests get queued up to get response. This leads the server to become inactive and fail to respond. In the Slowloris attack, partial HTTP connections requests are processed at the server end; as result, the server fails to respond to client requests [11]. HTTP fragmentation attack puts the HTTP connections on hold for longer to bring down the server. Attackers divide the legitimate HTTP packets into several smaller fragments and send each fragment to server with a time-delay in which server gets timed-out [11]. Thomas Lukaseder et al. [17] defined the slow POST attack and highlighted its capability to upload a request entity in the form of text files, while in general request is transmitted with a header containing IP addresses. The slow POST attack is known as slow Body HTTP attack. In slow reading attack, criminals generate large number of requests to demand a variety of resources from a single server. After transmitting requests, the criminals create congestions in channels to keep busy server to response with significant delay [17].

6.6 DDoS attacks on OSI layers

The OSI model refers to an ISO standard used for worldwide digital communications. It is a communication framework in which protocols and interfaces are arranged to facilitate quick communication. Criminals either intercept to communications or break the connections established among legitimate parties to create obstacles in the information interchange. The DDoS quick guide [18]summarizes the most common DDoS attacks that are triggered to different layers of OSI model to conduct different categories of crimes. The following *table 6.1* summarizes all these attacks with their corresponding layer on which these take place [19]:

Layer name	Traffic transmission	Functions of layers	Protocols and standards	Popular DDoS attacks on OSI layers
Application layer	Data Transmission	Virtual terminal management, File Transfer, File Access, File Management, Mail services	FTP, HTTP, POP3, SMTP	PDF GET requests, HTTP GET, HTTP POST, Reflection/ Amplification Attacks, Application Request Flood, Database Connection Pool exhaustion, Resource exhaustion.
Presentation layer	Data Transmission	Formatting and delivery of Information, Encryption, Decryption, Compression	SSL, AppleTalk Filing Protocol, Telnet,	SSL Exhaustion, Criminals use SSL to tunnel HTTP attacks to disrupt functioning of server.
Session layer	Data Transmission	Session Management, Token Management, Synchronization, Works as Dialog controller.	Logon, Logoff	Criminals exploit flaws in Telnet server and in installed applications to make server unresponsive.
Transport layer	Segment Transmission	Connection Control, Segmentation and Reassembling, Flow Control, Error Control	TCP, UDP	SYN Flood, UDP Flood, TCP spoofed and Non-Spoofed Flood, TCP Connection exhaustion, IPSec Flood, Slow Transfer Rate, Long Lived TCP.

Network layer	Packet Transmission	Fusion of multiple networks, Routing, Logical addressing, Fragmentation.	IP, ICMP, ARP, RIP	ICMP Flooding, Smurf Attack, IP/ICMP Fragmentation
Data Link layer	Frame Transmission	Data packets generation, Framing, Adds source and destination address, Access Control, Flow Control	(Point-to-Point Protocol) PPP, 802.3, 802.5	MAC Flooding
Physical layer	Bits Transmission	Establish connections, Fix data transmission rate, Communicate about the direction of data transmission.	100 Base-T, 1000 Base-X	Congestion on channels to block receiving of bits.

Table 6.1: *DDoS Flooding Attacks on OSI Layers*

6.7 Cyberwar

The development of internet and revolution in information technology present the risk of cyberwar. Catherine A. Theohary et al. [20] defines Cyberwar as a state action on other state that becomes equivalent to armed attack or military action in cyberspace. This technology-based action can lead a military response from opposition with a proportional kinetic use of forces. The term Cyberwar refers to utilization of internet and networking technologies to destroy the enemy nation's computers and the IT infrastructure to cause considerable amount of damage as similar as in case of traditional military operations with soldiers armed with fire-arms and missiles. The internet technologies are being used as cyber weapons. Therefore, nations are preparing themselves for cyber battlespace [21]. These nations conduct cyber espionage and cyber reconnaissance to steal the crucial information about enemy countries and to check their skills and abilities in cyberspace, respectively. Nations are now more concerned about cybersecurity and want to protect their critical national infrastructures to ensure the uninterrupted services for their citizens. Therefore, they have started to develop offensive cyberwar capabilities and national strategies [21]. Cyberwar has now been converted into buzzword as it is more common and deals with various kinds of conflicts such as political conflicts, economical conflicts and military conflicts with an international dimension [21]. Cyberspace acts as a theatre for these conflicts.

6.7.1 Why cyberwar is attractive?

Cyberwar is conducted to freeze computers with networked devices, to fail crucial servers to dead communication infrastructure and to thwart technical strategies applied to achieve data assurance. Fred Schreier [21] mentioned several reasons due to which cyberwar is preferred. These reasons are as follows:

- The cyberwar becomes economical for nations as it does not require massive troops and weapons.
- To begin cyberwar, entry cost is low as it requires only a computer and internet access.
- Cyberwar can be started silently from anywhere on a global scale.
- Tools mostly used in cyberwar are software, can be purchased easily or downloaded from the internet.
- The massive availability of malicious tools and their delivery to anyone without any restrictions.
- Lack of technological, financial and legal barriers to the dispersion and utilization of malicious tools and services.
- Cyberspace hides the criminals due to its anonymous nature and makes the origin detection difficult.
- The cyberspace delivers disproportionate power to insignificant actors and criminals.
- Cyberwar is profitable and saves lives.
- In Cyberwar, it is difficult to assess damages.
- No need to participate in combat operations.
- Cyberwar does not use battlefield, but leaves long-lasting adverse impacts on opponent countries.
- Cyberwar can be conducted with single click on computer.

- It is difficult to prevent cyberattacks and settle down cyberwar as these require skilled hardware and software engineers with sound knowledge and experience in networking and finding such people is difficult.
- Rapid expansion of IT infrastructure creating countless opportunities for cybercriminals.
- Cyberwar is a way to attain a bloodless conquest.

6.7.2 Key terminologies

Cyberspace is newly evolved fifth battlefield for countries after land, sea, air and space [21]. It comprises all the IT infrastructures of all the countries across the world to make them as a whole. Cyberspace can be considered as a laboratory where malicious software is developed, vulnerabilities are created, and attempts to damage opponents' IT infrastructure are made to disrupt the services of critical national infrastructure of any country. As a result, Cyberwar occurs in cyberspace. The following *Table 6.2* elaborates some key terms that are frequently used in reference to Cyberwar:

Term	Explanation
Cyber Power	This refers to the capability of a nation to control the IT system, computer network and digital interconnected infrastructure in and through cyberspace [12].
Cyberterrorists	Cyberterrorists can be defined as state-sponsored actors who use cyberspace and conduc torganized cybercrimes to meet the objectives of a country for which they work [20].
Cyberspies	These refer to persons who secretly steal proprietary information used by governments or private organizations for financial and political benefits [20].
Cyberthieves	These are the persons who conduct cybercrime to have monetary benefits [20].
Cyberwarriors	These are skilled hardware and software engineers who protect computer systems and its associated devices, IT infrastructure and communication infrastructure against cyberattacks and empower the nation to plan strategies against malicious threats.

Cyberactivists	These are miscreants who conduct cybercrime for pleasure, not for monetary benefits.
Cyber-weapons	Cyber-weapons are malicious programs and code with the help of a system is penetrated and breached, an IT infrastructure is hacked or damaged and may cause cyberwar among the nations.
Cyber hooliganism	Cyber hooliganism represents widespread form of cyber conflict that receives a huge public attention[21].
Cyber espionage	Cyber espionage refers to a close watch on enemies' computers and their IT infrastructure to know their secrets, intensions, and capabilities [21].

***Table 6.2**: Cyberwar terminologies*

Cyberspace has now been converted into warfighting domain. Countries achieve their political and strategic goals without military operations. The state-sponsored cybercriminals attempt to damage critical national infrastructure such as government, power, health, transportation, financial, safety, economical, education, and so on to maintain supremacy across the world.

Conclusion

People are adopting internet technologies to satisfy their variety of needs and sharing confidential information without worrying about severe dangers and loopholes in hardware and software design, and serious deficiencies in infrastructural design of internet. Basically, internet was designed for trustworthy academician and researchers for knowledge sharing and interruptions in delivery of services were rare. Now, scenario has been changed, internet covers all the nations and incorporates legitimate users as well as criminals to satisfy their wide range of political and economic needs. This chapter begins with COTS software and provides the detail on how these are helpful to criminals to breach systems and to compromise the security of digital infrastructure. The internet infrastructure has been examined and assessed to determine inherent vulnerabilities and to identify problems that make tracing and tracking process difficult to find the true crime origin. Further, CITRA architecture has been explained to automate tracing process without human intervention. We also present a detailed study about DDoS flooding attacks and classify them as per their application levels. We have examined the OSI layers for their functioning and determined which layer receives what kind of DDoS flooding attack. Finally, we have covered an overview of Cyberwar and detailed the reasons for its popularity.

Points to remember

- The **COTS** software means **Commercial-off-the-shelf software**. These refer to readymade software products that are available in the market for commercial use without any modification.
- COTS software neither require technical expertise for installation nor need customization to avail services.
- Vulnerabilities in hardware, software and infrastructure are converted into opportunities by criminals.
- COTS are installed on millions of computers so each system contains vulnerability and invite criminals for exploitation and conducting crimes.
- The vulnerability life cycle represents the state of vulnerabilities in its life time.
- Whenever the developer knows about the vulnerabilities, he releases modification and configuration change code popularly known as 'patches' to tackle with underlying flaws and corrects them.
- Internet is not just like a telephone system that facilitates communicating parties tracking and billing capability.
- The Internet structure does not facilitate tracking and tracing user behavior.
- The internet lacks central security mechanism.
- Cybersecurity suffers with cross multiple administrative, jurisdictional and national boundaries.
- The internet is world's common and biggest information resource and incorporates billions of computers and networked devices, cabling and networked infrastructure scattered across the world.
- Tunneling basically refers to a protocol that facilitates secure transmission of data from one network to another network.
- Wrapping of private network data packets inside outer packets is generally known as 'encapsulation.'

- Encapsulated packets protect malicious packets and help them to pass to their target while tracing mechanism only registers the details of public network packets.
- The Cooperative Intrusion Traceback and Response Architecture (CITRA) is an agent-based system that facilitates better coordination among its components such as routers, firewalls security management unit and sensors.
- CITRA uses Intrusion Detection and Isolation Protocol (IDIP) for quick and centralized reporting of malicious intrusion events and to generate immediate effective response to these intrusions.
- Discovery Coordinator determines the complete path of attack and generates optimal system response.
- In the CITRA architecture, GrIDS helps to remove redundancy and to prepare detailed reports at discovery coordinator with unique records.
- EMERALD is a distributed scalable tool suite to identify malicious activities, to track the path of malicious packets transmission, and to locate the source of malicious traffic.
- With flooding attack, the attackers attempt to disrupt legitimate users' network connections by exhausting with a heavy traffic load.
- Attackers hide themselves and achieve anonymity through the use of reflectors.
- Reflectors refer to intermediary nodes with capability to launch amplification attacks to increase the traffic load at channels and to consume victim bandwidth.
- A HTTP flood attack is a special kind of attack in which a server becomes unresponsive when high volume network traffic is diverted in the form of countless queries.
- HTTP flooding attacks are launched with GET and POST requests. The GET request is used to receive static contents like images and text from server while with the POST request, we receive dynamic contents like database records.
- When session connection requests rate from attacker becomes higher than the rate of legitimate users, the session flood attack occurs.
- Faulty application attacks under asymmetric flooding attack use the poor design structure of websites and improper database design to disrupt the server.

- HTTP fragmentation attack puts the HTTP connections on hold for longer to bring down the server.
- Cyberwar can be defined as state action on other state that becomes equivalent to armed attack or military action in cyberspace.
- Cyberspace acts as a theatre for conflicts such as political conflicts, economical conflicts and military conflicts.
- Cyberwar is conducted to freeze computers with networked devices, to fail crucial servers to dead communication infrastructure, and to thwart technical strategies applied to achieve data assurance.
- Cyberspace is newly evolved fifth battlefield.

MCQ

1. **COTS software represents:**
   a. Commercial-off-the-shelf Software
   b. Commercial-on-the-shelf Software
   c. Commercial Taxation Software
   d. Commercial Trading Software
2. **Tunnels are used to:**
   a. Achieve secure retransmitting of Data frames
   b. Transmit private network packets to public network
   c. Decrypt network packets
   d. Avoid cryptography
3. **Which of the following is required to achieve Tunneling?**
   a. Polymorphism
   b. Inheritance
   c. Encapsulation
   d. Virtualization
4. **CITRA stands for:**
   a. Coordinated Intrusion Traceback and Response Architecture
   b. Co-related Intrusion Traceback and Response Architecture

   c. Common Intrusion Traceback and Response Architecture
   d. Cooperative Intrusion Traceback and Response Architecture

5. **MAC Flooding occurs at:**
   a. Data Link Layer
   b. Network Layer
   c. Transport Layer
   d. Session Layer

6. **IDIP stands for:**
   a. Intrusion Detection and Intrusion Prevention
   b. Intrusion Detection and Isolation Protocol
   c. Initial Detection and Initial Protection
   d. International Discovery Internet Protocol

7. **INFOCON stands for:**
   a. Information Operation Connections
   b. Informative Operational Connections
   c. Information Operations Condition
   d. Informative Open Connections

8. **VoIP stands for:**
   a. Vulnerable operations in Internet Protocol
   b. Voice Operations in Internet Protocol
   c. Vulnerability of Internet Protocol
   d. Voice Over IP

9. **SIP stands for:**
   a. Session Initiation Protocol
   b. Secure Internet Protocol
   c. Single Instruction Protocol
   d. Session Integration Protocol

Answer

1. a
2. b
3. c
4. d
5. a
6. b
7. c
8. d
9. a

Questions

1. What are COTS software and how these are dangerous to network security? Explain.
2. Explain Vulnerability Life Cycle in detail?
3. Internet does not facilitate tracking and tracing mechanism? Elaborate your view.
4. Internet infrastructure lacks central security mechanism? Explain.
5. What do you mean by 'Tunneling'? Describe the role of encapsulation to achieve 'Tunneling'.
6. Explain the following:
   - Graph-based Intrusion Detection System (GrIDS)
   - EMERALD
   - Reflection-based flooding Attacks
   - Cyber Power
7. Describe the major shortfalls in Internet infrastructure?
8. Explain Cooperative Intrusion Traceback and Response Architecture (CITRA) in detail with its major components?
9. Explain CITRA Correlation Tools in detail?

10. Differentiate the following:
    - ICMP flood Versus DNS flood
    - Cyberterrorists Versus Cyberthieves
    - Cyberwarriors Versus Cyberactivists
    - Cyber hooliganism Versus Cyber espionage
    - Session Flooding Attack Versus Request Flooding Attack
11. Describe DDoS Flooding attacks taxonomy in detail.
12. Cyberspace is considered fifth battlefield. Explain.
13. What do you mean by Cyberwar? How is it different from traditional war? Explain in detail.
14. What are the major reasons that attract towards Cyberwar? Explain.

References

[1]A Report, *"COTS implementation"*, available at:**https://www.questica.com/news/6-steps-successful-cots-implementation.**

[2] Howard F. Lipson, *"Tracking and Tracing Cyber-Attacks: Technical Challenges and Global Policy Issues"*, Carnegie Mellon University, November 2002.

[3] William A. Arbaugh, William L. Fithen and John McHugh, "Windows of Vulnerability: A Case Study Analysis", December 2000, available at:**http://www.cs.umd.edu/~waa/pubs/Windows_of_Vulnerability.pdf**

[4] Karen Kent, Murugiah Souppaya, *"Guide to Computer Security Log Management"*, Recommendations of the National Institute of Standards and Technology, NIST National Institute of Standards and Technology, Technology administration U.S Department of Commerce.

[5] Natalia Stakhanova, Samik Basu, Johnny S. Wong, *"A Taxonomy of Intrusion Response Systems"*, IOWA State University, 2006.

[6] Dan Schnackenberg, Harley Holliday, Randall Smith, Kelly Djahandari, Dan Sterne, *"Cooperative Intrusion Traceback and Response Architecture (CITRA)"*, Proceeding of the DARPA Information Survivability Conference and Exposition (DISCEXII'01), 2001.

[7] S. Staniford-Chen, S. Cheung, R. Crawford, M. Dilger, J. Frank, J. Hoagland, K. Levitt, C. Wee, R. Yip, D. Zerkle, "GrIDS: A Graph Based Intrusion Detection System for Large Network", In Proceedings of the 20th National Information Systems Security Conference, volume 1, pages 361–370, October 1996.

[8] *"A report, "Complex Event Processing"*, available at: **https://complexevents.com/stanford/cep/**.

[9] Peter Neumann & Phillip Porras, *"EMERALD: Event Monitoring Enabling Responses to Anomalous Live Disturbances"*, National Information Systems Security Conference, October, 1997.

[10] Dan Sterne, Kelly Djahandari, Brett Wilson, Bill Babson, Dan Schnackenberg, Harley Holliday and Travis Reid, *"Autonomic Response to Distributed Denial of Service Attack"*, Recent Advances in Intrusion Detection, RAID 2001, pp 134-149.

[11] Saman Taghavi Zargar, James Joshi and David Tipper, *"A Survey of Defense Mechanisms against Distributed Denial of Service (DDoS) Flooding Attacks"*, IEEE Communications Surveys & Tutorials 15(4), November 2013.

[12] *"A Report from RioRey, "Taxonomy of DDoS Attacks"*, **http://www.riorey.com/types-of-ddos-attacks**, 2006.

[13] Supranamaya Ranjan, Ram Swaminathan, Mustafa Uysal, Antonio Nucci, Edward Knightly, *"DDoS-Shield: DDoS-Resilient Scheduling to Counter Application Layer Attacks"*, IEEE/ACM Transaction on Networking, 2008.

[14] Usman Tariq, ManPyo Hong, Kyung-sukLhee, *"A Comprehensive Categorization of DDoS Attack and DDoS Defense Techniques"*, Advanced Data Mining and Applications, ADMA 2006.

[15] A Report, *"HTTP flood attacks"*, available at:

https://www.ionos.com/digitalguide/server/security/http-flood-attacks/

[16] Ang Chen, Akshay Sriraman, Tavish Vaidya, Yuankai Zhang, Andreas Haeberlen, Boon Thau Loo, Linh Thi Xuan Phan, Micah Sherr, Clay Shields, Wenchao Zhou, *"Dispersing Asymmetric DDoS Attacks with SplitStack"*, HotNets '16: Proceedings of the 15th ACM Workshop on Hot Topics in Networks, November 2016.

[17] Thomas Lukaseder, Lisa Maile, Benjamin Erb, and Frank Kargl, *"SDN-Assisted Network-Based Mitigation of Slow DDoS Attacks"*, April 2018.

[18] A Report, *"Attack Possibilities by OSI layer"*, DDoS quick guide, CISA, Defend today secure tomorrow, October 2020.

[19] A Report, *"DDoS Attack Types Across Network Layers of the OSI model"*, Arbor networks, The security division of NETSCOUT. Available at: **https://www.inforte.com/wp-content/uploads/2018/06/DDoS-ATTACK-TYPES.pdf**.

[20] Catherine A. Theohary and John W. Rollins, *"Cyberwarfare and Cyberterrorism: In Brief"*, CRS Report, congressional research service, March 27, 2015. Available at: **https://fas.org/sgp/crs/natsec/R43955.pdf**.

[21] Fred Schreier, *"On Cyberwarfare"*, DCAF horizon, 2015 Available at: **https://www.dcaf.ch/sites/default/files/publications/documents/OnCyberwarfare-Schreier.pdf**

[22] A Report, *"Network tunneling"*, available at: **https://support.betternet.co/hc/en-us/articles/360022556111--What-is-Network-tunneling-**

[23] Lillian Ablon, Andy Bogart, *"Zero Days, Thousands of Nights: The Life and Times of Zero-Day Vulnerabilities and Their Exploits"*, RAND Corporation, 2017. Available at: **https://www.rand.org/content/dam/rand/pubs/research_reports/RR1700/RR1751/RAND_RR1751.pdf**.

Index

J

L

M

T

U

V

W

Printed in Great Britain
by Amazon